THE AMERICAN
CATHOLIC REVOLUTION

The American Catholic Revolution

How the Sixties Changed the Church Forever

MARK S. MASSA, S.J.

OXFORD
UNIVERSITY PRESS

2010

OXFORD

UNIVERSITY PRESS

Oxford University Press, Inc., publishes works that further
Oxford University's objective of excellence
in research, scholarship, and education.

Oxford   New York
Auckland   Cape Town   Dar es Salaam   Hong Kong   Karachi
Kuala Lumpur   Madrid   Melbourne   Mexico City   Nairobi
New Delhi   Shanghai   Taipei   Toronto

With offices in
Argentina   Austria   Brazil   Chile   Czech Republic   France   Greece
Guatemala   Hungary   Italy   Japan   Poland   Portugal   Singapore
South Korea   Switzerland   Thailand   Turkey   Ukraine   Vietnam

Published by Oxford University Press, Inc.
198 Madison Avenue, New York, New York 10016

www.oup.com

Oxford is a registered trademark of Oxford University Press

Library of Congress Cataloging-in-Publication Data
Massa, Mark Stephen.
The American Catholic revolution : how the sixties changed
the church forever / by Mark S. Massa.
p.   cm.
Includes bibliographical references and index.
ISBN 978-0-19-973412-2
1. Catholic Church—United States—History—1965–
I. Title.
BX1406.3.M375 2010
282'.7309046—dc22   2010001485

1 3 5 7 9 8 6 4 2

Printed in the United States of America
on acid-free paper

To Nick Lombardi, S.J.,
amicus in Domino

In the past, D. H. Lawrence claimed, our civilization's "dirty little secret" was sex. But the church's secret, hidden away in official teaching, minimized when it could not be ignored, was *change*. Other things came and went, captive to history. But the gates of hell would not prevail against the church, and the gates of hell often looked like history, or the latest products of history—"modernism," science, rationalism. We did not deal with such fads. What was sound in them the church had always possessed. [Thus] the experience of change came to Catholics as a form of personal crisis.

Garry Wills, *Bare Ruined Choirs:*
Doubt, Prophecy, and Radical Religion

CONTENTS

PREFACE: "SOMETHING IRREVERSIBLE HAS HAPPENED"

On the morning of November 12, 1962, the great French theologian Yves Congar stood dumbstruck in the vast basilica of St. Peter's on the Vatican Hill in Rome. More than two thousand bishops had just voted on a document that would permanently change the way the Catholic Church would celebrate its public worship. By the extraordinarily lopsided vote of 2,162 to 46, they had officially approved the new document on liturgy and worship, _Sacrosanctum Concilium_, which would be published in the United States as "The Constitution on the Sacred Liturgy." Congar, a canny reader of church politics as well as a world-class theologian, recognized revolution when he saw it. "Something irreversible has happened and been affirmed in the Church," he uttered in astonishment to those around him.[1]

Two years later the implementation of that document would begin the American Catholic revolution. But that revolution, like the broader cultural decade during which it emerged, cannot be reduced to simply chronology. The "American sixties" is itself a chronological term that might be better understood as cultural shorthand for the emergence of four social movements during the course of that tumultuous decade. These four seminal movements were the appearance of both the civil rights and feminist movements, each of which challenged the assumption that white males were (and should be) the determinative voices in the culture, and the appearance of two protest movements centered on the issues of free speech and U.S. military involvement in Vietnam. Both of these latter movements blossomed into myriad other "protest" impulses (against college curricula focused on "dead white males"; against the prohibition of certain hallucinatory drugs; against inherited traditions of political and military "reality") that became incarnated in everything from rock music to popular TV shows.

Many American Catholics, to be sure, took full part in those four movements. But individual Catholic participation in the movements of the decade was not itself the cause of the American Catholic revolution in any simplistic or deterministic sense. And that is the case for three reasons.

First, the Catholic purchase on the cultural revolution of the sixties involved incorporating and balancing international with national loyalties in ways that were unique from the larger cultural story. For instance, the Catholic debate over sexuality in the sixties emerged not with the appearance of proto-feminist arguments about women's rights over their own bodies, but with the promulgation of a papal letter on birth control sent from Rome. It was the publication of Pope Paul VI's encyclical *Humanae Vitae* in 1968 that set off the American Catholic debates over reproductive freedom and sexuality, not the publication of *Our Bodies, Our Selves,* the founding document of American feminist sexuality. And that Catholic debate over sexuality was conducted in the arcane language of Catholic natural law—arcane, anyway, to non-Catholics—and not in the distinctively American argot of individual rights and personal freedoms that marked broader cultural debates.

Second, the American Catholic revolution certainly dates from the sixties but represents a unique phase of that decade because it was focused on and conducted in the language of theology and religious belief, not constitutional rights, cultural norms, or political ideology. From first to last, the American Catholic revolution was defined by debates about Roman Catholic belief, worship, ethics, and citizenship. Perhaps part of the reason why the Catholic sixties remain comparatively understudied, then, is precisely because they seem, to some students of the past, "denominational" rather than cultural. But such a dismissal in fact impoverishes our understanding of the larger cultural event of "the sixties" precisely because for many Americans, and not just American Catholics, that era was refracted through religious no less than political, social, and cultural issues. It is one of the problems of American cultural history as a discipline that religious issues within American culture tend to be given short shrift, if they are studied at all. But such a prejudice (and I would certainly label it as such) in fact *hides* important cultural, political, and social impulses by simply pretending they are not present at all. This book attempts to right that silence by offering a story important in itself, but also crucial for understanding the larger cultural narrative. To that extent the American Catholic revolution is important for anyone attempting to understand the sixties in America, whether they are Catholic or not.

3) Third, the American Catholic revolution remains distinct from the larger story of the sixties because it follows a somewhat different chronology from the broader American story. It begins not in 1960 (the opening of the decade), nor even in 1961, seemingly a promising date, as it marked the election of America's first Catholic president, John F. Kennedy. Instead the Catholic sixties began in 1964, which was when the first (and arguably most dramatic) implementation of the reforms of the Second Vatican Council (the reform of the celebration of the Mass) reached American shores.

Beginning the emergence of the American Catholic Revolution in 1964 offers the first important clue for understanding the story that follows: this book is not a chronological history of Catholicism in the United States. Chronological histories are important for students beginning the study of history: this event helped to cause that one, which in turn gave birth to a third. Chronology is thus a useful, but not—from the standpoint of this story, anyway—a particularly insightful method for getting at the big picture of what happened in the past, or why what happened might be important for *us*. Indeed chronologies can contribute to that deadening sense, reportedly voiced by Henry Ford, that sees history as "just one damned thing after another."

There are a number of other useful historical approaches that might have been utilized for narrating the events described in this book. An institutional history of Catholicism in the United States during the 1960s would have focused on the leadership and official structures of the Catholic Church during that decade—on how the leaders of the Church acted or reacted to challenges posed by the free speech, antiwar, and feminist movements, as well as to the challenges posed by the reforms of Vatican II, and how well (or badly) they met the challenges thus posed. Institutional histories are crucial, but they get at just one side of the story narrated here.

An approach often called "history from below" would start not at the top of the institutional ladder (with bishops and theologians), but at the bottom, with that 98 percent of Catholic believers without whom, as Cardinal John Henry Newman once wryly remarked, the Church would look pretty silly. A book employing this method would have examined how ordinary Catholics understood their world to have been changed by the maelstrom of ideas and events, both in the Church and in the larger culture around them, which defined the sixties. This approach to narrating the past has been brilliantly applied in the past few decades in several landmark scholarly studies focused on faith on the ground, in the everyday language of believers who never studied theology or held high positions of authority in the institution. But this study is built on the firm conviction that the only way to understand the origins of the American Catholic Revolution is to recount that story from a much broader historical perspective than can be offered through the story of everyday piety and belief, however fervently practiced or believed.

Yet another form of history from below might have looked at how marginalized demographic groups within the American Catholic community—women, Hispanics, immigrants from Southeast Asia—changed their social location both within the larger cultural community of North America and within the Catholic Church as a result of the dynamism of the sixties. But such an approach to the events narrated here—valuable and needed for understanding all the ramifications of what took place in the American Catholic community in the years after Vatican II—would still need a broader perspective of why such marginalized groups themselves took that precise moment to move social markers. What did Vatican II *do* (in concert with other cultural and intellectual forces) to sponsor such a turnaround after 1964 within a community that had, for well over a century, largely defined itself as duty-bound to "pay, pray, and obey"?

All these historical approaches are useful for constructing a meaningful sense of how the past has impacted the present. But the story narrated is the product of what is usually called "the history of ideas," and that is the second important clue for understanding the structure and purpose of this book.

A history-of-ideas approach to the past presumes that beneath the multifarious events taking place in any age, influencing dominant personalities and shaping popular opinion, there are overarching ideas or ideologies that give meaning and direction to the flow of events. Thus a history-of-ideas approach to the Protestant Reformation would take as its organizing principle the idea of reform itself, which, as recent scholarship has shown, began considerably before sixteenth-century Protestant figures such as Martin Luther and John Calvin. Indeed the evolution of that idea of reform made Luther and Calvin possible, not the other way around. Without the development of the reformist impulse within late medieval Catholicism, sixteenth-century reformers would have been perceived as speaking nonsense, and would today appear in the footnotes rather than in the titles of works studying the early modern period. Likewise such an approach to the American Revolution would craft its account around the growth and evolution of dominant ideas, such as individual rights and democratic government, which had developed in British culture in the decades after the English Civil War and the Glorious Revolution of 1688. These ideas, such an approach would argue, defined a political and social context that made it possible for such figures as Tom Paine, Samuel Adams, and Thomas Jefferson to attract discontented colonists to a cause that would have been unthinkable just fifty years previously.[2]

In both of these examples, ideas would not be considered causative factors, but rather explanatory ones. That is, the ideas of reform and individual rights would not be presented as *causing* the Reformation or the American Revolution in any deterministic sense; they would instead be presented as *explaining* how all the individual events and figures, which seem diffuse and unconnected when examined at close range, can be put together to form a meaningful story. In such an approach to narrating the past, the validity of the overarching idea or ideology presented as crucial for understanding the story can be judged only by how well (or badly) it succeeds in offering a coherent narrative, helping the reader to see a larger meaning.

3   The idea that is crucial for understanding what the American Catholic Revolution was about, constituting the third key for understanding this book, is *historical consciousness*. At its most basic level, historical consciousness is the recognition that everything changes, and that historical events and figures need to be contextualized within their specific times and cultures in order to be understood. Looking at the past from the perspective of historical consciousness means attempting to understand how people who lived four hundred or a thousand years ago were different from us, and how their real world was different from ours. This approach attacks the assumption that Luther and Calvin were just like us, only dressed differently and without indoor plumbing. Historical consciousness assumes that as sixteenth-century figures, Luther and Calvin lived in a universe that was at least as different from ours as it was similar.

This insight may sound like a penetrating glimpse of the obvious, but it was anything *but* that to many Catholics in the United States in 1964, who fervently believed that what they did on Sunday mornings was pretty much what Jesus' own apostles did in the first century and that Catholic teaching was unchanging simply because it was unchangeable. Many Catholics in 1964 lived in a hermetically sealed universe when it came to their faith and religious practices, mistaking the doxology at the end of their prayers ("as it was in the beginning, is now, and will be forever") for a description of the timelessness of their theology and worship. It was this very sense of timelessness and frozen perfection that the historical consciousness of the Catholic sixties assailed and made permanently problematic.

As Garry Wills recognized with such clarity and intellectual elegance in 1971—in the midst of the period examined by this book—while Western civilization's "dirty little secret" might very well have been about sex, what "the church's secret, hidden away in official teaching, minimized when it could not be ignored, was *change*" itself. Most Roman Catholics, including Americans, took as axiomatic that their twentieth-century version of Christianity was timeless and eternal, sharing in the timeless nature of the God-man who had handed the keys to the Kingdom of Heaven to St. Peter, the first pope. Thus the very idea that Peter might not (and indeed could not) be a pope in any modern sense shocked (and probably still shocks) Catholics unaccustomed to thinking of their faith in historical terms. It was precisely for this reason that Wills so cannily observed that the "experience of change came to Catholics as a form of personal crisis." This book is about both that experience of change and the crisis it caused. But the one addition this study makes to Wills's brilliant insight is to argue that the crisis he recognized so clearly was communal as well as personal.

The fourth and final key for entering into the narrative that follows is the law of unintended consequences. This law, pressed by such brilliant historians of the Catholic past as John O'Malley, simply observes that historical events have consequences separate from (and even sometimes quite opposed to) the intentions of the historical actors who set those events in motion. These unintended consequences are just as important as intended ones that did not come to pass and have the same historical validity. Indeed it is possible that they are considerably more important.

This, too, might sound like a quite disembodied and minor historical insight, but it has important implications. Many participants in the Second Vatican Council have claimed that some of the results of that Council (liturgical experimentation, for instance) were unintended and are thus invalid, or at least less valid than the intentions of its participants. What I propose is that although it *is* quite important to understand the intentions of the participants at the Second Vatican Council, its reforms, once promulgated, took on a life of their own, and their results cannot be judged simply by how closely they hewed to original intent. Church reform, like everything else in history, has its own dynamism, which cannot be contained by initiators. Change happens, whatever the intentions of historical actors, even infallible ones. And thereby, as they say, hangs a tale.

THE AMERICAN
CATHOLIC REVOLUTION

A Brief History of Catholic Time

MISS HAVISHAM'S HOUSE

Few if any of the three thousand bishops, curial officials, and observers sitting in St. Peter's Basilica on the morning of November 12, 1962, guessed that they were participating in an event that would end Tridentine Catholicism, that hermetically sealed brand of Counter-Reformation belief and practice that had defined Roman Catholicism for four centuries. They were assembled on one of Rome's famously damp autumn mornings to formally vote on a document that would be the first to issue from the epochal church council convened by Good Pope John XXIII in January 1959. This first fruit of their deliberations aimed to reform the Church's worship (its "liturgy," in official Catholic-speak).[1]

The "Constitution on the Sacred Liturgy" had been completely revised three times by various subcommittees of liturgists, bishops, and theologians, and when the working draft of the document was finally presented to the assembled bishops of the council, 328 amendments to its contents and structure—surely some kind of indoor record in the annals of Church history—had been suggested on the floor of St. Peter's. But the long windup turned out to be well worth the effort: on that November morning in 1962 the official version of that document (*Sacrosanctum Concilium*) was accepted by the council fathers by a vote of 2,162 to 46. They could hardly have predicted that this decree, touching the folks in the pews in more immediate and understandable ways than any other decree to emerge from Vatican II, would soon set off the "wars over the Mass," the (literally) parochial version of the larger "wars over the Church," and let loose the typhoon of historical consciousness among unsuspecting believers.[2]

The formal promulgation of the council's decree on the liturgy, the act that made it universal Church law, took place a little over a year later, on December 4, 1963. That promulgation was followed by an *Instruction* on

September 29, 1964, which set out the practical details of implementing the decree at the parish level, where the arcane language of theology took on flesh in a way that ordinary Catholics could see and understand. This *Instruction*, which set the first Sunday of Advent 1964 (less than three months away) as the date by which the decree was to be applied to parish worship, revealed in detailed and practical ways the revolution in Catholic worship that would shortly take place. Sacred actions that Catholics had believed were intrinsic to the liturgy itself, and which they (mistakenly) believed went back to the earliest days of Christianity, were now changed or abolished. The readings from scripture, as well as the "Gloria" and the "Lord's Prayer," would now be either read by lay people or recited by the entire congregation in their own language, rather than in the ancient and (more or less) universal language of Church Latin. The folks in the pews would now be encouraged, and even expected, to respond corporately and uniformly to the prayers of the priest, rather than participate "mystically" in the service through the silent recitation of private prayers and devotions. John Henry Newman's famous observation after the First Vatican Council, "There has seldom been a council without great confusion after it," was inadequate to describe the reaction to the 1964 *Instruction*.[3]

The *Instruction* implemented changes greater in scale than anything seen in centuries. Pius V's *Missale Romanum* of 1570, which had cleaned up various accretions that accumulated in the Mass of the Roman Rite over the course of a millennium, froze Catholic public worship for four centuries. Indeed if Vatican II can be rightly described as "the most important event in the history of the Roman Catholic Church since the Protestant Reformation," then the liturgical reforms mandated by the council were the most shaking changes experienced by Catholics on the parish level in modern times.[4]

Most Catholics before Vatican II took it for granted that what they did on Sunday mornings looked like what the Church had always done: the sacred (if sometimes misunderstood) drama of the Mass was understood as timeless, like the words *in saecula saeculorum* that ended all the prayers read by the priest. The drone of Latin with sudden sounds of Greek (*Kyrie eleison*) witnessing to the earliest days of Christianity; ancient titles applied to the Bishop of Rome (*Summus Pontifex*), along with an ancient familiarity of address harkening back to the less formal worship of house churches ("Paul our Pope, and Laurence our Bishop")—all of these lent credibility to the belief that the Mass of the Roman Rite was a ritual not only of ancient provenance, but something outside time altogether.[5]

The American Catholic bishops, under the progressive leadership of Detroit Archbishop John Dearden, worried about the effect of the implementation of the liturgical changes even before that implementation began, worries expressed in a public manner unusual for the U.S. hierarchy, which had always attempted to keep episcopal concerns out of public view. The resolutely progressive *National Catholic Reporter* (then in its first year of existence) reported a month before the mandated changes were to go into effect, "The American Bishops' Commission on the Liturgical Apostolate has warned that there is 'the greatest possibility of scandal . . . in the new English usage in the Mass.'"[6]

Indeed many Catholics arriving at Mass on that first Sunday of Advent in 1964 found it "a strange house, littered with signs of alien occupancy." Centuries-old taboos and childhood memories of nuns' injunctions were suddenly (and for many traumatically) overturned. Catholics were now asked to do things against which elaborate inhibitions had been built up all their lives. A significant part of the older Mass celebrated since Trent had taken the form of a ritual focused on a thing untouchable in both a metaphorical and a physical sense: a sacred dance focused on the sacred wafer, the Host, which Catholics believed *was* Jesus under the appearance of bread, the "bowings, liftings, displaying, and hidings of it." All of that now seemed banished with the sound of guitars, the sudden appearance of banners, and an easy familiarity with the "bread of celebration" that left a number of Catholics reeling between confusion and feelings of betrayal. One disgruntled parishioner complained that his parish had a fellow who stood in front of the church and told them "when to stand, when to sit, when to kneel. It made me so mad that I couldn't think about anything else. . . . I found another parish where they don't have an interlocutor saying 'Gentlemen, be seated.'"[7]

Over against the rigid and quite precise rubrical directions of the Mass celebrated by most Catholics since 1570, the new rite outlined in the September *Instruction* opened up a number of choices, alternatives, and variations, especially in the first part of the Mass, the Liturgy of the Word. Concretely this meant that more of the details shaping what would actually go on in the front of the church were left to the judgment of the individual pastor and would not be predetermined for every celebration. Perhaps most dramatically, and certainly first in the order of new things noticed on just entering the church building, the altar, which formed the locus of attention, was now to be pulled away from the wall, so that the priest would face the congregation rather than stand with his back to the faithful—a simple logistical move that, while restoring the liturgical practice of the twentieth century to the tradition of the early Church, overturned a style of worship that had been practiced for a thousand years. Who, many Catholics would soon ask, was being addressed in the rite? And on whose side was the priest: representing the congregation before God, or standing *in persona Christi* ("in the person of Christ") for the gathered people? Moreover the logistical rearrangement also meant that priests had to clean up their acts liturgically, as now the entire congregation (and not only the altar boys and, presumably, God) could detect goof-ups in the choreography of the celebration. Among other things, this dealt a death blow to generations of altar boy stories, a revered Catholic adolescent form of urban legend about liturgical snafus.[8]

But other, equally significant (if less obvious) changes would greet worshippers during the course of the new rite. In contrast to the quiet organ music serving as background noise, most parish Masses would now be punctuated by regular (if weakly sung) congregational hymns. Within twenty years of the "changes" (as some disgruntled Catholics referred to them), over 90 percent of all Sunday Masses in the United States had at least some congregational singing. Although such an innovation might appear minor or insignificant to non-Catholics, hymn singing itself, and the nature of the hymns sung, emerged in the decade after the close of Vatican II as one of the most heated points of battle between Catholic conservatives and progressives. To devout Mass attendees, accustomed to the familiar and comforting world of Catholic popular devotions focused on the Virgin Mary and one's "household saints"—devotions such as saying the Rosary and lighting candles before the statues of one's most depended-on friends of God while the priest murmured his Latin prayers at the altar—the sudden intrusion of congregational singing appeared foreign, even suspiciously Protestant. No longer would parishioners offer the familiar round of inaudible petitions and thank-yous to the saints for favors sought and received, against the solemn if inaccessible background of the Church's "Great Prayer," to which the priest was the only person paying full attention. Now everyone was to participate fully—and prayerfully.[9]

The immediate response to the changes in most parishes in the United States at the end of 1964 and in the early months of the new year appears to have been dutiful compliance, with surprisingly few episodes of outraged sensibilities. Catholics, whatever else they might have had in common, were accustomed to obeying Church authorities dutifully. It is unlikely that there was much preparation for the changes at the parish level.

A pastor in a suburban New Jersey parish announced the week before the new liturgy was introduced, "As some of you are probably aware, there will begin next Sunday the implementation of a series of changes in the Mass issued by the Holy See." After outlining with breathtaking brevity some of these dramatic changes, the pastor ended by noting, "We realize that this will be difficult for many of you, but realize that this is the will of the Holy Father, the Vatican Council and his Excellency [the local bishop], and we know we can count on your fine cooperation just as we have so many times in the past."[10]

Father Gommar De Pauw, a Belgian-born priest in the Baltimore archdiocese, founded the Catholic Traditionalist Movement just eight weeks after the new liturgical reforms began to be implemented. The first (and arguably the most famous) liturgical protester of the sixties, De Pauw claimed that his conservative crusade had the backing of thirty American bishops as well as high-placed Vatican officials. But De Pauw went considerably beyond simply questioning the timetable or the aesthetics of the new rite: he denounced the "new Mass" as a betrayal of a thousand years of worship in the Western Church by "extremist advisors to the bishops." Among the extremists he named at a news conference on Easter Sunday 1965 were Gregory Baum, Hans Kung, and John Courtney Murray, a group unlikely to agree on anything, much less a unified undermining of the orthodox worship of the Western Church.[11]

The publicity generated by figures like De Pauw made good copy in both the religious and the secular press, and some uninformed readers might have believed that the first Sunday of Advent had unleashed a near universal tide of complaints among the Catholic faithful. But in fact many Catholics—especially priests, liturgy enthusiasts, and many lay people—felt that the new "semireformed" Mass was well overdue and did not go far or fast enough. The very week the changes were introduced, Monsignor J. D. Conway, functioning something like a clerical Ann Landers in his weekly column in the *National Catholic Reporter*, "The Question Box," answered an inquiry from a distraught reader with a touch of impatience: "My earliest memories of high mass center around the meaningless and threateningly endless repetition of Latin words, sung to cheap and gaudy music by a mediocre choir while the congregation sat in silent boredom."[12]

Both De Pauw and Conway, and many others on a broad spectrum between them, would have agreed with Yves Congar that "something irreversible" had happened in the life of the Church, as indeed it had. But the full meaning of that irreversibility was buried underneath startling new debates on a number of fronts about the meaning(s) of being Catholic. And an important factor complicating a full understanding of what exactly had been irreversibly changed was the law of unintended consequences, which the historian John O'Malley has utilized in making some incisive judgments about the council.

O'Malley has quite cannily observed that the efforts by many of the bishops at the council to modernize and renew the Church were balanced by an equally conservative call to return *ad fontes*, to the original wellsprings of the faith as found in the early Church and the Church Fathers. From O'Malley's point of view, two different (and to some extent opposing) impulses sparked the reforms coming out of the council, one looking forward to conversation with the modern world (*aggiornamento*) and the other looking backward to the ancient (and presumably purer) sources of belief and worship in the early Church (*resourcement*). As O'Malley notes, "Although these two words express almost diametrically opposed impulses—the first looking forward and the second backward—they are both geared to change." But even granting that the two groups had very different understandings of what *change* in the Church would look like, both were committed on a profound level to the organic unity of the tradition itself. None of the bishops at the council had any intention of rupturing the fundamental continuity of the Catholic tradition:

> In the opening oration at Lateran V (1512), Egidio da Viterbo in an often quoted axiom expressed the mind-set that prevailed in councils up to Vatican II: we are to be changed by religion, he insisted, not religion by us. The bishops of Vatican II surely subscribed to that principle, but they would interpret it in an unprecedentedly broad way.[13]

But as O'Malley further argues, actions in history can have unintended consequences, and the reception and interpretation of *Sacrosanctum Concilium* in the American Catholic community provides us with a textbook example. It is arguable that the majority of Vatican II's bishops who voted so overwhelmingly for the liturgical changes understood their actions to be in continuity with Trent and Vatican I. But as O'Malley wryly notes, "All that being said, change happens." The law of unintended consequences might help us to understand why, despite the bishops' intentions, there were radical discontinuities in the North American Church.[14]

For the first time in their history, ordinary Catholics now addressed how "relevant" their religious symbols and worship should be. For the first time in the lives of many adult Catholics, questions of what eucharist and prayer actually meant were presented as real, live issues that could be debated in print and at public meetings. The forces of modernity, so long held at bay outside the strong fortress of the Church, now pounded at the door and demanded attention. Quite suddenly Catholics came to utilize new prefixes in describing each other. "Liberal" and "conservative," "progressive" and "traditionalist" now appeared before the noun *Catholic* to describe how people stood on the liturgical reforms. Such prefixes were largely unknown in the pre–Vatican II world, where "lapsed" was the only adjective added to define divisions within the faith community.

Whole forests have been decimated to provide pages for books accounting for the sometimes fractious debates over liturgy that emerged after 1964. Some of these accounts have attempted to situate the new liturgy as emerging seamlessly from liturgical reforms set in motion at the beginning of the twentieth century by Popes Pius X and Pius XII, as well as by Pius Parsch in Austria, Dom Virgil Michel at St. John's Abbey in Collegeville, Minnesota, during the 1920s, and Martin Hellriegel at his "liturgically correct" church in St. Louis during the 1940s and 1950s. Others have critiqued the liturgical changes as a hasty and ill-thought-out quick fix for the perceived and overstated threats of modernization and secularization in Western Europe and North America. Still others, O'Malley most convincingly, have argued that the reforms represented a fragile truce between two groups having very different understandings of "change" in the Church, a fragile truce with unintended consequences. My own sense is that O'Malley has gotten it right. Seen through the lens of his law of unintended consequences, the responses to the new liturgy implemented by the 1964 *September Instruction* were, finally, less about ecclesiology, theology, or even liturgy, than about history. The battles might be best understood as being about change itself. Quite apart from the intentions of the bishops, *Sacrosanctum Concilium,* as Garry Wills has so memorably noted,

> let out the dirty little secret, in the most startling symbolic way, the fact that the *church changes.* No more neat a-historical belief that what one did on Sunday morning looked (with minor adjustments) like what the church had always done, from the time of the catacombs. All that lying eternity and arranged air of timelessness (as in

Mae West's vestmented and massive pose) was shattered. The house with arrested clocks, like Miss Havisham's Satis House, collapsed, by reverse dilapidation, out of death's security into uncertain life.[15]

✔ THE DIRTY LITTLE SECRET

For centuries Roman Catholicism had defined itself in largely institutional terms, focused on the person of the Supreme Pontiff, the Bishop of Rome, and those clergy and laity in union with him. While minor reforms in worship, Church law, and the celebration of the sacraments certainly occurred in the four centuries after the Council of Trent, most Catholic leaders (and most of the faithful as well) understood the Church as a "perfect society" (in the words of Cardinal Bellarmine) that largely stood above the battles of historical change and accident. The Church was alarmingly visible, specific, and unchanging, known by its structure and government and possessing the fullness of authority to judge ideas and nations. *Tu es Petrus*—"You are Peter"—the Sistine Chapel Choir sang as the pope was carried into St. Peter's Basilica on great feasts. Ambiguity, change, and disjunction were almost nonexistent here.[16]

Vatican II appeared to privilege a different, significantly more fluid model of the Christian community's identity in history, a model that seemed to sponsor the kind of historical *disjunction* that few of the council's participants had foreseen or wanted. Eschewing both the rigid definitions and the juridical categories that had reigned in Church documents for centuries, Vatican II showed a marked preference for biblical metaphors and historically contextualized language. Thus, in what is widely considered their most significant theological document, *Lumen Gentium* ("The Dogmatic Constitution on the Church"), the council fathers began their theological consideration of "Church" not with a discussion of the structures and government of the central hierarchy centered on the pope, but with the notion of the Church as a "people on pilgrimage," with whom God communicates in love and judgment. Indeed *Lumen Gentium* offered a quite remarkable discussion of Christ's holy Church as the "People of God": "Among all nations there is but one People of God, which takes its citizens from every race, making them citizens of a kingdom which is of a heavenly and not an earthly nature."[17]

In the view of some historians of postconciliar Catholicism, such language helped to ignite a battle over Catholic identity throughout the

1960s and well into the next several decades. The "Dogmatic Constitution" provides something like the smoking gun for understanding the unrest and debates of the decades after the council. "The people of God," in such an interpretation, came to embody the egalitarian promise of the council's theological *aggiornamento*, with disastrous results for an understanding of the Church as a static, perfect society. But the problem with this interpretation is that it presumes both that ordinary Catholics, even well-read ones, read and understood the theological implications of Roman documents, and that Church leaders fully understand, and can control, all the historical implications of the documents they issue. Both of these historical presuppositions, I think, are problematic.

The "Constitution on the Sacred Liturgy" made concrete to ordinary Catholics ("in the pews," literally, in this case) the theological changes being implemented by Vatican II, something that the theologically more significant "Dogmatic Constitution on the Church" could never achieve. And it accomplished this by reshaping patterns of worship that defined how ordinary Catholics encountered God, the Church, and prayer. Catholics were now asked to adjust to a new awareness, a historical awareness, that even the most sacred religious symbols, the eucharist no less than the texts of scripture, evolve over time and bear the marks of that historical evolution. The very idea that many previous popes had endeavored so strenuously to eradicate from Catholic consciousness—that no religious symbol drops down from heaven or springs to its perfect, complete form from the lips of Jesus and the apostles—was now being advanced by an ecumenical council endorsed by the Supreme Pontiff himself. Like the opening of the windows to let in the streaming sunlight into Miss Havisham's house, which instantaneously destroyed the timeless, death-defying world of her jilted wedding day decades before, all of that former secure world was now gone. Things change.

If the debates within the American Catholic community set off by the decrees of Vatican II were actually based on the unintended consequence of allowing, or even encouraging, Catholic believers to face the long-delayed implications of historical development and contingency, then the battles suddenly become more important and the stakes become higher. The centuries-long ambivalence about history and change now had to be played out yet again, but with considerably less certainty about the probability of success for the "continuity" side of the argument. What if, as appeared to be the case in the light of the new historical consciousness unleashed by Vatican II, *ruptures* defined the development of the tradition at least as much as, and perhaps more than, continuity? What if the efforts of the liberals to reconcile Catholic Christianity with the scientific, sociological, and ideological insights of modern culture, efforts roundly condemned by Pius X and his successors through the middle of the twentieth century, actually represented the side of the angels? What if it turned out that the dogmas the Church taught as revealed truths were not immutable, but were human efforts to capture a divine encounter forged in history, bearing the marks of that process? What if the institutional structures of the Church were not of divine origin, but were subject to perpetual evolution?

The implications of letting historical consciousness out of the bag spread considerably beyond liturgy and institutional structures. Theological arguments offered in the language of natural law—the argot in which the Western Church had argued some of its most important teaching on sexuality, money, and war for centuries—were now seen as problematic by many American Catholic theologians precisely because of natural law's classicist, unchanging presuppositions about human nature and social reality. Upholders of those self-same classicist categories viewed any attack on them as an attack on the faith itself. The traditional categories of ordained and nonordained, and especially the roles of women in the Church, now came to be seen by many faithful Catholics as embodying often embarrassing presuppositions of cultural worlds gone forever, and not categories dropped from heaven. Others viewed even the questioning of an all-male priesthood and the hierarchical selection of bishops as doubts propagated by the Evil One.

From the vantage of a new millennium, the efforts of *both* American Catholic liberals who sought to explore the ramifications of a brave new world created by Vatican II and of the conservatives who sought to reclaim Vatican II for the side of continuity and timeless truths must be seen as embodying issues of considerably more importance than the arrangement of church furniture, the makeup of parish councils, or even questions of married clergy and women priests.

Writing at the time, Bernard Lonergan, the brilliant Canadian Jesuit theologian, identified most clearly the stakes involved in the ecclesial battles being fought in the North American Catholic community. In a very brief paper delivered at a seminar sponsored by the Canon Law Society of America in 1967, Lonergan addressed two very different understandings of the role of law in the Church. But in outlining those two conceptions of law he also sketched with breathtaking brevity and clarity two worldviews that were just then beginning to clash within the American Catholic

Church. It was this "background sketch" that made Lonergan's eight-page paper, "The Transition from a Classicist World View to Historical Mindedness," into a blueprint for understanding the battles within the American Church during the final quarter of the twentieth century.

Lonergan argued that, underneath the battles then being fought about how much law should figure in contemporary debates about ethics and the Christian life, there were two quite distinct worldviews—"total mentalities," in his words—informing and determining the actual positions being taken:

> One may be named classicist, conservative, traditional; the other may be named modern, liberal, perhaps historicist (though that word unfortunately is ambiguous). The differences between the two are enormous, for they differ in their apprehension of man, in their account of the good, and in the role they ascribe to the Church in the world. But these differences are not immediately theological. They are differences in horizon, in total mentality. For either side to understand the other is a major achievement, and when such understanding is lacking, the interpretation of Scripture or of other theological sources is most likely to be at cross-purposes.[18]

Lonergan observed that, for the classicists, reality consisted of unchanging human essences and social truths that remained "substantially the same thing" throughout history (though he immediately added, "I am not sure that the word 'substantially' means anything more than that things are the same insofar as you prescind from their differences"). For classicist believers, "human nature" and "right action" were static, resting on eternal laws whose author was God, whose purposes and intentions for humankind could be appropriated through rational study of an immutable "natural law." But to term this approach to reality "theologically conservative" was only partly to understand it. This stance was actually pretheological, a framework shaping one's "total mentality" long before concrete questions of theology ever arose, a lens through which specific theological questions would be seen. Believers holding this worldview would not look kindly on the call for theological change or development: "It seems unlikely [that those who see reality in this light] will arrive at a law demanding the change of laws, forms, structures, [and] methods, for universals do not change; they are just what they are defined to be."[19]

But Lonergan then announced, in two simple phrases, what might be taken as the death knell for the uncontested dominance of a two-millennia-old classicist understanding of Catholic thought and practice: "[The static conception of reality] is no longer the only conception, or the commonly received conception; and I think our Scripture scholars would agree that its abstractness, and the omissions due to abstraction, have no foundation in the revealed word of God."[20]

Over against that static worldview Lonergan sketched the "commonly received [modern] conception," which did not look to "some stock of ideal forms subsistent in some Platonic heaven" to understand the common meaning of history and its direction. Rather believers looking at the world through this second lens felt no need to appeal to some changeless realm of static truths untouched by historical change to proclaim the Christian story. And however ambiguous the word *historicist* might be, Lonergan proceeded to lay out its presuppositions as essential to a modern faith. In this worldview, which represented the future of religious faith, the historical process itself provided the key to understanding all human meaning, even meaning claiming to disclose transcendent realities superior to the historical process.[21]

This second approach to understanding reality had, in Lonergan's estimation, won the day in the West since the eighteenth century, so much so that to be "modern" meant to understand the human project as developing over and in time. The idea that there existed, somewhere either in history or above it, a perfect and timeless model of perfection that could serve as the yardstick for measuring human goodness or rightness appeared not only naïve but nonsensical to modern people:

> There are modern languages and modern literatures, consciously developed by turning away from Latin and Greek language and literature. There are modern mathematics and modern science, and they differ not only in extent but also in their fundamental conceptions from Greek conceptions. . . . In every case modernity means the desertion, if not the repudiation, of the old models and methods, and the exercise of freedom, initiative, creativity. . . . So to modern man it seems self-evident that he has made his own modern world and, no less, that other people at other times either have done the same or else have made do with a world fashioned by bolder ancestors and inertly handed on.[22]

In Lonergan's view, then, the real issue underlying many of the Church debates in the years immediately after the close of the Second Vatican

Council had little to do with worship, law, or episcopal authority; it had to do with how the gospel message should be understood and proclaimed in a sea of history that was now seen to touch and shape everything. In light of the historical consciousness (quite unintentionally) freed within the Church by Vatican II, it could now be recognized that human nature and human values were "not fixed, static, immutable, but shifting, developing, going astray, and capable of redemption." That being the case, the gospel of that redemption had to be framed in the context of "historicity, which results from human nature," for "it is on this level and through this medium of changing meaning that divine revelation has entered the world, and that the Church's witness is given to it." Lonergan thus announced to fellow believers in the mid-twentieth century that Christian theology was put in an impossible situation when the best of modern thought was perceived as an impossible challenge to it. Catholics could no longer ignore the results of historical consciousness.[23]

Bernard Lonergan, a world-class theologian but hardly a household name among rank-and-file Catholics in North America either then or now, thus outlined a much broader context for understanding what the debates just then heating up in the North American Church were really about. The real battle, as the title of his presentation so succinctly (and deceptively simply) put it, was "the transition from a classicist worldview to historical-mindedness."

If Lonergan's brilliantly succinct identification of the real issue behind the heated exchanges between American Catholics in the 1960s and 1970s makes those battles look simple, or preordained toward certain outcomes, nothing could be further from the truth. If the transition from a classical to a historicist worldview *was* in fact the central issue, then the chances of conservatives winning the post-council debates by simply proving continuity between Vatican II and previous ecumenical councils seemed remote, at best. No matter what the (essentially conservative) intentions of the person who originally called that council (Good Pope John XXIII), or of the overwhelming majority of Catholic bishops who approved the reforms of the council, events in history have their own logic. After the actual experience of change on the ground, the unsettling new historical consciousness unleashed by the council's reforms could not be stopped by anything so simple as an appeal to the intentions of the council's participants, or to some purported "law of continuity" within the tradition that existed above the realm of historical experience. Indeed one of the most secure pillars of

that tradition was the revered fourth-century axiom *Lex orandi lex cre-*
dendi, "The law of praying grounds the law of believing." Change the
experience, which the Second Vatican Council did with breathtaking
historical innocence, and what the belief means changes with it.

But the transition to a historical consciousness initiated (however
unwittingly) by Vatican II hardly offered an easy victory for the side of the
liberals either, for the new worldview appeared to promote a kind of historical relativism that Catholicism in the late nineteenth and early twentieth
centuries quite understandably recognized as raising unsettling questions
about the stability and authority of revelation itself. If the tradition was not
changeless, static, and always perspicacious, that is, meaning what it says
and saying what it means everywhere and at all times, where could
believers find solid ground to stand on in the evil day? Was the final, and
most distressing, implication of historical consciousness what Pius X and
others had always feared in their condemnation of modernism: that *every-*
thing in Christianity was relative and historically conditioned, and no part
of the sacred tradition survived the acids of modernity intact? Was the
gospel itself just another historically conditioned project, soon to be displaced by a better message? How could either conservative or liberal Catholics live with the implications of such historicism come home to roost?

Frederick McManus and *Worship* in the United States

LEX ORANDI LEX CREDENDI

Most theologians in the twenty-first century would agree that the redefinition of the Church as the "People of God" in the *Dogmatic Constitution on the Church* had the most far-reaching effect on twentieth-century American Catholicism of any of the reforms coming out of the Second Vatican Council. But from the standpoint of ordinary Catholics one could make an almost water-tight case that the most immediate and dramatic decisions of the council, far and away, were embodied in the "Constitution on the Sacred Liturgy." The theological revolution resulting from the astonishing near unanimous vote on that document might be taken as proof positive, if one had a providential view of history at least, that the Holy Spirit had other motives from those of the bishops sitting in the nave of St. Peter's Basilica.[1]

But despite scattered evidence of frustration, disaffection, and wistful yearning for the old Mass, the widespread fears of rejection and nonreception among the faithful appeared to be unfounded. Most North American Catholics overwhelmingly—and surprisingly quickly—came to support what would come to be known as the new Mass. According to the best data at our disposal, within five years of the closing of the council, between 85 and 87 percent of practicing Catholics in the United States said that they preferred the new Mass to that celebrated according to the sixteenth-century *Missale Romanum*. And the strongest support for the new liturgy came almost immediately from parish priests. Such widespread support for the liturgical changes on the part of both clergy and laity, in fact, was the mirror image of the widespread nonreception of Paul VI's encyclical condemning birth control, *Humanae Vitae*, issued four years later.[2]

Such an overwhelmingly positive reception of Church teaching that so dramatically reshaped the ritual practices that had largely defined Catholic identity for centuries is both counterintuitive and not surprising. It is counterintuitive because most Church historians would agree with the observation, made by the great German scholar Hubert Jedin in his magisterial (and multivolume) study of the Council of Trent, that the implementation and positive reception of reforms promulgated by ecumenical councils usually take one to two centuries to achieve widespread popular acceptance. On the other hand, the liturgical restoration undertaken by *Sacrosanctum Concilium* was hardly surprising to anyone familiar with the history of the liturgical movement in Europe and the United States.[3]

But even allowing for the liturgical reform movement in the Roman Church, which had been building since the beginning of the twentieth century, the rapid and overwhelmingly positive reception of the new Mass by American Catholics was not inevitable. It is precisely here that the figure of Frederick McManus is crucial to the story of the reception of the new English liturgy. It has been said of *Worship,* the liturgical journal in which McManus regularly published, that "in proportion to its circulation, no Catholic magazine ever exercised so great an influence on American Catholic life." And a strong argument could be made that no single American Catholic played so crucial a role in shaping the liturgical reforms in the decade after Vatican II as Frederick McManus.[4]

McManus, a priest of the archdiocese of Boston, trained as a canon lawyer and serving as the editor for the *Newsletter* of the Committee on the Liturgy of the National Conference of Catholic Bishops during the crucial reception years of 1965–75, was himself an insider at the national level of the Church in the United States. It is thus not surprising that he was positioned to play a crucial role in shaping the reception of *Sacrosanctum Concilium.* Indeed it was this very insidership that would make him into an object of vilification by traditionalist Catholics deeply critical of the vernacular Mass.[5]

What is surprising about McManus's important role in the reception of Vatican II's liturgical reforms is the fact that he utilized relatively arcane monthly columns about rubrics and canonical liturgical guidelines to help broker a fairly radical historical consciousness about the liturgy. That historical consciousness allowed the readers of McManus's columns to understand how and why history makes different demands on Church worship at different cultural periods. Indeed McManus made that consciousness seem self-evident and logical, so that the vast majority of his readers embraced his understanding of the rationale for the liturgical changes readily and with passion. Those *Worship* articles, read by thousands of parish priests, diocesan liturgical officials, and lay people charged with doing something radically new ("liturgical planning"), played a crucial role in mediating the overwhelmingly positive reception of the liturgical reforms in the United States. But more important for our purposes, those carefully argued and historically based articles also mediated something new for Catholics in the United States: a consciousness that the liturgy, like everything else, changes, so that what the faithful did on Sunday mornings was both continuous *and* discontinuous with the house liturgies of the early Christians. While this may sound banal today, such a consciousness was quite radical in mid-twentieth-century American Catholicism, as it opened the door to an awareness of even broader changes and discontinuities.[6]

"RESPONSES"

Ordained for the diocese of Boston in 1947, Frederick McManus was appointed diocesan master of ceremonies (a sign that he was on the escalator going up in archdiocesan politics) just a year later. In 1951 he began studies at the School of Canon Law at the Catholic University of America (CUA), where he quickly earned three consecutive degrees in canon (Church) law in short order. In 1958 he was invited back to the university to teach canon law in the program he had sailed through with such ease and brilliance. His intellectual skills and organizational acuity were such that, after a four-year stint teaching at the Boston archdiocese's seminary in Brighton, Massachusetts, he was invited back to Catholic University to become dean of the canon law faculty in 1967, dean of graduate studies and vice provost in 1974, and eventually academic vice president of the entire university. In the midst of his many teaching and administrative activities, McManus was asked to take over the editorship of *The Jurist*, arguably the premier canon law journal in the English-speaking world, in 1959, a position he dutifully retained while fulfilling his other duties.[7]

Having worked on preparations for the upcoming council well before the bishops began meeting, McManus was invited to Rome in 1962 as a *peritus*, a scholarly expert serving as a resource for the bishops working on the Conciliar Commission on the Liturgy, a position in which he served for three years. While in Rome McManus was one of a handful of nonbishops invited to the organizational meeting of the International Commission on English in the Liturgy (ICEL) in October 1965, a body whose work every Catholic in the English-speaking world knows intimately, even if he or she has never heard of ICEL, as the prayers and readings of the Mass in the United States are the products of their meetings. His hard work and superb knowledge of Church law led to his being named a consulter on the committee organized to implement *Sacrosanctum Concilium* from 1964 to 1970, a critically important position that he held during the crucial years of the reception of the new liturgy in the United States. It was during those years on this committee that McManus became editor for both the *Newsletter* of the Committee on the Liturgy of the National Conference of Catholic Bishops (1965) and an associate editor of *Worship* magazine (1968).[8]

Much of what is now called "liturgical studies" was, in the years immediately before and after the Second Vatican Council, actually the province of canon lawyers concerned with arcane questions about the distinction between the "licit" and "valid" celebration of the sacraments whose guidelines ("rubrics") were minutely spelled out in the *Missale Romanum* of 1570 and other liturgical books. That McManus the canonist had broad influence in interpreting the Vatican Council's liturgical changes was thus hardly surprising. His first publication, which appeared in 1953, the year before he finished his doctoral dissertation, was a clean text and commentary on the new *Ceremonies of the Easter Vigil* just promulgated by Rome. He expanded this guide to the Easter Vigil in 1956 to include a very useful guide for priests, published by the St. Anthony Guild Press as *The Rites of Holy Week*. The following year he published an even more accessible booklet to be used by lay worshippers, *The Peoples' Holy Week*. Thus, well before the Second Vatican Council even met, McManus had emerged as an important, authoritative voice in demystifying the official worship of the Church for the folks in the pews.[9]

But it would be McManus's regular writing in *Worship* that would extend his influence well beyond the province of canon lawyers and bishops in the years after Vatican II. *Worship* magazine, published out of the largest Benedictine monastery in the United States, St. John's Abbey in Collegeville, Minnesota, had been started as *Orate Fratres* ("Pray, brothers") by the great liturgical scholar Dom Virgil Michel, and had quickly emerged as the premier Catholic publication focused on the liturgy in the English-speaking world.[10]

McManus began a regular column, titled "Responses," in 1957, four years before the Second Vatican Council even began meeting. His first contribution, "Scripture Readings in English," offered scrupulously correct canonical advice grounded in a sophisticated historical sense and sound pastoral instincts. Halfway through this first column, on how and when English versions of the epistle and gospel should be read, McManus detoured from his arcane discussion of Church ritual to address the simple question of when the Introit (the opening scripture verses of a Mass giving the tone of the celebration that day) at solemn and Sunday Masses should be sung by the choir. He answered unhesitatingly, "while the celebrant is processing." Many circumstances, he noted, "over many centuries have contributed to a general misunderstanding of the character of the Introit." McManus allowed that, as various liturgical guides over the course of centuries differed among themselves, it was clear that the Church's worship had lost its way on this particular part of the rite. But after unraveling the torturous historical record of the Introit's intonation, McManus stepped back from the tangled history of these rubrics to observe that the significance of the Introit, like all the guidelines on liturgical prayer, must be situated "in our desire that every element of the Mass should genuinely fulfill its *function*." It would be this pragmatically pastoral understanding of liturgical rubrics, informed by the simple historical understanding that things changed (sometimes radically) in how the Church worshipped over the course of millennia, that would prove to be so decisive in giving McManus the central role he would play in the next decade.[11]

In his next column McManus supplemented his historical understanding of Catholic worship with an equally historically informed emphasis on the central role of the *entire* community in celebrating the eucharist. This second column addressed the tension between singing during the procession of people coming forward to receive communion and the need for "private thanksgiving" by those who have already received communion. Well before the emphasis on community in worship that resulted from the Council's liturgical reforms, McManus observed:

> It is surely important to urge and commend private and personal prayers of preparation and thanksgiving for communion. . . . But that these should replace the common table prayer of the Christian people (the Our Father), the united song of the faithful approaching the sacred banquet (the communion antiphon and psalm), or the Church's public prayer for the effects of holy Mass among us all (the post-communion prayer) is surely an inversion of values.[12]

That was it: the practice of private prayer during communion, which defined how many American Catholic parishes observed the rite—a practice that many American Catholics in the mid-twentieth century believed dated from the earliest days of Christianity—was simply dismissed as bad practice (or even as an "inversion of values") arising out of a misunderstanding of what the rite was actually about. Best just to scrap historical accretions like these, which had become attached to the rite (and were considered sacred by many of the faithful), to let the structure of the rite be revealed as it should be understood.

McManus kept offering well-grounded pastoral and historical advice on liturgical issues like these in the years just after the Second Vatican Council and just as *Worship*'s readership was booming: the journal grew from 12,500 subscribers in 1963 to 20,000 in 1967–68. Thus, though hardly a popular periodical in comparison with *Reader's Digest* or *Our Sunday Visitor*, *Worship* was nonetheless perceived as being something like the Cadillac of English-speaking periodicals focused on liturgy, and many pastors turned to it to understand how they might explain to their good-willed but confused parishioners why they were implementing the liturgical directives touching on matters they believed had been in place since the apostles.[13]

Well before the first Sunday of Advent in 1964 McManus addressed the question of whether it was permitted for parishes to erect an altar *versus populum* (facing the people). Citing a previous Vatican "Instruction" of September 3, 1958, he argued in a January 1959 column that such liturgical "innovation" was in fact not new at all, but had a long and venerable history, witnessed by the fact that the principal churches of Rome (including St. Peter's Basilica) had been constructed for precisely this kind of celebration. From a historical standpoint, then, such liturgical practice "had considerable tradition in its favor." But, he went on to argue, historical precedent in itself was not decisive on such matters, as the Church had celebrated its sacraments in a number of ways, none of which was "apostolic" in the sense of "going back to apostles." All such "historical" arguments, in any event, involved a fair amount of winking at historical evidence. A far better argument, McManus observed, could be found in the meaning of what was done during Mass. Far better, he thought, to look at

> the Canon itself. Its words directly concern the worshipping community: they express its unity with Christ and the celebrant in the offering of sacrifice, and yet they are unheard and unintelligible to the faithful. Perhaps the celebration of Mass with the celebrant facing the people, even if done only on occasion, may help to involve the people in the sacred action, and move them to that inward participation which the words demand.[14]

On the eve of the council itself McManus penned a column on the "new code of rubrics," noting that most parishes in the United States lagged far behind on implementing the kind of lay participation being undertaken in Europe and envisioned even by the Vatican, especially with regard to the use of "popular missals" for use by lay people at Mass. Experimentation with such missals for the laity, however, shouldn't slavishly follow the rite laid out in the Missal of 1570, which was a flawed "functional handbook" directing priests how to celebrate Mass, its strengths (such as they were) more than counterbalanced by a number of historical shortcomings. Most problematically, the 1570 Missal lacked an explicit *epiclesis,* a calling down of the Holy Spirit on the bread and wine on the altar, so that many Orthodox Christian theologians had felt for centuries that the "Roman Liturgy" it outlined was invalid, or at least incomplete. The last thing the laity needed to renew their appreciation for the Church's liturgical life was popular missals modeled on the Missal of 1570. The defects of that missal, which had made historically and theologically questionable developments sacrosanct, "need not be copied in popular missals," McManus wrote. Far better, he thought, to ignore the historical mistakes canonized in that book and start anew.[15]

McManus's "Responses" columns from 1962, while he was still in Rome advising the bishops, noted that the daily liturgical life of the bishops at the council had profoundly influenced the bishops themselves. He dramatically contrasted the opening session of the council, which had been "overweighted with baroque music and lengthy ceremonial—almost an argument for liturgical innovation," with the "daily low mass celebrated with full participation by all present." This daily experience of worship in which everyone participated, shorn of many historical additions that obscured the central action of the rite, was quite striking, and potentially quite important:

> There is a certain satisfaction, again merely in the externals, in seeing Mass offered at a simple altar, with the celebrating bishop facing the congregation, with all responding and reciting ordinary chants and the Lord's Prayer. To some this may appear to be a startling innovation; to the vast majority it is surely only the outcome . . . of a wholesome liturgical reawakening in the Church.[16]

McManus's personal impressions, written in Rome, would be expanded two years later into a three-part commentary on the "Constitution on the

Sacred Liturgy" then being implemented in the United States. In a sixty-page commentary in the May 1964 issue of *Worship* he offered an extended close reading of the conciliar text, beginning with the observation that the authority of the new Constitution would "depend on the custom and usage it inspired." Its real authority, as opposed to its "validity" as the product of an ecumenical council, would depend on how the document was received and practiced by Catholics in the pews. Its usage, in other words, would ultimately determine its authority for subsequent generations. Such a seemingly "progressive" interpretation of the document's authority, McManus argued, was actually rooted in the Church's own law:

> In fact, the Code of Canon Law itself acknowledges that custom is the best interpreter of laws (Canon 29). It is only through usage, through the practice of the Christian people, that there will be real growth in the understanding of the Church's laws. This is a vital thing, the very opposite of legalism and literalism.[17]

This "vital thing, the very opposite of legalism and literalism," in interpreting the authority of *Sacrosanctum Concilium* was taken up in part II of his commentary, a forty-page article published in the September 1964 issue of *Worship*. McManus opened this article by observing, "[The] purpose of the restoration and reform of the rite of Mass is intended to make it pastorally efficacious to the fullest degree." The test of that effectiveness was how much it helped the laity understand what the liturgy was about and how much it fostered "their easier participation with devotion and action." The historical form of the rite, so understood, was actually quite secondary, as forms were not ends in themselves: their purpose was to foster a lived experience in a vibrant historical community. To that extent, tradition itself might be judged according to how well it met—or didn't meet—the needs of living, breathing people.[18]

This "receptive" test for measuring the efficacy of the council's liturgical reforms was further embodied in McManus's extended discussion of the role of the homily in the new liturgy. The new emphasis on the homily preached after the gospel reading of the day "corrects the unfortunate impression that the homily is somehow or other an interruption of the Mass," he wrote. On the contrary, the priest's homily on the readings of the liturgy sought to "evoke a response from the faithful, both in the actual liturgical celebration and, just as important, in the actual living of the Christian life."[19]

Likewise, in commenting on the restored "Prayer of the Faithful" at the end of the Liturgy of the Word, McManus emphasized that the Constitution on the Liturgy itself insisted on the participation of everyone in it. This, too, was in fact a restoration of a "practice common to almost all rites but the Roman—and the Roman Rite had known the usage until the fifth century." This restoration might very well serve as a "bond of unity, especially with the Oriental rites, but also with Protestant liturgies which preserve the 'bidding prayers.'" Catholic Christians of the Roman Rite had been deprived of this important part of the liturgy for reasons that were now irrelevant. But the new context of worship provided by the council allowed Roman Catholics, for a host of new historical reasons, to reinstitute the prayer.[20]

But arguably McManus's single most important and influential article for pastors was an extended, two-part article titled "The New Rite of Mass" published in the January and March 1965 issues of *Worship*. This one-hundred-page guide to the new liturgy just then being implemented in parishes across the United States became the American pastor's essential reading, utilized not only to navigate the new guidelines, but also to explain to the faithful *why* the new Mass had been established and *what* its dynamics were about. McManus began by observing that "if the new rite seem[ed] complicated to the priest," it nonetheless offered an important opportunity for the faithful, for if the priest "works out his role very carefully, the members of the congregation will be taking part in a service that is vastly clearer and more meaningful." The hard work on the part of pastors in implementing the dynamics of a new form of the Mass would be more than rewarded by a

> more natural, human and even spontaneous approach by the clergy to the manner of celebration, together with an awakening of deeper participation of the people which is conscious and genuine. To achieve such results will not be easy, and they are impossible of attainment merely by the formal observances of rules and rubrics.[21]

Beginning with the (now eliminated) "Prayers at the Foot of the Altar," McManus sought to contextualize the reasons for the new rubrics both within the ancient liturgical tradition of the Western Church of the first thousand years and within a new appreciation of the need to invite Christians to a full and conscious "response" in celebrating their Christian vocation in the world. The former (historical) emphasis in his commentary sought to set the changes then being implemented in the United States within a much broader context, in the process illustrating by many examples how the purportedly timeless liturgy of Catholicism had in fact changed over the course of centuries. But the latter emphasis in McManus's extended commentary focused on how the Church must always be reshaping its public worship to meet new historical challenges. This impulse was picked up in an October 1965 article in *Worship*, "The Implementation and Goals of Liturgical Reform," a paper read at Clergy Day at St. John's Abbey the previous August. McManus opened by noting that all liturgical reform was itself simply the first difficult step toward grappling in every age with the profound Catholic insight *Ecclesia semper reformanda* ("The Church is always in need of reform"). Such reform was itself "an admission of past weaknesses, defects, and limitations." And Church history offered graphic examples of those weaknesses, defects, and limitations. Those who sought a timeless Church, free of history's challenges and pitfalls, had best look elsewhere than to the history of Catholic worship.[22]

The motto that the Church always needed reforming, first used a century before Luther and the Protestant Reformers, bore witness to an even more ancient and revered Christian understanding of *Church* that was tied to history and its contingencies. That more ancient understanding was much closer to understanding the Church as a people on pilgrimage (the Second Vatican Council's preferred metaphor) than to Cardinal Bellarmine's understanding of the Church as an institution in, but not necessarily of, history. *Ecclesia simper reformanda*: things change, and thus the Church itself and its liturgy must always change too. Only such reform could set up the context for a Christian life and form of worship that was credible and compelling. As John Henry Newman had observed a century before Vatican II, "In a higher world it is otherwise, but here below to live is to change; and to be perfect is to have changed often." Indeed, the Church, having lived for a very long time, had changed more often than mid-twentieth-century Catholics knew.[23]

RECEPTION AS AN ECCLESIOLOGICAL— AND HISTORICAL—REALITY

The successful reception of the reforms of Vatican II in the United States, and more particularly the reception of the "restored liturgy" implemented on the first Sunday of Advent in 1964, was the result of many factors reaching back decades. But that having been said, Frederick McManus played a crucial role, arguably *the* most crucial role played by any single individual, in mediating the extraordinarily positive reception of the new Mass in the United States.

McManus's accessible and historically informed commentaries on the new liturgy mandated by the Second Vatican Council were presented in a form that hard-pressed pastors could both understand and present to perhaps anxious parish groups, a form that privileged sound historical and theological reasons for the changes. The new liturgy as McManus presented it was a living work, the opposite of timeless formalism and ritualism—a work borne by the whole Church.

McManus's historically rooted, pastorally oriented, and canonically exact commentaries in the pages of *Worship* over the course of a decade fraught with potential landmines prepared the ground for the overwhelmingly positive reception of Vatican II's "Constitution on the Sacred Liturgy" in the United States. His was the wise, measured, and authoritative voice that allowed American Catholics to recognize the truth of their own Catholic identity in the reforms mandated by the council, in the process making the distance between what they had always done on Sunday mornings and the rubrics of the new Mass seem like an invitation to enter into a richer understanding of what it meant to be Catholic.

Further, McManus's deft historical contextualization of the new liturgy within the evolving tradition of the Western Church allowed American Catholics to see in the council and its reforms their place in a long history of reform, the simple fact of which the vast majority of Catholics in the United States (including bishops) were unaware. Indeed the emphasis McManus placed on "popular usage" allowed Catholics to see that the changes they were asked to incorporate into their worship patterns were hardly novel or a break with tradition; they were instead a welcome return to an ancient tradition of regularly incorporating new forms and prayers into the central liturgical act of the Church at prayer. He invited his readers, in other words, into the realization that the teachings of general councils were binding not because a particular Church official or body asserted it, but because it was true to what Catholic worship was supposed to be. The outward form of the rite was changed *precisely to remain true to* an action Jesus had commanded at the Last Supper. Such an understanding of Catholic tradition was presented less as a changeless set of actions than as the ongoing development of that tradition in light of the actual lived experience of Christians in the world. The reception of the liturgical changes mandated by Vatican II could thus be understood—and actually experi-enced—as inviting the body of believers to express themselves in new ways. Just part of the elegance of McManus's mediatory role in eliciting a largely favorable response from the folks in the pews was his deft and understated manner in making all of this seem proper, and even self-evident.

What neither McManus nor his readers could understand at the time was that his compelling commentaries on the strengths of the new Mass, in the very process of neutralizing the idea of continuous historical change within the Church, promoted something radically new: the idea that his-torical consciousness itself could now be a legitimate stance within the Roman Church. This was, we can safely say, neither intended nor foreseen by McManus, himself a cautious canonist dedicated to careful scholarship and closely reasoned arguments based on historical precedent. Just part of the irony of McManus's role in helping to craft such widespread accep-tance of the new rite was the fact that this erudite Church lawyer quite unwittingly helped to give birth to the Catholic sixties, a birthing process that began on the parish level with the implementation of the new Mass.

McManus's intentions notwithstanding, we can see in his carefully rea-soned columns in *Worship* a compelling instance of the law of unintended consequences: what his sedate and arcane articles on the liturgy actually embodied was a short course for pastors and parish liturgy planners on the value of historical consciousness, or at least a painless way of seeing that "change happens," even in the Church, which they, in turn, passed on to congregants and Confraternity of Christian Doctrine teachers. However obvious such a truth may seem now, it was a revolutionary idea within American Catholicism. Gone was the death-defying sense of Catholic wor-ship promoted by the Missal of 1570, that the Mass was something outside of time altogether. Gone was the sense of mid-century American Catholics that what they did on Sunday mornings was, with the exception of a few details, what had gone on in the catacombs of Rome in the second and third centuries. Gone was the fortress-like sense of Catholic Christianity and its acts of prayer standing above the battle-scarred plains of history—in history surely, but hardly of it.

All of that was now washed away by changes that would have seemed quite impossible just a few years before: banners, guitar music, the sudden disappearance of beloved statues of household saints from side altars into basement closets.

In the decades since the implementation of the changes in the Mass, a nomenclature has developed within American Catholicism to describe the range of receptions accorded the liturgical implementation: "progressives" were those who much preferred the music of the St. Louis Jesuits to the motets of Palestrina; "restorationists" were those who sought a recovery of the glories of the Latin Mass of 1570. There is enough truth in these (essentially political) labels to warrant their carefully limited use in the Catholic ecclesial context. But seen from another context, these monikers also obscure at least as much as they explain. How was the movement from plainchant to folk tunes, in itself, "progress"? Progress toward what? And what, exactly, was being "restored" by returning to a language of worship that few if any in the congregation understood? Incomprehension? Respect for what was mysterious, or at least obscure? How, and why, was that worthy of restoration?

What the category of historical consciousness allows us to recognize is that beneath the aesthetic, pietistic, and stylistic preferences informing the various receptions accorded the new liturgy lay something deeper, something far more important in understanding the real meaning of Vatican II. What this category allows us to see is that what was being received (or resisted) was the idea of change itself, and the historical consciousness that accompanied that change. Seen thus, what conservatives found so distasteful and disquieting was the very idea that the older, static, and timeless way of understanding Catholic Christianity (a stance labeled "classicist" by Bernard Lonergan) was being abandoned for an understanding of Catholicism in which history and change would play starring roles. The bishops attending the Second Vatican Council had themselves believed—wrongly, as it turned out—that reforms could be implemented in Catholic worship while leaving the superstructure of belief and identity largely untouched. Such a belief implied that these changes were quite secondary to the seemingly impervious, unchanging nature of "the Faith." Karol Woytila, himself a participant at Vatican II, would attempt just this—an attempt to put the historicist genie back into the bottle—several decades later when he was elected Pope John Paul II. An important part of his effort would be an attempt to claim the Second Vatican Council for the side of continuity and static truth. Nothing essential or important in the belief and practice of the pre–Vatican II Church, John Paul would assert, had changed as a result of the council. Things were as they had always been, and those Catholics who claimed otherwise missed the real spirit of the council.

But genies, religious and otherwise, have a bad habit of not obeying orders to go back into their bottles. Such was assuredly the case of the genie of historical consciousness in the years after 1964. If things *really* change in the Church, as the liturgical reforms seemed to show with dramatic clarity to the discomfiture of some and the satisfaction of others, then an entire way of understanding Catholic Christianity changed with that realization—a realization to which the adjectives *liberal* and *conservative* hardly begin to do justice. The reception of the pope's letter regarding birth control just a few years later, in 1968, proved just that.

Humanae Vitae in the United States

HUMANAE VITAE AND GOD'S ETERNAL NATURAL LAW

Just four years after the promulgation of Vatican II's Constitution on the Sacred Liturgy in the United States, Pope Paul VI ended years of discussion and study among Catholics by issuing a new encyclical on human sexuality and birth control, *Humanae Vitae* ("On Human Life"). The encyclical was a complex and quite sophisticated theological reflection on both sexuality and the duties of Christian marriage. The structure of the encyclical was complex and sophisticated as well. The introduction noted that modern science, with its advances in controlling human fertility, "gives rise to new questions" that required Catholics to enter into a "new and deeper reflection upon the principles of the moral teaching on marriage." It was here, early on in *Humanae Vitae*'s extended reflection on contraception, that the letter reminded readers that it was both the duty and the right of the pastors of the Church—and especially of the chief pastor of the Church, the pope himself—to deal with such questions. This was so because the Church had received from Christ the responsibility to interpret "the entire moral law—not only the law of the Gospel but also the natural law, which are both the expression of God's will for man's moral life." No one, it is safe to say, on any side of the debates that would shortly break out, could take exception with anything argued up to that point.[1]

The encyclical's lush and elegiac second section, exploring the doctrinal principles that must underlie moral decisions in light of the scientific advances on human fertility, began with the unexceptional observation that all moral decisions had to contextualize biological, psychological, demographic, and sociological perspectives within a much broader and richer context of the nature of human persons, keeping always in mind the high vocation to which human beings were called. At this point the encyclical offered a quite beautiful and extended reflection on the love of husband and wife, drawing on teaching offered in the Second Vatican Council's "Constitution on the Church in the Modern World," *Gaudium et Spes.*

Indeed the pope would state at a public audience a month after the encyclical's promulgation, in August 1968, that he quite consciously "adopted the personalist concept which is proper to [*Gaudium et Spes*'s] doctrine on conjugal relations, and which gives to the love that generates and nourishes it the preeminent place that befits it in [any] evaluation of marriage." Thus, relying on the rich language regarding Christian marriage that had suffused one of Vatican II's most famous (and popularly received) documents, the pope announced that genuine love and respect between partners in marriage naturally flows into "*responsible* parenthood." Indeed it was the use of that word "responsible" that gave first readers of the document hope that the pope was about to overturn current Church teaching on contraception; the exercise of responsible parenthood, the pope declared in Article 10 of the encyclical, requires that husband and wife "recognize their duties toward God, toward themselves, toward the family, and toward society, in a correct hierarchy of values."[2]

Up to this point the encyclical could have moved in a number of possible directions: toward a change in the Church's teaching regarding contraception (based on a theological argument about "responsible parenthood" leading couples to limit childbirths); toward a reaffirmation of the norms of the past (in light of couples' "duty toward God"); or toward some new position on a spectrum between the two poles (population or food crises underscoring the need for limiting childbirths as part of Christian responsibility). There had in fact been some intimations earlier in the encyclical of the direction in which the pope's argument was heading. But the boom was lowered at the very end of Article 10, which declared that married couples

> are not free to proceed completely at will, as if they could determine in a wholly autonomous fashion the honest path to follow; but they must conform their activity to the creative intention of God expressed in the very nature of marriage and its acts, and manifested by the constant teaching of the Church.[3]

Thus, while the ostensible focus of the entire encyclical was on "the most serious duty of transmitting human life" (as its opening sentence announced), the debates it generated came to focus quite specifically on three articles: 11, 12, and 14. Article 11 was the first full declaration that the pope intended to stand with the Church's teaching in the past: "[The Church,] calling men back to the observance of the norms of the natural law, as interpreted by her constant doctrine, teaches that *each and every* marriage act must remain open to the transmission of life." Article 14 elucidated that "constant teaching" with an alarmingly specific attention to actions before, during, and after the sexual act that the encyclical described as "intrinsically disordered":

> It is not licit, even for the gravest reasons, to do evil that good may follow therefrom; that is, to make into the object of a positive act of the will something which is intrinsically disordered, and hence unworthy of the human person, even when the intention is to safeguard or promote individual, family, or social well-being.[4]

Parts of the encyclical had in fact argued, following the arguments of Vatican II's "Constitution on the Church in the Modern World," that due respect had to be given to the interpersonal dimension of marriage, which recognized the fact that sexual relations between married couples embodied a range of important values and "goods," goods that included the expression of mutual affection, comfort, and fidelity between spouses. But Articles 11 and 14 of the encyclical insisted that, even allowing for the interpersonal dimension, sexual relations between spouses could never be judged *just* from the standpoint of comfort and mutual affection.

It was Article 12 that held together the theological arguments contained in Articles 11 and 14. Article 12 announced, "This teaching is founded on the *inseparable connection, willed by God and unable to be broken by man on his own initiative, between the two meanings of the act: the unitive meaning and the procreative meaning.*" Viewed with the 20-20 vision of hindsight, it is now clear that there were two phrases in Article 12 that helped cause the perfect storm the encyclical unleashed: the first was this description of the connection between the two meanings of sexual relations in marriage as "inseparable"; the second was the very last sentence of Article 12, in which Paul VI observed, "We believe that the men of our day are particularly capable of seizing the deeply *reasonable* and human character of this fundamental principle."[5]

No Catholic moral theologian in 1968 would have denied that there was an intrinsic and sacred connection between conjugal love and procreation. What many (and possibly the majority of) moral theologians in the United States did question was the "inseparable" nature of that connection in each and every act of sexual intercourse—and more specifically the natural law arguments offered to explain and justify that inseparability in "each and every act." Indeed far from "seizing the deeply reasonable and human character" of these arguments, many American Catholic moral theologians in 1968 felt that the theological arguments seemed implausible, or at least appeared dated, and easy to refute. Were these the best arguments available, many asked, to justify what many Catholic married couples had come to view as an oppressive Church teaching? And what about the role of "responsible parenthood," which the encyclical itself had praised so extensively?

But other, political questions also dogged the reception of the encyclical. Precisely because it was issued in the wake of the Second Vatican Council's more biblical and less hierarchical understanding of the Church as "the People of God," the very manner of the encyclical's promulgation seemed problematic to many theologians and lay Catholics in the United States. In issuing *Humanae Vitae*, Paul VI had overridden the majority opinion of a blue-ribbon international committee which his much-loved predecessor, Pope John XXIII, had appointed. The majority on that committee had favored a change in Church teaching that would allow some forms of contraception. Further, the question of the nature of the encyclical's authority as definitive Church teaching was complicated by Monsignor Ferdinando Lambruschini, who introduced the encyclical at a Vatican press conference on July 29, 1968, by announcing to those present that an "attentive reading of the encyclical does not suggest the theological note of infallibility."[6]

But the rough reception accorded Paul VI's birth control encyclical was hardly lightning in a cloudless July sky. Warning signs had been gathering for quite a while that arguments like those offered in *Humanae Vitae* were in danger of being dismissed as implausible, or at least as being in danger of being intellectually incomprehensible.

In 1964, four years before *Humanae Vitae*, the American moral theologian George J. Lynch (a Jesuit never accused of being a liberal) observed in the pages of *Theological Studies'* famed "Notes on Moral Theology" that there appeared to be a very real threat of schism among Catholic moral theologians over the Church's teaching on artificial birth control. Referring to the observations of fellow Jesuit moralist Gerald Kelley about the ecumenical problems posed by the Church's teaching on contraception, Lynch noted that this teaching was "based on a single principle—the fact of an established design which God Himself has written unchangeably into the natural structure of the conjugal act." This argument had been consistently affirmed by twentieth-century Catholic teaching, most recently by Pope Pius XII in his 1951 address to Italian midwives. But Lynch also observed that, despite the consistency and authoritative level of this teaching, it was becoming quite common to hear the "confident prophecy voiced intramurally" among his fellow Catholic theologians that the Church would soon change its official position on this complicated issue. And, he added with some concern, "it is not only lay 'liberals' who are lobbying the cause." Even some of his fellow Jesuit seminary professors were confessing that they also shared the most commonly voiced complaint regarding the Church's teaching on contraception, namely "that none of the rational arguments advanced in proof of the intrinsic evil of the practice is totally convincing. In honesty it must be admitted that the cogency of these arguments can be difficult to comprehend and even more difficult to communicate."[7]

In Lynch's estimation problems with the cogency of the rational arguments presented to condemn the practice was upsetting, of course, but not upsetting enough to warrant overturning current Church teaching. Lynch argued that the purpose of such rational arguments was not to discover the truth of the Church's teaching—that is, to discern whether or not the practice of contraception was intrinsically wrong—but "only the better to understand it for his own intellectual satisfaction. The truth itself we already have most securely from the constant and explicit teaching of the Church."[8]

Lynch was prescient in recognizing the chasm between the problematic arguments against contraception on the one hand, and the truth of the Church's teaching on the other. This conflict was a small cloud on the horizon that would soon cast a dark shadow over the entire American Catholic landscape. The reason for his worry about that small cloud, as Lynch well knew, was that Catholic moral teaching in the nineteenth and early twentieth centuries had presumed that, although the truths of the faith weren't necessarily "rational" in an Enlightenment sense, they were nonetheless *reasonable*; they were, in other words, capable of being "seized as deeply reasonable by the men of our day." Given the presence of faith on the part of the person receiving such teaching, the Catholic moral argument went, the believer could and should be able to understand the reasons adduced to justify the Church's teaching on moral matters. It was for *this* reason that Lynch's seemingly simple confession—that "in honesty it must be admitted that the cogency of these arguments can be difficult to comprehend and even more difficult to communicate"—now sounds more like the roar of distant guns than a simple plaint by a disgruntled academic.[9]

In the years before Vatican II Catholic moral theologians like Lynch understood their discipline as a science resting on the firmest evidence of all: an empirically knowable natural law that offered data for making moral decisions. God was the author of an eternal, immutable set of laws that governed the material universe as well as the moral actions undertaken within it. Indeed it might not be overstating the case to say that the moral science practiced by Lynch and his fellow Catholic moralists of the time operated on a principle very close to a moral naturalism, which posited an intrinsic connection between the external laws implanted by God in nature and the rules governing human right and wrong. This "science of moral theology" rested on an "objective moral order of immutable principles for all men and for all times and circumstances." The important things in the real world, in other words, remained ever the same throughout history, for everyone and at all times. Moral theology could thus justifiably call itself a science because it mined that objective moral order in a way very much like mineral scientists mining the earth to discover the physical properties of the natural elements.[10]

While this understanding of moral theology, resting on the reliability of reasonable laws built into the "facts of nature," might have been thought to be secure until the battles that were unleashed in 1968, cracks in its foundations had begun to appear well before the appearance of Humanae Vitae—and not only among "lay liberals," as Lynch himself had so discern-ingly noted.

Indeed the widespread nonreception by moral theologians of Humanae Vitae's arguments announced the presence of a historical consciousness among Catholic academics in a way analogous to the widespread reception of Vatican II's liturgical changes among lay Catholics. That historical con-sciousness made static and unchanging categories of right and wrong appear dated, forced, and (among many) implausible. The idea that God had implanted in the physical world "facts" of moral teaching that were as empirically discernible and verifiable as the laws of physics came to seem both intellectually naïve and theologically dangerous to many Catholic moralists by the mid-twentieth century.

Many of the American Catholic theologians who raised serious questions about the Church's stand on contraception in the years after 1968 argued that the model of natural law used to justify the teaching of Humanae Vitae rested on a simplistic and dated understanding of nature itself. Indeed many of the critics of Paul VI's encyclical would come to label its model of moral teaching "physicalism," as it attempted to adduce Christian morality from an outdated understanding of the physical structure of nature. This was problematic enough in itself, as it implied that the meaning and evaluation of human acts were somehow subservient to nonsentient physical laws in nature. To many moralists such an understanding of Christian morality risked relegating Christian moral teaching to being an afterthought to physical "facts" that were themselves amoral in meaning.[11]

But what made all of this even more problematic ("embarrassing" was the term some critics used) was the fact that Christian moralists who made such an appeal were using a model of the physical universe that most scientists by the end of the nineteenth century had simply discarded. The older model, usually labeled "Baconian," had understood science as the measurement of "hard" facts" (in the sense in which Lynch and his colleagues used the term), building on concrete and measurable physical components to construct a larger understanding of the universe in which each part remained stationary and knowable—like pinning butterflies to a board. But precisely that understanding of the physical universe had been abandoned after Darwin, Einstein, and especially Heisenberg, in favor of a much more porous and probabilistic understanding of the facts of nature. The newer understanding of the physical universe questioned whether the laws of nature *were* facts, at least in the sense of concrete truths that would always remain the same at all times and everywhere. The newer (post-Heisenberg) paradigm in physics, for example, understood light itself not as a discreet "thing" that always and everywhere behaved the same, but as sometimes manifesting the qualities of particles, and at other times waves. To that extent physicists ceased talking about the "facts" of the physical world in favor of discussions about the "probable activity" of particles and the "most likely" speed and direction of light waves. The "facts" of nature were thus the very opposite of "hard" data that always and everywhere remained the same. Thus Lynch's supposedly hard-nosed appeal to the facts of the moral universe seemed dated—perhaps embarrassingly so—if taken to be in any way analogous to how modern scientists understood the physical universe.[12]

Many Catholic moral theologians in the United States feared that the intellectual shortcomings (both as science and as theology) of such an understanding of the "science of morality" would breed a larger contempt for Church teaching in all of its forms. If the Church could be this intellectually dated on such an important question, they feared some would think, what else was it wrong about? If these ostensible "intellectual explanations" for moral teaching failed to convince Catholic moral theologians, what could one expect the theologically unsophisticated laity to make of it? Given the centuries-long dominance of that classical style of moral theology, its collapse came surprisingly quickly, and dramatically.

THE COLLAPSE OF THE "FACTS OF NATURE"

In 1964, the same year as the appearance of Lynch's article in *Theological Studies*, a Notre Dame law professor named John Noonan, who also happened to be a member of the international papal commission gathered by Pope John XXIII to study the question of the Church's position on birth control, finished the manuscript of a 533-page study that would be published under the title *Contraception*. John Ford, a Jesuit moral theologian and friend of Lynch, had pressed for Noonan's appointment to the papal commission as a scholar who would be "valuable to all of us." But Ford came to have second thoughts about his active support for the young law professor's presence on the Vatican commission when he received an advance copy of Noonan's manuscript, scheduled for publication the following year.[13]

Before actually reading Noonan's mammoth historical study, Ford believed that Noonan's work would supply important scholarly support for his, and Paul VI's, arguments against changing the Church's position on the topic. But in reaching the first of Noonan's famous (and unsettling) conclusions—that "it is a perennial mistake to confuse repetition of old formulas with the living law of the Church"—Ford realized that he would have to fly to Rome immediately to prepare for the blow Noonan's book would deliver to what would become the minority position on the papal birth control commission. Ford did just that, arriving in Rome in June 1964 for meetings with Vatican officials and with Paul VI himself. But even before he left for the Eternal City, Ford wrote to the pope's representative in Washington, D.C, the apostolic delegate Archbishop Egidio Vagnozzi, warning that Noonan's study seemed to raise unsettling questions about the viability and plausibility of older arguments that he and others, including Lynch and Kelley, had used to condemn contraception. In a breathtaking confession that now seems like the death knell of the approach to moral theology that had reigned in the Catholic Church for centuries, Ford simply announced, "We lack convincing arguments from natural law which are universally valid and universally admitted."[14]

Noonan, himself hardly a theological revolutionary, articulated the widespread sense, even among supporters of the Church's ban on contraception, that the older model of moral theology resting on the "facts of nature" could no longer do its job. And Noonan was not alone. A newer reading of natural law had already begun to spread among those whom it would be safe to describe as conservatives on the contraception question, a newer approach that achieved sophisticated form in the work of scholars such as Germain Grisez in the years immediately before and after the publication of *Humanae Vitae*.

Indeed Grisez himself was a major player in providing more plausible and flexible arguments in support of the Church's ban on contraception, recognizing well before the appearance of Paul VI's encyclical that it was difficult to argue that Christians could derive the *ought* from the *is*. That is, well before 1968 Grisez had begun to argue that the entire effort to derive moral principles (the *ought*) from the sheer facts of the physical universe (the *is*), as the older style of natural law had attempted, was a doomed project. Grisez therefore sought to lay out an altogether different set of arguments for intellectually buttressing the idea of natural law. In a brilliant work titled *Contraception and the Natural Law*, published in 1965, Grisez argued that human nature was less a "given" than a project undertaken in history toward certain "basic goods." Human nature, he thus argued with an eye toward more contemporary anthropological models of human evolution, was much better conceived as a fluid and progressive project rather than a static "thing." In one intellectual move Grisez thus pulled the intellectual rug out from under the feet of natural law moralists like Ford, Lynch, and Kelly. Human moral acts could not be judged as good or bad by simply studying physical acts. Moral theology was not a science that could mine the facts of the natural law, the way physical scientists could mine minerals in the earth.[15]

Indeed the "basic goods" that defined the morality of the human project could not be "proven" in any empirical or objective manner. Ethical meanings could not be rationally derived from the "data" of nature. Rather Grisez postulated certain "prescriptions" contained in natural law that were *undemonstrable* in any purely rational sense, but were nonetheless self-evidently necessary for ordering human life. These prescriptions included what he took to be self-evident truths, such as "Life is a good which is to be sought" and "Truth is a good which is to be sought." Precisely as "first principles of human action," such prescriptions could not be rationally proven in any observable sense by appeal to empirical acts, as moralists like Lynch and Kelly had come close to arguing. Rather Grisez argued that such prescriptions were self-evidently true to human reason. And precisely because they were part of the "radical, rational constitution of man, the goods they set for human action could not be directly attacked by man without his doing violation to his rational nature. To act against truth, to act against life, to act against procreation, was to deny part of man's rational nature."[16]

Grisez argued that one of these self-evidently true prescriptions, along with life and truth, was that "procreation is a good which ought to be sought." But in making precisely this argument about the good of procreation, Grisez was consciously distancing himself from the older Catholic natural law argument, which was that birth control was intrinsically disordered because it prevented the physical act from attaining its "natural end." Such an argument, he observed, was incapable of proof, since no rational argument could prove moral meanings from physical acts. Indeed the moral meanings of human acts could not be so simplistically discerned by human reason. No physical act in itself, such as shooting a gun at a person or taking material goods that another person owned, could in itself disclose, much less prove, the action taken as "intrinsically disordered," or indeed as intrinsically anything, at least morally. Indeed Grisez found such theological arguments both unconvincing and overly "naturalistic" in a naïvely simplistic way. He sought to find a more plausible intellectual model of natural law based on the moral obligation that human beings never act against essential or basic "human goods," which were undemonstrable from reason but were nonetheless self-evidently true and validated by universal human experience. The appeal, then, was less to human reason than to human experience.[17]

Grisez himself strongly supported Humanae Vitae's condemnation of contraception, but in his own arguments in support of the encyclical there was a noticeable intellectual distancing from its style of natural law reasoning. The malice of contraception, he argued, was not to be found in its violation of the fundamental structure of the conjugal act, nor even in the external act of using contraceptive devices. Its malice rested in involving the couple in a rejection of one of the most basic goods that defined human flourishing: the good of procreation. From Grisez's point of view the problem with arguments used by Paul VI's encyclical was that they appeared to presume that human beings could rationally discern the moral meaning of physical acts. But was the moral meaning of aiming a gun at another person always the same? What if the person holding the gun was defending children against a classroom intruder? A simple description of the physical activity of participants in such a scenario hardly uncovered a moral meaning analogous to a robber aiming a gun at unarmed passersby. The problem, from Grisez's point of view, was that such an argument wasn't plausible at all.

But Grisez also sought to distance his own support of the encyclical's teaching from a secondary line of philosophical argument utilized in condemning the grave moral evil that was contraception, and this was the phenomenological argument. This line of argument, intermingled with the classic natural law arguments, was less physicalist in analyzing the moral meanings of the physical act of married sexual intercourse. It was utilized most obviously in Article 12 of *Humanae Vitae*, which argued for two inseparable meanings of the sexual act, the unitive and the procreative, that the act itself (as an observable phenomenon) embodied. By focusing on the "intimate structure" of the conjugal act, which, "while most closely uniting husband and wife, capacitates them for the generation of new lives," it appealed less to the rational "ends" of the act than to the moral meanings of the "total giving" between spouses inscribed into the very structure of the act itself. But Grisez argued that it was very difficult, if not impossible, to argue that *every* historically conditioned human act could (or should) fully embody a single, much less total meaning that could determine its morality. All human acts, to the extent they were human, embodied a range of meanings, none of which could be taken as "total" in any final moral sense. And precisely because of that lack of totality, it was implausible to believe that each and every act of conjugal intercourse could embody the kind of "total giving" the encyclical seemed to make normative.[18]

Grisez's support of the encyclical thus witnessed to a widespread sense, even among its fervent supporters, that although its *teaching* regarding contraception might be accepted, the natural law arguments offered for that teaching were less than convincing. That sense of implausibility was shared by a number of American Catholic moral theologians who were far more critical of its teaching than was Germain Grisez. Thus Richard McCormick, in a widely read article in *Theological Studies* published shortly after *Humanae Vitae*'s appearance in 1968, offered a thoughtful and devastating extended reflection on its arguments.

McCormick, himself something like the dean of American Catholic moralists at the time and a professor at a seminary in the Midwest, observed that the encyclical's condemnation of contraception was, first of all, based on an embarrassingly dated understanding of biology: "It attributes a [moral] meaning to all coitus on the basis of what happens with relative rarity." How could the moral meaning of a physical act be derived from an end that the act achieved only rarely? He further noted that there was something close to a logical contradiction in the encyclical's allowance of what is usually called the "rhythm method" among Catholics, that is, of intentionally plotting the cycles of menstruation to determine the safe periods for coitus that would lessen the likelihood of pregnancy: "The encyclical seems unwittingly to imply a *factual* separation of the unitive and procreative aspects of individual coitus during the infertile period." Wasn't *any* separation of the unitive and procreative aspects of the sexual act precisely the stance condemned by the encyclical as "intrinsically disordered"? And if so, why was the factual separation of those two aspects allowable for the rhythm method, but not for other methods of controlling contraception? Was the use of a thermometer and calendar more "natural" than the use of a pill to achieve the same desired end? Further, McCormick agreed with Grisez that the encyclical's "physiological" criterion for measuring the moral meaning of human action was deeply problematic: "The criterion apparently inseparable from this analysis is an approach which measures the meaning of an act by examining its physiological structure." This seemed to McCormick deeply problematic as a moral standard for judging human (much less Christian) acts.[19]

But McCormick went considerably further than raising questions about the specific natural law arguments offered by the encyclical. He also offered an extended intellectual rumination on the crucial importance of *plausibility* in the Church's theological arguments explaining moral teaching: "If the analysis and argument used in an authoritative moral teaching on natural law do not support the conclusions [of that teaching], what is one to think of those conclusions?" This was precisely the dilemma of Catholic moral theologians like McCormick. The Catholic tradition of moral reasoning, which had relied for centuries on a natural law understanding of the *reasonableness* of morality, presumed that the human intellect could grasp the essential coherence and plausibility of the Church's stance on moral issues, as *Humanae Vitae* had declared in its own Article 12: "We believe that the men of our day are particularly capable of seizing the deeply reasonable and human character" of the inseparability of the unitive and procreative aspects of the marriage act. But Catholic moralists like McCormick could not, in fact, see how this very argument was deeply reasonable or even plausible:

> At the least, very many moral theologians will agree that there are serious methodological problems, even deficiencies, in the analysis used to support the conclusion [of the encyclical]. . . . It says in effect that the authoritative character of the teaching is not identified with the reasons adduced for it. On the other hand, it clearly implies that the certainty of the teaching cannot prescind from the adequacy of the analyses given. Establishing the proper balance is the problem we face.[20]

Widely respected within the American Catholic community both for his theological balance and for the depth of his mastery of the Catholic moral tradition, McCormick thus laid out two extremes that theologians had to avoid in considering official teaching. On the one hand, Catholic thinkers had to avoid the position that Church teaching was only as valid as the argument offered to explain it. This position made the pope simply another theologian, in the process destroying the ancient Catholic understanding that the pope received his teaching authority from Christ himself, as successor of St. Peter, to whom Jesus had entrusted the "keys to the Kingdom of Heaven." The pope's authority as teacher, in the traditional Catholic understanding of "magisterial" authority, did not rest on the sophistication of the pope's theological education or intellectual acuity, but on the promise of Jesus himself to be with the Church (and its leaders) always. On the other hand, McCormick argued that no Catholic theologian could claim that the authority of official teaching was *totally* independent of the arguments advanced to explain it. Such a position, which the mainstream tradition of Catholic moral theology had consistently rejected, made the pope into an arbitrary issuer of edicts. Indeed the Church had embraced the tradition of natural law after the thirteenth century to explain its moral teaching precisely *because* that tradition offered the promise of explaining—or even justifying—moral positions by an appeal to their *reasonability* within the stance of faith. Thus if *Humanae Vitae* was not infallible teaching, as Monsignor Lambruschini had stated at its promulgation, could the encyclical be accepted as valid completely independently of the reasons and arguments advanced to explain it? If that were the case, then the very possibility of faithful dissent from that teaching would be eliminated on principle. The problem with the latter option was that the papal tradition of authority had allowed for just such dissent since the Middle Ages.[21]

In McCormick's estimation the theological arguments offered in Paul VI's encyclical condemning contraception seemed not only doubtful, but intellectually threadbare. Like Grisez, an unlikely ally, McCormick observed:

> The vast majority of theologians will conclude that the analyses of *Humanae Vitae* build upon an unacceptable identification of natural law with natural processes. That is, they will assert that the argument does not justify the conclusion. . . . At this point, the theologian's docility will stimulate him to ask: can the intrinsic immorality of contraception be established in some more reasonable way, and on other grounds?[22]

"A SUPREMELY IMPORTANT, INTRINSIC, AND NECESSARY DUTY"

Richard McCormick's prediction that the majority of moral theologians would most probably conclude that Paul VI's natural law reasoning was unacceptable was something of an understatement. But his incisive recognition of the encyclical's "unacceptable identification of natural law with natural processes" was but the tip of a considerably larger theological iceberg, an iceberg Bernard Lonergan had described the year before the encyclical even appeared, which he identified as the "historicist" worldview. That new worldview, and the historical consciousness that defined it, represented an alternative, if not opposing, conception to the older classicist understanding of how the real world operated. That older conception had posited a static and immutable reality at the heart of *things*—the very word *things* bespeaking a *givenness* to the real world that human reason could recognize and organize into a science. But again, just as Lonergan had so presciently prophesied, that classicist worldview was "no longer the only conception, or [even] the commonly received conception." And many of the presuppositions of that older classicist worldview were to be found in Paul VI's encyclical "on human life": that judging the goodness and badness of human acts could be determined by rationally identifying the ends of physiological acts; that moral reality could be "objectively" determined because it rested on unchanging human essences and static social truths;

that God's purposes and intentions for humankind could be appropriated through the rational study of an immutable "natural law" found in the physical world itself. All of those classicist presuppositions now seemed problematic to many American Catholic moral theologians, both among those who supported the conclusions of the 1968 encyclical, whatever its arguments, and among those who did not.

McCormick called for establishing the plausibility of *Humanae Vitae*'s teaching on contraception "in some more acceptable way, and on other grounds." Literally dozens of Catholic moralists took up his call, from every imaginable point on the Catholic theological spectrum. But arguably the most balanced, thoughtful, and helpful contribution was offered a full decade later, in 1978, by an American Catholic theologian noted for his nonideological commitment to conversation and by his centrist position on most theological questions: Joseph Komonchak.

Komonchak, a professor of theology at the Catholic University of America (CUA), argued that a better model for grounding Church teaching than that found in Paul VI's 1968 encyclical could be found in how ecumenical councils like Vatican II proceeded. If nothing else, the overwhelmingly positive reception accorded to the reforms of Vatican II showed that frontloading process considerations—with free and open debate—had avoided the kind of divisive reception accorded Paul VI's teaching on contraception just three years later. Komonchak noted that in the process followed by Vatican II, the issues at stake were openly debated, and inadequate or prejudicial expressions had been challenged, with unconvincing arguments exposed and refuted. Chief among the strengths of this approach to formulating Church teaching was that it recognized the centrality of

> the relationship between doctrinal authority and theological reasoning. The classical view of the magisterium places an enormous emphasis on the formal authority of the pope and bishops, whose teachings are said to have an authority independent of, and superior to, the reasons they do or even can advance in support of them. But even here, it should be noted, the theological reasoning employed in the preparation and expression of a [given] teaching has great significance for the interpretation of the teaching itself, and even for an evaluation of its authority.[23]

Komonchak thus took up precisely the point McCormick had made: that many of *Humanae Vitae*'s supporters argued that the encyclical should be welcomed by the faithful because of Jesus' promised "aid of the Spirit" in guiding the teaching of the Church, however faulty or clouded human understanding may be in perceiving the plausibility of that teaching. Such aid of the Spirit was indeed welcome, Komonchak observed, but in no way excused the pope or any other teacher in the Church from utilizing the most plausible theological explanations in presenting and interpreting Christ's message in history. On the contrary, he argued, "the intrinsic necessity of theological reasoning in the magisterial process should also mean that it is *not* illegitimate to ask of an authorized teacher: 'Why do you teach this? How did you arrive at this conclusion? How is [this teaching] related to the central truths of the gospel?'"[24]

While allowing that theological reflection on the role of "receiving" Church teaching by the faithful was still in its infancy, Komonchak nonetheless observed that it was inadequate, and profoundly un-Catholic, to reduce faithful reception of Church teaching to simple silent obedience. Indeed the Catholic understanding of Church teaching had always emphasized "the necessity of its theological reasoning, which is why Pope Paul [VI] recently spoke of this [reasoning] as a 'supremely important, intrinsic, and necessary duty of the ecclesial magisterium.'" Indeed Komonchak observed that Paul VI himself had declared both before and after issuing *Humanae Vitae* that Church teaching, what Catholics termed the *magisterium,* "must have theological reasons behind what it teaches."[25]

From Komonchak's point of view, the problem with Paul VI's encyclical was "*not* in its effort to derive a moral imperative from an understanding of the physical structure of the reproductive process." On this point at least Komonchak was closer to the pope than either McCormick or Grisez. Rather the problem with the encyclical's intellectual arguments was its *incoherence in applying those arguments*. As Komonchak read the encyclical, its most fundamental teaching was that "what God has established for the reproduction of the race must always be respected." This position, he observed, would reasonably seem to imply not only that each and every conjugal act, during both fertile and infertile periods, had to remain open to the transmission of new life, but also that this teaching had to be *internalized* by faithful Christian couples. That is, this fundamental teaching must be observed by couples in both form and intent. But that fundamental position, taken by the pope, would seem to be "as directly contravened by [intentional] systematic abstinence during fertile periods as it is by other artificial procedures. If, however, the restriction of intercourse to infertile periods is permissible, it is difficult to see why other measures may not also be permitted."[26]

As Komonchak read the encyclical (agreeing with McCormick on this point at least), the allowance of "natural" family planning (the rhythm method) appeared to undercut the very thing that made moral acts *moral*: the *intention* of the couple to hold the unitive and procreative aspects of their marriage act together. If the very intention of their lovemaking was to separate those two aspects of coitus, however open they might be toward having a child should their efforts prove futile, it was difficult to see why other forms of birth control, based on other "natural" methods of contraception, such as the pill, might not also be considered legitimate if the couples involved were equally open to new life should their contraceptive methods prove a failure. In Komonchak's view, the encyclical would have had more intellectual coherence if it had forbidden *all* forms of contraceptive practice, including purportedly "natural" methods like the rhythm method. But failing such a new prohibition, *Humanae Vitae* undercut its own intellectual arguments in explaining why contraception was "intrinsically disordered."[27]

Janet Smith offered the closest analogue to Komonchak's "centrist" analysis from the "Catholic Right" in a collection of articles she edited titled *Why "Humanae Vitae" Was Right*. In her article "Pope John Paul II and *Humanae Vitae*," Smith took up the efforts of Paul VI's much revered successor in the Chair of Peter, John Paul II, to explain why the 1968 encyclical *was* correct in its teaching regarding contraception, however flawed the arguments offered to explain that teaching. Smith herself confessed at the outset of the article that traditional Catholic natural law defenders of *Humanae Vitae* often found John Paul's "defense" of that teaching "hard going, because he does not explicitly use Thomas's method or vocabulary." And she allowed that the 1968 encyclical had followed the Thomistic pattern of "linking eternal law, natural law, and human law" in constructing an argument that held that human behavior must follow "the laws of nature, which are the laws of God." But she then confessed that John Paul had simply ignored that manner of linking natural law with human morality in favor of utilizing the phenomenological "language of the body" to talk about human sexuality and contraception. For Pope John Paul, she noted, the body was the "expression of the human person." Thus in his *Reflections on "Humanae Vitae*," John Paul had argued that human beings must use "the expression of the body honestly, and that there must be a correspondence between what our bodies do and what . . . true lovers intend."

Such an argument, Smith observed, showed that "there is more than one way to get to Rome, more than one way to discover and teach the truth."[28]

But Smith also confessed that John Paul's defense of the encyclical's condemnation of contraception was anomalous in terms of its avoidance of the arguments pressed by the encyclical itself: "There is something in his manner of proceeding which is somewhat foreign to Thomists." John Paul II's approach in fact consistently *avoided* Thomistic natural law terminology and argumentation, instead using "common language to analyze human experience, and by means of this analysis to unfold basic truths of existence." This consistent avoidance of natural law argumentation by the pope is never explained or justified by Smith; she only notes that John Paul

> does not begin with the principles of natural law. The pope's entry is different; he starts with a statement of value which he expects all to accept. He starts with the principle that man has an intrinsic value, and that it is never right to treat him as a means to an end. His foremost concern is how each and every act we perform conforms with what is in accord with what human dignity demands.[29]

In Smith's view, John Paul II's *Reflections on "Humanae Vitae,"* sought to buttress the teachings of the 1968 encyclical, but attempted to do so by using "first principles" very different from those offered by the encyclical itself, and also different from those offered by Germain Grisez. Further, she noted that the pope never explicitly repudiated the natural law arguments offered by the encyclical, but rather incorporated the presuppositions of those arguments into a newer, "personalist" approach. The end result was something considerably different from the arguments offered in 1968: a "language of the body" that offered a different rationale for the condemnation of contraception. John Paul II's condemnation of contraceptive practice was based on the

> central Catholic doctrine which he reiterates: that man and woman are not just souls within bodies, but that the human person is the union of the soul and the body. . . . The argument in [John Paul's] *Reflections on Humanae Vitae* is that we must use the expressions of the body honestly, and that there must be a correspondence between what our bodies do and what we, as true lovers, intend. It is in this context that John Paul II uses the phrase "language of the body."

He wants to teach us what the truth is we should be expressing with our bodies in our sexual relationships.[30]

Much like the argument advanced by George Lynch four decades earlier, Smith's presentation of John Paul II's defense of the encyclical appeared to presuppose that such a defense was not undertaken to discover the truth of Church teaching, but only to understand it for our intellectual satisfaction. But Smith's often brilliant exposition of a more plausible rationale for the teaching of the 1968 encyclical sought to provide precisely an argument thar might be "universally valid and universally recognized" by believers—perhaps even seen as "deeply reasonable." But this very fact witnessed to her sense, shared by many defenders of *Humanae Vitae*, that the arguments adduced for its teaching were less than accessible, or convincing, to many of its readers.

"MORE THAN ONE WAY TO GET TO ROME"

One could make a fairly strong argument that the most prophetic voice within the guild of American Catholic moral theology in the twentieth century was John Ford. Ford had, quite presciently, observed to the Apostolic Delegate in 1964, four years before the appearance of *Himanae Vitae*, that, in terms of the arguments used by the Church to condemn contraceptive practice, "we lack convincing arguments from natural law which are universally valid and universally admitted." Ford, himself a lifelong supporter of the Church's stance on contraception, utilized his considerable mastery of the art of neoscholastic casuistry to make certain that the teaching of the 1968 encyclical would remain normative Catholic teaching. His recognition of the implausibility, or at least the intellectual thinness, of the natural law arguments utilized by the Church in the years before the "birth control encyclical" (and utilized by that encyclical itself) correctly portended a fierce, four-decades-long battle within North American Catholicism over precisely the question of the validity of the theological arguments offered to support this teaching.

It is now common practice in rehearsing these intramural and oftentimes quite acrimonious debates to label defenders of the encyclical's teaching, such as Ford and Grisez, conservatives and to refer to theologians who questioned the plausibility of the encyclical's teaching, such as McCormick and Komonchak, liberals. The use of these essentially political labels may be understandable, but it actually hides as much as it reveals. There is nothing in Grisez's radical rethinking of the Catholic natural law tradition that can be reasonably termed conservative in itself, nor is there anything in Komonchak's quite balanced and historically grounded ecclesiological reflections that can really be termed liberal or progressive, especially given his constant appeal to a universal council of the Church whose teachings had been promulgated by the very pope who had issued the 1968 encyclical. Thus those who ascribe the rocky reception of the encyclical in the North American Church to a cabal of leftist theologians challenging papal teaching authority actually miss the deeper energies that fueled the debate. The encyclical certainly *did* unleash widespread debates about ecclesial authority and the meanings of assent to magisterial teaching on the part of the Catholic faithful. But the critical response to *Humanae Vitae* on the part of so many Catholic theologians cannot be dismissed so easily with an appeal to the "paranoid style of history," which tends to ascribe bitter historical conflicts to plots by institutional and social malcontents.[31]

What all of these postencyclical theological efforts actually reveal is a widespread sense, along a wide spectrum of Catholic moralists, that the older static and classical concepts and arguments from neoscholastic natural law could no longer provide a believable substructure for Catholic moral teaching. It was precisely the "timeless" categories presupposed in those natural law arguments in the encyclical—timeless categories of science, evidence, and even of moral reasoning—that now appeared naïve, or at least dated and implausible. The decades-long attempts by Catholic thinkers as diverse as Richard McCormick, Germain Grisez, Joseph Komonchak, and Janet Smith to respond *reasonably* (and thereby critically) to the encyclical's teaching demonstrates a fairly diffuse sense of intellectual unease with its arguments. Something deeper and more fundamental can thus be glimpsed in these efforts to respond to the encyclical precisely as responsible Catholic theologians to the chief teacher in the Church: the sense that historical consciousness was now the coin of the realm among many, if not most, Catholic thinkers in North America. The timeless categories of classical thought that had served the Church so well for so long now served the Church badly, an evaluation shared even by defenders of *Humanae Vitae*. The failure of Church leaders to understand this would lead to a deep fissure within the household of faith itself, a fissure with tragic consequences. Among the most famous of these battles would be played out at the Catholic University of America, in what would come to be termed the "Charles Curran Affair."

4

The Charles Curran Affair

LOYAL DISSENT AND THE "RESPONSE TO HUMAN LIFE"

On the very afternoon on which *Humanae Vitae* was formally published, July 29, 1968, Father Charles Curran, a rising star in the field of moral theology teaching at the Catholic University of America (CUA) in Washington, D.C., obtained a copy of the full text.[1] He immediately convened a meeting of his colleagues at Caldwell Hall, the faculty residence for priests on campus, during which they read the encyclical and drafted a response to it. This impressively quick work was followed by another of astonishing transcontinental alacrity, especially in an era before the Internet and faxes. Those present at the Caldwell Hall meeting were commissioned to call colleagues across the country to invite input on the final wording of a statement they intended to make public the following morning. Thus it was that by 3 a.m. on the morning of July 30 the group of CUA theologians had obtained a number of suggestions for "cleaning up" the final version of the text, as well as eighty-seven signatures of other theologians supporting the document. In addition to these, the one hundred members of the Association of Washington Priests would likewise issue a public statement that they intended to support the "dissenting position" crafted by Curran and several dozen other scholars. Several hours later, Curran himself presided at a press conference at the Mayflower Hotel in Washington. Thus began l'affaire Curran, one of the more interesting episodes in the history of American Catholic theology in the twentieth century.[2]

Judged by the standards of other protest documents produced in the United States in the 1960s, the statement handed out to the press at the Mayflower Hotel was a rather tame affair, hardly the theological "revolt" that the press so breathlessly predicted in its coverage of the morning's events. Indeed the document handed out to the press that morning began with a blunt confession: "As Roman Catholic theologians we respectfully acknowledge a distinct role of the hierarchical [teaching office] in the Church of Christ." The signatories went to some pains to point out that "many positive values concerning marriage are expressed" in *Humanae Vitae*. But the statement also observed that the "Christian tradition assigns theologians the special responsibility of evaluating and interpreting pronouncements of the magisterium in light of the total theological data operative in each question or statement." It was in this docile spirit that the theologians who had signed the statement offered some "initial comments" on Paul VI's encyclical.[3]

The first of these comments was that, because the encyclical did not purport to be infallible teaching, it was instructive to note that "history shows that a number of statements of similar or even greater authoritative weight have subsequently been proven inadequate or even erroneous." This historical observation was followed by examples of "authoritative" teaching that had subsequently been determined to be erroneous: the Church's condemnation of interest-taking on money, the condemnation of the idea of freedom of conscience for non-Catholics in Catholic countries, and the condemnation of the "right to silence" on the part of accused parties in judicial proceedings. Although few readers of the statement at the time, either in Rome or at the Mayflower Hotel, took much notice of this brief list, one could easily read it as witnessing to the kind of historical consciousness Bernard Lonergan had outlined the year before, a consciousness almost literally unintelligible to those inhabiting a classicist universe. For those who still lived in such a static universe—and there were many both in Rome and in American episcopacy who held on to that way of seeing the world—the very possibility that the Church could change its mind about important matters (especially sexual matters) was a position from which "average" believers had to be protected.[4]

But it was in paragraph 4 of the statement that the dissenting theologians, as they were soon to be labeled by both Rome and the American press, offered the first of their substantive criticisms. In light of the Second Vatican Council's privileging of the "People of God" metaphor to describe the Church, a metaphor broadly egalitarian in spirit, what did the encyclical's appeal to the "Church's experience" to condemn contraceptive practice *mean*? If the experience of real lay people had been ignored in offering the encyclical's position on contraception, what did it mean to say that "the Church" understood its moral tradition to prohibit contraception? That appeal seemed at best hollow and at worst like an effort to defend yet another teaching that many Catholic Christians now took to be "inadequate, or even erroneous":

> The encyclical consistently assumes that the church is identical with the hierarchical office. No real importance is afforded . . . the life of the church in its totality; the special witness of many Christian couples is neglected. . . . Furthermore, the encyclical betrays a narrow positivistic notion of papal authority, as illustrated by the rejection of the majority view presented by the commission established to consider the question, as well as by the rejection of the conclusions of a large part of the international Catholic theological community.[5]

But the most substantive criticism offered in their document was aimed squarely at the "specific ethical conclusions contained in the encyclical." In the opinion of the theologians who had signed the document, those conclusions were based on "an inadequate concept of natural law"; indeed the very fact that there *were* other, less static and classical approaches to natural law was totally ignored. In fact advocates of other kinds of natural law teaching "come to different conclusions on this very question." Further, the dissenting academics pointed out a number of serious theological *and* scientific problems in the encyclical. There was in *Humanae Vitae* an overemphasis on the "biological aspects of conjugal relations as ethically normative," as well as an undue stress on sexual acts "viewed in themselves and apart from the person and the couple." But there was also a new element in their list of criticisms, an element focused on the idea that church teaching couldn't remain static if it was really to faithfully bear witness to the eternal truths of the gospel. In their minds, the experience of Vatican II had proved precisely this point, which Paul VI's encyclical seemed to ignore. Indeed, just below the surface of their statement there seemed to lurk the fear that Paul VI sought to identify Catholic Christianity with a static understanding of truth that was now largely discredited among the vast majority of Catholic theologians. In their view, *Humanae Vitae* seemed to presuppose

> a static worldview which downplays the historical and evolutionary character of humanity in its finite existence, as described in Vatican II's pastoral constitution on "The Church in the Modern World.". . . In actual fact, the encyclical demonstrates no development over the

teaching of Pius XI's "Casti Connubii," whose conclusions have been called into question for grave and serious reasons.[6]

Viewed within the context of later Catholic responses to the encyclical, the statement of dissent released at the Mayflower Hotel that July morning appears measured, respectful, and even rather conservative. Compared with, say, the editorial in the August 17 issue of *America* magazine published two weeks later, which offered a deeply unflattering comparison between Paul VI and President Lyndon Johnson, the Mayflower press release appeared downright docile. "Breaking with the past," the *America* editorial observed, "is always difficult; but not breaking, in these times, appears equally hazardous." Just as President Johnson had wisely decided not to run for reelection, the editorial implied, perhaps the time had come for the pope to do something similar and simply step aside for a new pope more in tune with the times. John Noonan, himself a member of the papal commission formed to investigate the question of contraception, observed in a much commented-on interview in the *National Catholic Reporter*:

> [It is,] to say the least, surprising that what is alleged to be the design of God could only be discovered in the utmost secrecy of a military character and without subjecting the statement of the alleged design of God to the scrutiny of [those] moral theologians who are experts in the matter, or the comment of the faithful who would be expected to carry out the orders given.[7]

Pat and Patty Crowley, the Chicago couple who served with Noonan on the papal commission, likewise weighed in after the encyclical's appearance. They voiced their deep disappointment that Paul VI had decided to listen to a very small minority of ("frightened") members of the commission to offer teaching that seemed to them largely negative and scolding, especially given that there was such a need for "a more positive pedagogy on marriage." Likewise Michael Novak, a public intellectual who would eventually switch sides in the intramural battle within the American Church, confessed his own intellectual confusion over the encyclical's condemnation of contraceptive devices like the pill while allowing the rhythm method as a legitimate approach to Christian contraception. Why, Novak asked,

> is it "unnatural" to block the spatial flow of the sperm so that it does not fertilize the ovum, and yet not "unnatural" to time the placement

of the sperm so that it does not fertilize an ovum[?] In either case human intelligence is directing the process so that the ovum will not be fertilized. In the first case a physical spatial object is inserted in the process; in the second case an equally physical temporal gap is deliberately inserted in the process. I do not understand why spatial objects are blameworthy, while temporal gaps are not. Both are equally "natural" (or "unnatural").[8]

Literally dozens of other responses, many far harsher and more pointedly critical of the pope's letter than these, appeared within weeks of the encyclical's appearance. But the reader of these responses, many offered by respected scholars who had spent their academic lives studying the Church's tradition of moral theology, can also detect a disconnect in the debate that followed. The two sides that formed literally within hours of the encyclical's appearance often seemed to be arguing past each other, using the same words, appealing to the same Catholic tradition of moral reasoning, invoking the same revered authors, but never really connecting. Indeed one quickly gets the sense that the debate involved something deeper, something considerably more fundamental than the moral status of contraceptive practice within the Roman Church.

Some scholars have posited that what was really going on in the escalating exchange of words was a debate about the relationship of Church teaching to academic theology, or more exactly the relationship of belief to the explanations offered to justify that belief. Could and should the faithful demand, or at least expect, reasonable explanations of the doctrines offered by hierarchical teachers in the Church? And if those teachers couldn't offer explanations that were convincing, or at least plausible, what claim did that teaching have on the consciences of the faithful? Other scholars have interpreted what would soon be termed "the Curran Affair" as being about a rearguard action to put a halt to the democratic impulses unleashed by Vatican II, and thus an attempt to recentralize authority in Rome, and especially in the papal teaching office. In this interpretation of events, Paul VI (and others far more conservative than he in the Roman Curia) now feared that too many people were claiming a voice in offering "definitive readings" of Church teaching, potentially confusing and scandalizing the faithful, and thus a clear line had to be drawn in the theological sand. Still others have explained the Curran Affair as being about two competing magisteria (or teaching authorities) within the Church, a tension that had been present since the Middle Ages but that now came to a head in the buoyant atmosphere after Vatican II. Many theologians took the council's more democratic metaphor for explaining the reality of the Church ("the People of God") to be a belated recognition of their own central role in explaining the faith to the Church itself. But what if the professional theologians, charged with explaining official teaching to both laity and Church leaders not trained in theology, found significant reasons for dissenting from the interpretation of doctrine offered by the pope and bishops? What exactly was the duty of those theologians in such a position of intellectual dissent? Was it to their own consciences, which St. Thomas Aquinas himself had argued? To "teach with the Church," as popes in the nineteenth and early twentieth centuries understood to mean "in accordance with the teaching of the papacy"? Or was their duty to sponsor a public debate about the disputed teaching and to caution Rome that its interpretation of doctrine was implausible? Yet others have interpreted the bitter exchanges that would shortly follow as being about the fear that the Church would change its mind on important moral questions. If the Church could change its position about something as important as this, what other teaching might eventually be changed?[9]

All of these explanations get at important aspects of the debate that quickly came to focus on the person of Charles Curran himself, a priest in good standing of the diocese of Rochester, New York. But all of these explanations also miss something important, indeed something crucial, for explaining the bitterness, the emotion, and the sense of disconnect one finds in the debates that dominated the next decade of American Catholicism. Why was it that the dramatic changes introduced by Vatican II in the celebration of the Mass—changes many bishops had feared would scandalize and alienate Catholics who believed that the Church had always worshipped in the way they were then accustomed to—had gone so well, while the Church's simple reiteration of teaching on an issue many had considered a settled question for half a century sparked what the press termed a revolt? Why, too, did Charles Curran, a celibate priest with no personal horse in the race of contraception, emerge as the center of the storm rather than, say, respected married couples like the Crowleys of Chicago, who had been important players on the international Catholic scene since John XXIII appointed them to the commission to study this very question?

Positing historical consciousness as the real issue in the bitter debates over birth control offers a number of compelling explanations for understanding what ensued. First, scholars such as Curran and Noonan had developed a well-honed historical sense in their studies of the Catholic moral tradition, which attuned them to the fact that Catholic teaching on significant moral issues not only could but indeed had developed and changed over the course of its long history. Though not "historicists" in the strict sense of believing that the history of any phenomenon was all that was needed to understand it, they nonetheless had encountered enough examples of significant change in Church teaching to warrant Noonan's famous statement that it was a "perennial mistake to confuse repetition of old formulas with the living law of the Church." In other words, moral theologians like Curran simply knew too much history to believe that the Church had remained the same on every aspect of its moral teaching over the course of centuries.

Second, historical consciousness helps to explain the ferocious tone of the bitter battles between liberals and conservatives in the decade after 1968. Alarmed Church leaders and conservative theologians, who thought of Catholic doctrine and moral teaching in timeless, static categories, recognized that something very different, and possibly heretical, was being offered in the theological challenges of the "Mayflower Statement." What they did not agree on was the source and meaning of those challenges. Some saw it as the reappearance of "modernism," a form of Catholic intellectual progressivism denounced by Pope Pius X in 1907. Others argued that the challenges rested on a deep-seated form of philosophical "relativism," which denied the possibility of ever achieving certitude on any moral or theological question (i.e., "Everything is relative"). Still others argued that the challenges to ecclesial teaching posed by scholars like Curran proceeded from an overemphasis on individual freedom that was rampant in American popular culture, "infecting" American Catholicism with a distrust of all forms of authority—even Church authority. The very fact that those who grew increasingly alarmed by the widespread rejection of "authoritative teaching" after 1968 couldn't agree on the source of that rejection contributed to the frantic feeling that the very foundations of Catholic moral and theological teaching were being attacked, and perhaps not by mere flesh and blood. As historical studies of other eras of Church history have shown so convincingly, the absence of a clear understanding of the reasons for theological disagreement, under some conditions at least, leads not to fierce debate but to witch hunts.[10]

Third, seeing historical consciousness as the impulse for these disagreements allows us to understand the stakes as both sides came to understand them. Lovers of the seemingly eternal verities offered by Catholic

Christianity believed—too sanguinely, it turned out—that the triumph of a static, unchanging approach to Catholic theology and morality had been definitively won well before the twentieth century. Questions about the mutability of belief, they believed, had been faced and defeated by a long and revered line of popes and councils starting early in the nineteenth century. The sudden appearance of widespread revolt among the clergy themselves on points of teaching supposedly settled by the hierarchy seemed like willful disobedience, or even personal betrayal.

Dissident theologians pressing their discontent with static teaching felt that a mature and historically attuned awareness of change—change in the world, in science, and in Church teaching—had been put off long enough and needed to be addressed in a formal, even public way. The Second Vatican Council had seemingly legitimized acknowledgment of that fact for Catholic Christians, and especially for Catholic theologians. Offering old answers in new situations, as many felt that *Humanae Vitae* attempted to do in offering the same arguments in 1968 that Pope Pius XI had offered to the Church decades before, simply would not do. The times presented new critical challenges, and the Church needed to offer new critical answers, some of which would undoubtedly be *discontinuous* with teaching offered in the past, thus avoiding that "perennial mistake" of confusing repetition of old formulas with the living law of the Church. And no one believed such a repetition to be a mistake more fervently than the Reverend Charles Curran.

MORAL THEOLOGY AND ACADEMIC FREEDOM

The "Mayflower Statement" released to the press on July 30 may indeed have been an unlikely document to begin a revolution, but the fact that Charles Curran quickly emerged as the leader of the revolt was somewhat less surprising. At the age of thirteen Curran had entered a high school seminary in the diocese of Rochester, from which he graduated as valedictorian. From there he had entered St. Bernard's Seminary ("called, not always affectionately, 'The Rock'"), which he later described thus:

[Our life] was regulated by the bell, and our days were essentially unvaried: early rising, meditation and mass, breakfast, a short break, classes, examination of conscience in church, lunch, recreation, more classes, rosary and spiritual reading in chapel, dinner, study time, night prayer in chapel, and lights out before ten. . . . I was quite happy in this routine. I was devout, even adding additional devotional practices.[11]

Every year the diocese of Rochester sent two of its seminarians to Rome to study for ordination at the North American College. The "NAC," as the college was called by its students and alumni, had the reputation among American priests generally as a hothouse for promising seminarians training to be bishops by seeing firsthand how the home office was run in Rome. Curran, a brilliant student who had carried most of the academic prizes in both his high school and college seminary classes, was unsurprisingly one of the two in his year chosen to go to Rome. He thus spent the years 1955 to 1961 living at the NAC and taking courses at the Jesuit-sponsored Gregorian University, where lectures were delivered in Latin to an international student body, many of whom would soon be bishops, diocesan chancellors, or seminary professors back in their home dioceses. These future Church leaders were thus exposed to some of the most influential theologians teaching in the Eternal City. Among the heavy hitters teaching at the Gregorian at the time was the German Jesuit Franz Hurth, who was reputed to have been the primary author of Pius XI's 1930 encyclical condemning artificial contraception. Curran would later recall, "Even as seminarians we were aware that Hurth was the primary author of all of Pius XII's addresses and papal pronouncements on moral theology." Curran was a student of Hurth's in very large lecture classes whose dynamics not only militated against any give and take between professor and students, but positively discouraged any such discussion. Even so, Curran, the brilliant and eager young seminarian clearly destined for academic prominence, occasionally talked to the formidable German professor outside of class.[12]

In contrast to Hurth was fellow German Jesuit Josef Fuchs, who taught Curran's course on sexual morality. Though strongly supporting Catholic teaching in the area of sexual morality, Fuchs nonetheless offered a somewhat different approach to the subject than Hurth. Fuchs emphasized the intrinsic relationship of sexuality to the whole of Christian life, seeing sexuality as part of the life of discipleship itself, and not just a potential arena of sinful activity that had to be confessed to a priest. Curran observed, "Some of my classmates at the North American College got to know Fuchs much better than I did at the time, but later I became quite friendly [with him.]" This later friendship with Fuchs in fact would be emblematic of the theological direction in which Curran was moving. Years later (in 1968, to be exact), while visiting the Catholic University of America to give a lecture, Fuchs was happy to see that Curran had matured in his theological views, telling him, "I can remember when you were as rigid as a telephone pole."[13]

Curran was ordained a priest in Rome in July 1958, after which he was informed by his bishop that he would stay in Rome to study for a doctorate in moral theology in order to return to "The Rock" to teach seminarians himself. At the time Curran had just finished reading an Italian translation of a two-volume work on moral theology, Bernard Haring's *The Law of Christ*, and decided that he wanted to approach the Catholic moral tradition in a similar way. Haring had proposed a "person-centered" approach to understanding morality rather than an "act-centered" one. That is, rather than measuring moral right and wrong by lists of actions taken or avoided, he proposed a holistic approach to understanding the Christian life that brought together morality, spirituality, scripture, and the sacraments. Haring's approach was thus less centered on individual acts than on what kind of *believer* performed those acts. How were specific actions emblematic of the faith life of a believer, and how were they embodiments of a life of discipleship? Curran's decision to undertake a career in moral theology after the manner of Fuchs and Haring coincided with other, broader impulses taking shape in his mind and heart. As Curran himself remembered it later:

> I had already begun to move beyond the pre–Vatican II neoscholastic approaches to Catholicism. As a seminarian in Rome I had become quite conscious of the human side of the church, and had begun to recognize the significance of historical development in both theology and the life of the church. Pious Catholics visiting Rome would occasionally comment that it must be a great privilege to study in Rome and have such an opportunity to grow in faith. . . . But by the time I left Rome in 1961, I was conscious that the church was not only human but sinful. I was still a very committed Catholic, but I recognized the pilgrim nature of the church—that it is always in need of reform, an important concept which Vatican II brought to the fore.[14]

Ever the brilliant student, Curran wrote two dissertations while in Rome. But it was his doctoral dissertation at the Alfonsian Academy on a

seemingly arcane topic, "The Concept of Invincible Ignorance in Alphonsus Liguori," that is most pertinent to later events. And the implications of
what he discovered in researching his dissertation on Liguori were anything but arcane. Indeed one might argue that his research profoundly
influenced his later role as the leader of the faithful opposition to *Humanae Vitae*. Curran recognized that during the eighteenth century there had
been, as there were in the 1960s, sharp disagreements between "reliable"
Catholic authorities as to the gravity and even the moral meaning of specific acts. What some Catholic moralists in the time of Alphonsus Liguori
had declared to be intrinsically sinful and disordered, other, equally
"sound" Catholic authorities had viewed as morally neutral. Thus the static
understanding of Catholic moral theology, which had informed Curran's
approach to Catholic moral theology when he had arrived in Rome as a
seminarian, was simply not borne out by the historical record. Studying
Liguori led Curran to believe that the subjective aspect of human acts can
be just as important as the "objective facts" in judging the morality of
human activity. As St. Alphonsus himself had discovered centuries before,
the intentions and worldview of penitents coming to confession had to be
taken into account in judging the rightness or wrongness of human acts,
no less than the actions themselves.[15]

In September 1961 Curran returned to St. Bernard's Seminary to teach
moral theology. But he returned to his alma mater a changed man.

> My six years in Rome, especially my last two in doctoral work, signif-
> icantly colored my approach to moral theology. First, I rejected the
> narrow scope of the [nineteenth-century] manuals of moral the-
> ology, with their focus on training confessors in the sacrament of
> penance. Moral theology had to deal with the whole of the Christian
> life, especially the call to continual conversion, as Bernard Haring
> insisted. . . . I had also become aware of historical consciousness, with
> its recognition of the importance of the particular, and the recogni-
> tion of the historical embeddedness of every human thinker and
> knower.[16]

Surprisingly, given the static understanding of moral theology that pre-
vailed in those years just before the Second Vatican Council, the other
priests on the faculty of St. Bernard's both welcomed their young colleague
and encouraged him to write about his newer approach to Christian morality
for a larger audience. And Curran did just that, producing work that led

to a growing list of important speaking engagements, starting with his
invitation to speak at an ecumenical gathering of Protestant and Catholic
theologians (the first of its kind) at Harvard University in 1963. This led to
a 1964 lecture to the Catholic Club of Harvard, in which he argued, using
Catholic natural law reasoning, that the Church had to reverse its official
teaching banning contraception practices.[17]

But Curran's swift rise to prominence was not greeted by everyone. The
auxiliary bishop of Curran's Rochester diocese, Lawrence Casey, grew
increasingly concerned about the young priest's lecture series at St. Bernard's
Seminary. After bringing in the likes of Bernard Haring, Gustave Weigel,
and Roland Murphy—all prominent theologians and scripture scholars
who unapologetically applied historical methods to the Catholic theological and scriptural traditions—Curran was informed by Casey that the
series would be discontinued. Likewise in early 1965 Curran was called
into the seminary rector's office and "warned" about his teaching, specifically his teaching that the Church needed to change its position on contraception. At that same conference he was informed that "it would be better
if [he] did not give talks in parishes." The tensions reached their culmina-
tion in July 1965, when Bishop Casey informed him that he could no longer
teach at the seminary. But Casey also offered to write to Bishop William
McDonald, then rector of the Catholic University of America, offering
Curran's services there if they were needed. Within a week McDonald had
written to Curran, welcoming him to his new position on the faculty that
coming fall.[18]

Curran immediately took to the more academic and research-oriented
atmosphere of CUA, which allowed him much more time to do research
and write. He used one of his doctoral seminars during the spring 1966
semester to write a paper for the annual meeting of the Catholic Theological Society of America on the subject of masturbation. The nineteenth-
century manuals of theology used by Catholic priests to guide them in
hearing confessions had taught that masturbation always involved "objectively grave matter"; that is, masturbation was always a mortal sin that,
under normal circumstances, cut off a person from God's grace. Curran,
basing his argument on contemporary psychological and scientific data
about the psychosexual development of individuals, as well as on
St. Thomas Aquinas's own sophisticated arguments about what constituted
"grave sin," argued that one had to make a distinction between "objectively grave matter" (actions that in themselves were grievously sinful) and
subjective culpability (the degree of guilt on the part of the person doing

the action). He argued that masturbation did not always involve serious sin, as one had to take into account the context, the intention of the person, and the person's psychological development. Curran's paper was received well at the conference that June, but it also served notice to theologians who thought of Catholic moral teaching as an already determined set of correct answers that the young moralist just recently arrived at CUA was someone who would need to be watched.[19]

Curran's paper proved to be a prophetic statement of where his research was leading him, and over the course of the next several years he began producing scholarly articles and talks that critiqued traditional (neoscholastic) natural law approaches to understanding human sexuality. Intrinsic to this ongoing critique was his growing sense of the inadequacy of natural law's static understanding of human nature, which presumed that human nature was always and everywhere the same. He also grew increasingly impatient with the way Catholic teaching had "absolutized" the biological or physical aspect of human sexuality. Why, he asked, does *every* physical act have to embody the entire range of meanings that all human acts could possibly embody? How could finite, contingent human acts, undertaken in history without knowing all the factors influencing human intentions or the circumstances of the actors, be read through the lens of such absolute meaning? This seemed at best highly improbable as the basis for reliable teaching, and at worst a benighted attempt to hold on to past answers simply because they were old.[20]

Further and far more damaging in Curran's estimation to natural law's ability to actually answer contemporary moral questions, the older approach to morality seemed to naïvely assume that natural law had rationally and scientifically proven its case. But in fact the arguments of the older approach were shot through with outdated understandings of philosophical causality and embarrassingly dated scientific reasoning, and bore the marks of their own historical time and place. Thomas Aquinas's brilliant synthesis of natural law in the thirteenth century—the supposedly "unimpeachable authority" to which natural law moralists appealed in grounding its moral pronouncements—itself simply represented a historically conditioned end product of generations of scholarly communal discernment. Thomas's use of Aristotle to frame the medieval Church's teachings on morality was an appeal to the best science of the day, the newly rediscovered corpus of Aristotle, in order to provide an intellectually respectable groundwork for explaining the experience of Christian people. But by the middle of the twentieth century neither the majority of scientists nor the majority of the Christian people found such scientific reasoning plausible—or even understandable. "Obviously," Curran later wrote, any moral teaching that ignored the experience of the majority of the Christian faithful, or offered moral teaching that was difficult for the faithful to understand or justify, flew in the face of the Catholic tradition of moral reasoning, a tradition that had always allowed that

> the experience of individuals and groups, and perhaps even of the whole community, can be wrong (consider, for example, the former Christian position on slavery); but the experience of the Christian community is an important source of moral wisdom and knowledge. In a sense, Catholic theology has always recognized this reality in its acceptance of the role of the *sensus fidelium*—the sense of the faithful. The church must always value the experience of people, even though that experience may sometimes be wrong.[21]

Such criticism of the Church's approach to morality, offered well before the appearance of *Humanae Vitae,* augured a prophetic role for Curran in the reception of Paul VI's encyclical on contraception.

FIRED

In a sense, then, the Curran Affair began several years before the actual appearance of Paul VI's encyclical, although the summer of 1968 was the moment when the affair permanently linked Curran's name to the fractious American reception of Vatican sexual teaching, specifically on birth control.

Early in the fall of 1966 CUA's rector, Bishop McDonald, called Curran into his office to express his (and others') anxiety about Curran's membership on the board of directors of a group ominously named Institute for Freedom in the Church—ominous, at least, from the rector's point of view. McDonald also voiced an anxiety generated by the university's board of trustees about Curran's increasing prominence in liberal periodicals such as the *National Catholic Reporter,* which portrayed the Rochester priest as something like the "ringleader" of a group of young American theologians challenging the traditional classicist approach to Catholic moral theology. But despite these anxieties voiced and duly noted, Curran continued to publish widely and to produce perceptive studies of the Catholic moral tradition. He likewise became well-known among the university's graduate students as a lively and engaging teacher. He thus applied for academic promotion to the rank of associate professor early in 1967, a promotion both he and his academic colleagues presumed would be a pro forma exercise in academic hoop-jumping. As if on cue, Curran's application for promotion was unanimously approved by his department in February 1967 and seconded by the university's academic senate (the facultywide body set up to guarantee that deals were not being struck on the departmental level on personnel issues) the following month. But on April 17, 1967, Curran was called into the office of the rector, who had hired him just two years previously, to be informed that the university's trustees had voted not to renew his contract. Indeed two of the most prominent bishops on that board—Patrick O'Boyle, archbishop of Washington and ex officio chancellor of Catholic University, and Cardinal John Krol, archbishop of Philadelphia—would later be revealed as the primary players in the effort to rid CUA of Curran, an effort abetted by no less a personage than the pope's own representative to the United States, Apostolic Delegate Egidio Vagnozzi. As Curran would later write, "The Vatican wanted to make an example out of a liberal priest, and I was to be the one."[22]

Archbishop Vagnozzi later boasted to journalist Roy Meachum that he had been instrumental in Curran's firing, although his role as the pope's man in Washington in the events of 1967 has proved to be difficult to reconstruct. What seems to be unimpeachable fact is that Vagnozzi asked another professor at Catholic University, the conservative scholar Father Francis Connell, for an evaluation of a book Curran published in 1966, *Christian Morality Today*. Connell's reply confirmed the apostolic delegate's sense of growing unease with Curran's theological trajectory. Connell wrote that

> it is incredible that a book like this could be published by a Catholic priest, especially by one who holds the important function of a teacher in the chief pontifical university of America. It is filled with errors. Unless something is done soon by ecclesiastical authority to remedy this situation, great harm will be done to the church.[23]

Washington's Archbishop O'Boyle was also in communication with Connell, who had written to the archbishop about Curran's paper on masturbation. That paper, Connell argued, would "without doubt induce thousands of young persons" to sinful activity, activity seemingly supported by the Catholic University of America, which employed Curran. This possibility horrified O'Boyle, who then formed a committee of three trustees—Cardinal Krol of Philadelphia, Archbishop Hannan of New Orleans, and the rector of CUA himself—to investigate Curran's writing on this subject, an investigation undertaken without Curran's knowledge or input. Krol made a report of the committee's findings to an April 10, 1967, meeting of the university's trustees, who then voted, twenty-eight to one, not to renew Curran's contact.[24]

Much of this backstory to the vote would not come out until much later, but McDonald did communicate to Curran at their meeting the week after the vote the growing unease of the board with regard to his scholarship. Curran's response was hardly one of a cowed or intimidated academic. After hearing McDonald out, Curran angrily replied that he found the entire process leading to his nonrenewal both secretive and dishonest, "and dishonesty in the church had to stop." He flatly informed McDonald that perhaps the best response was to make public the process followed by the board of trustees, a threat that made McDonald "so flustered that he never gave [Curran] the letter he had prepared." But events made it unnecessary for Curran to personally go public. On the very next afternoon the entire faculty of theology met (without Curran present) and voted unanimously to send a telegram to every bishop on the board, demanding that the trustees' vote be rescinded immediately. That evening every seat in CUA's McMahon Auditorium was filled with students who had come to hear Curran's colleagues describe the events roiling the faculty. "If there is no room for Charlie in the Catholic University *of* America," Curran's colleague Daniel Maguire told the assembled students, "there is no room for the Catholic University *in* America." Later that week two nuns (wearing traditional habits) carried those words on a banner in protest marches on campus, a picture captured by the *New York Times* and printed in its "Week in Review" section the following Sunday.[25]

Two days after Curran's meeting with McDonald, two thousand students, some of them seminary students from the various houses of study sponsored by religious orders on the edge of campus, gathered in front of the rector's office to demand a hearing, while the entire theology department met again. The unanimous resolution passed at that meeting declared, "Under these circumstances we cannot and will not function unless and until Fr. Curran is reinstated. We invite our colleagues in other schools of the university to join us in our protest." The faculty of every division of CUA, save for the small School of Education, agreed with their theology colleagues, so that the very next day something literally unimaginable to the institution's founders happened: the Catholic University of America went on strike.[26]

Much to the chagrin of both the rector and most of the board, the strike immediately became national news, in some cases (as in Washington and New York) being featured on the front pages of newspapers of record. Two highly visible cardinals in the American hierarchy, Lawrence Shehan of Baltimore and Richard Cushing of Boston, publicly denounced the board's action against Curran as intemperate and not in keeping with the character of a university, statements undoubtedly confirming the fears of Apostolic Delegate Vagnozzi (and of Vatican officials in Rome) that the American Church as a whole had a devotion to personal freedom and self-determination that needed disciplining.[27]

Curran would later recall that he received numerous statements of support and encouragement from colleagues and students during the days of the strike; a sign he frequently saw carried by students around campus read "Even my mother supports Father Curran." Not surprisingly, given the cultural climate and Curran's widespread support among Catholic scholars nationally and within CUA's faculty, a resolution to the strike, and a victory, was achieved a few days after the faculty shut down the university. The following Monday Cardinal O'Boyle and Rector McDonald emerged, looking weary, from a meeting with the theology department to address a large crowd gathered in front of the library. They announced that the board had voted to reverse their decision of the previous week and that Curran's promotion to associate professor would become effective the following September.[28]

In a real sense the 1967 strike at Catholic University represented an American Catholic analogue to protests at Columbia, the University of Wisconsin, the University of California at Berkeley, and a host of other academic institutions occurring at the same time. Indeed it preceded some of those more famous landmarks of the free speech movement. CUA's strike was actually more noteworthy because it involved both political and religious impulses that transcended the North American context: it involved the question of the rights and duties of a pontifical university faculty answerable, finally, not just to a North American body, but to the Vatican itself. And it was the faculty, not just students, who sponsored this memorable incident in the battle over due process and free speech, a fact that makes the entire episode the more remarkable.

In the short run, the "party of hope" (as Emerson had termed the perennial progressive cause) seemed to have won: Bishop McDonald resigned as rector of the university in November 1968, and the new university statutes adopted in 1969 announced in their opening paragraph that Catholic University was "essentially a free and autonomous center of study, [supporting] an atmosphere of academic competence where freedom is fostered and where the only constraint upon truth is truth itself." It was *then,* after these extraordinary and unprecedented events at a university owned by the Church, that the battle over contraception began.[29]

BIRTH CONTROL AND ITS (EPISCOPAL) DISCONTENTS

Curran's bona fides as a leader of the loyal opposition at the Catholic University of America were thus earned well before the appearance of *Humanae Vitae*. But however well prepared for his role, he could not but have felt uncomfortable by events immediately after the press conference at the Mayflower Hotel.

On August 1, just a few days later, Archbishop John Dearden of Detroit, a moderate widely respected among American bishops (and president of the U.S. Bishops Conference), issued a statement declaring, "We the bishops of the Church in the United States, unite with [Paul VI] in calling upon our priests and people to receive with sincerity what he has taught . . . and to form their consciences in its light." If this was what Curran and the other signers were going to encounter from Church leaders on their side, what might they expect from their opponents? They would discover very shortly. At a special (and hastily organized) meeting of the trustees on September 5, Cardinal James McIntyre of Los Angeles, one of CUA's trustees, introduced a long resolution declaring that Curran and other supporters of the Mayflower Statement had expressed "opinions in obvious conflict with the known and practiced teachings of the Church as held for centuries, and recently reiterated and confirmed by the Holy Father." In McIntyre's estimation Curran and the others who had signed the statement had violated the profession of faith required to receive contracts from the university and should therefore be terminated.[30]

But in issuing his recommendation for Curran's disciplining and termination, McIntyre had not taken stock of the mood (or the makeup) of the recently reorganized board of trustees. As a direct result of the 1967 strike, changes had been introduced in both the leadership of the board (the chair now being a layperson, Dr. Carroll Hochwalt of St. Louis) and its makeup, with a number of laymen now serving as voting members. It was thus that McIntyre, O'Boyle, and other episcopal members of the board learned, undoubtedly to their fury, that tenured professors in American universities could not be terminated without a formal hearing before their peers. And that hearing process was spelled out in exacting detail in the guidelines of the American Association of University Professors (AAUP), the faculty union whose guidelines even the Catholic University of America followed. At the end of that very long day, at nine o'clock, in fact, Dr. Hochwald read to the press a statement prepared by the board, a statement that embodied the tensions within the newly structured board itself. On the one hand, the board fully recognized its "responsibility arising from its authority to grant Pontifical degrees in the sacred sciences, and fully adheres to the teaching authority of the Pope." On the other hand, the board also reaffirmed "the commitment of the Catholic University of America to accepted norms of academic freedom in the work of teaching, and to the due process protective of such freedom." The board had therefore voted to direct the acting rector of the university to "institute through due academic process an immediate inquiry as to whether the teachers at this University who signed the recent statement of dissent have violated by their declarations or actions . . . their responsibilities to the University." The resolution was thus no resolution at all—at least for a while.[31]

The acting rector duly directed the academic senate to set up the inquiry according to the guidelines mandated by the AAUP, an exacting and complicated series of committee meetings. Finally, in January 1969, Curran and the other faculty signers of the Mayflower Statement appeared before the duly constituted inquiry board. Curran and others present had been in regular contact with the national AAUP office throughout the fall, and with their help submitted a 250-page statement to the inquiry board, explaining their actions and justifying their dissent on the basis of commonly received Catholic interpretations of noninfallible teaching. Intrinsic to the argument of this voluminous brief was a historical approach to doctrine. The brief argued that many noninfallible teachings—offered as "definitive" statements by the Church at various points in its long history—had in fact later been judged wrong and were either rescinded or allowed to lapse into something like canonical death. In a real sense, then, historical consciousness itself was the "interpretive key" for reading the long and detailed set of arguments offered in the brief. This accounts for its failure to convince many on CUA's board, despite its perspicacious appeal to the "plain facts of history." Such plain facts, for those who saw the teachings of the Church as timeless and impervious to historical change, were beside the point, however obvious they might appear to Curran and his academic colleagues.[32]

But the inquiry board, made up entirely of academics, *was* convinced by the historical and theological arguments of the brief, and in its final report submitted to the university's academic senate declared unanimously that the actions of the Mayflower professors represented

> a responsible theological dissent from the teaching of the Encyclical *Humanae Vitae*, and this dissent is reasonably supported as a tenable scholarly position. The release of [their] statement cannot be regarded as contrary to the accepted norms of academic procedure. Neither the timing, the content, nor the means of securing circulation and concurrence of colleagues are to be regarded as extraordinary or improper in light of current academic practices. The alternatives of either repressing the statement or of adopting a policy of concerted silence would have been more truly improper.[33]

On the basis of this unanimous report tendered to them, the academic senate in turn unanimously approved the inquiry board's report and sent it to the trustees, who were meeting in Houston on April 12–13, 1969. Many of the bishops on the board, still the largest single group of trustees, were angered by the recommendation resulting from the inquiry. To them the issue was not about historical precedent or the development of doctrine, issues that seemed to them academic in both a literal and a metaphorical sense. The real issue for them was *who* had the ecclesial authority to pronounce on Church teaching, and about the *manner* in which that teaching could and should be challenged. If any Catholic, following the lead of the "Mayflower dissidents," could publicly challenge Church teaching, the result would be institutional chaos. But the understandable fears of some of the trustee bishops were not shared by all of their fellow trustees, even on a board answerable, finally, to the pope himself. Thus, the resulting action of the board reflected its own internal tensions. The official report declared that the trustees of the Catholic University of America had voted to "receive" the report from the academic senate exonerating Curran and his faculty colleagues, but also voted not to act on that report immediately. The board therefore appointed a five-member committee of trustees, headed by Cardinal Krol, hardly a neutral presence in the entire affair, to examine the report and make recommendations for the next meeting of the board, which would occur on June 15, 1969.[34]

At that June meeting, a fractious one reflecting the divisions roiling the American Church on these very issues, the trustees finally issued a press release declaring that they accepted the report of the faculty inquiry board "insofar as it pertained to the *academic propriety* of the conduct of the dissenting faculty members." But the release also announced, undoubtedly reflecting the sentiments of some of the bishops on the board, that the trustees intended to initiate a different kind of inquiry—an inquiry into the *manner* of the protest, which was carried out by theologians who were duty-bound to pass on the faith of a national Church in union with Rome. The purely formal issue of academic dissent of university professors was one thing; such public dissent on Church teaching by ordained clerics publicly taking the hierarchy to task was quite another. The board therewith remanded this question of *ecclesiological*—as distinct from *academic*—dissent, not to another committee of academics at Catholic University, but to a standing committee of the U.S. Conference of Catholic Bishops, the Committee on Doctrine.[35]

But the lateral hand-off intended to mollify some of the bishops among the trustees was foiled by a fellow bishop, Cardinal John Dearden, head of the Bishops' Conference. Recognizing a rat's nest when he saw it, he refused to allow that standing committee of the Bishops Conference to become embroiled in what was quickly becoming an internal family quarrel among American bishops. Dearden directed the bishop in charge of that committee to form a three-person team to study the matter, a political move that led to yet another standoff. The three-person team of bishops issued a final report declaring that the CUA theologians (like all academics) needed academic freedom to pursue their craft, but also opining that the dissent manifested by Curran and his colleagues was "not sufficiently sensitive to the pastoral implications of their actions." This report, in due course, was also "received" by the Catholic University trustees at their November 1969 meeting but never formally approved. Thus the standoff remained for over a decade—a standoff that might serve as a useful metaphor for the entire U.S. Catholic Church in 1969.[36]

Curran himself believed that Archbishop, now Cardinal, O'Boyle lay behind the board's effort to distinguish between the strictly academic propriety of the dissidents' conduct and the propriety of such behavior by priests and seminary teachers taking on their duly constituted hierarchical superiors in public. Curran's suspicions have strong circumstantial evidence in their favor. While the Catholic University events were hurtling to their institutional resolution—or, more properly, irresolution—O'Boyle himself was involved in an unseemly and much publicized wrestling match with a number of priests of his own diocese.

One hundred priests of the Washington archdiocese had issued a public "statement of conscience" supporting Curran's July 30, 1968, dissent from the Vatican's position on birth control, an action they had undertaken without O'Boyle's permission. It was one thing to have a bunch of priests and academics at Catholic University perform such antics in public, as problematic and disobedient as O'Boyle believed such activity to be. It was quite another to allow such antics from the priests of his own diocese, answerable (canonically, at least) to him as chief shepherd of the District of Columbia. O'Boyle called each of the signers of that statement of conscience to his chancery office—usually not a welcome "invitation" for any Catholic priest, in the best of circumstances—to answer charges in the context of a formal canonical hearing. On September 30, 1969, O'Boyle imposed "canonical penalties," including suspension from being able to perform priestly functions, on forty priests in his own diocese, including his aged confessor of many years, the Jesuit Horace McKenna. O'Boyle's heavy-handed "pastoral inquiry" into the actions of his own diocesan priests was remanded to Rome, from which, finally, in 1971, the Vatican's Congregation for the Clergy issued an ambiguous report resolving the matter. The Congregation for the Clergy failed to reprimand O'Boyle for any abuse of power, but it also failed to demand any kind of retraction from the priests who had signed the public statement of conscience. But by that time, three years after the tumultuous events of 1968–69, only nineteen priests remained of the forty whom O'Boyle had disciplined. Most of the others had left the Catholic priesthood, themselves being, arguably, the worst-treated victims of the Charles Curran Affair.[37]

A COMMUNITY OF FAITH DIVIDED AGAINST ITSELF

It is instructive to read the various irresolutions of the Curran Affair between 1967 and 1969 as emblematic of a more basic unresolved tension within the American Catholic community itself. But defining that tension is more difficult than would at first reading appear. It cannot simply have been a tension between theologians and bishops, as the actions of Cardinal

Dearden and the Vatican Congregation for the Clergy illustrate. Nor is it especially helpful to categorize that tension as being between theological liberals and conservatives, as O'Boyle's disciplining of his own rather conservative confessor and the public support offered to Curran by Cardinals Sheehan and Cushing, themselves hardly liberals on sexual matters, witness. The tension at the heart of the Curran Affair hardly demonstrated a revolt of the laity against clerical oppression in the bedroom. At almost every stage of the various battles, most of the actors on both sides of the debate were ordained clergy, and sometimes bishops, who had no personal stake (one presumes, anyway) in the matter of birth control.

Examining the escalating skirmishes of the Curran Affair from the safe distance of a new millennium offers the disconcerting sense that both sides intuited that something larger, something transcending questions of sexual teaching, was in the offing. That intuition, in tandem with the assertion of Pope Benedict XVI forty years later that there was no "before and after" in the history of Church councils, offers the student of the Curran Affair another, hopefully clearer lens for viewing those debates. In an odd kind of way, Benedict XVI's claims may be correct, but not in the way he intended: the historical consciousness that powered so many of the arguments of Curran's side of the debate was, in fact, not new. In this, at least, Pope Benedict was correct. Indeed historical consciousness had emerged in the eighteenth century during a sprawling succession of intellectual movements collectively known as the Enlightenment. The awareness of the contingency of events and ideas in history had never dissipated or decreased, despite its submergence within the Roman Church, largely as a result of a harrowing series of intellectual witch hunts undertaken by Popes Pius IX and X in the early twentieth century, witch hunts now known collectively as the Modernist Crisis. But what *was* new was a widespread sense among large sections of Catholic clergy and laity alike that the worldview resulting from that consciousness was the true one, or at least the one through which most North American Catholics now saw their lives. In an age of rapid scientific progress, appeals to static immutable truths no longer made much sense. The timeless, unchanging character of that older worldview, so seemingly real for many generations of Catholic believers, now appeared shoddy and full of holes, intellectually embarrassing, and worst of all irrelevant. The passionate appeals of Cardinals Krol and O'Boyle to the timeless truths of Catholic teaching fell on deaf ears belonging to Catholic theologians who were far more familiar with the Catholic theological tradition than the harried bishops of large and administratively demanding dioceses.

Curran and those on his side of the debate believed that their academic rejection of the Church teaching regarding contraception simply gave intellectual expression to an already widespread lay rejection of Church teaching on sexual issues well before 1968. Read thus, Curran and his fellow theologians' intellectual rejection of *Humanae Vitae* represented the tip of a far larger iceberg, floating inexorably toward the hull of Holy Mother Church.

Curran and his fellow priests among the dissidents knew from long Saturday afternoons spent hearing the confessions of rank-and-file Catholics that the majority of the faithful (devout ones, who went to confession regularly) had decided long before the summer of 1968 that the Church had simply gotten it wrong on the "bedroom issues." They ignored that body of teaching, many with the tacit approval of their confessors.

As Andrew Greeley has persuasively argued since, American Catholics did not start practicing birth control in the late 1960s. On the contrary, national fertility studies, like those undertaken by the University of Michigan and Princeton, reported that in the late 1950s and early 1960s a very high percentage of women who described themselves as devout Catholics practiced some form of fertility control, usually after they decided that they had produced enough children. Indeed in the first study of Catholic practice, produced by the National Opinion Research Center at the University of Chicago in 1963, 50 percent of practicing Catholic women said it was "not wrong" to use some form of birth control to limit family size. This and other demographic data led Greeley to argue that the encyclical on contraception in 1968 actually "occasioned an experience of emancipation for the most devout of Catholic women—exactly the opposite of Paul VI's intention." Greeley's insight is probably right: the very fact that Paul VI had set up a commission to study the Church's position on contraception was read by many as proof positive that the Church's condemnation was not immutable. This realization (as Greeley saw) emancipated many practicing Catholics from worrying about a practice in which they had long engaged.[38]

The demographic data gathered by the National Opinion Research Center in the decade after *Humanae Vitae*'s appearance only served to confirm its initial findings about American Catholic practice from the early 1960s. According to surveys taken in 1973 (of all U.S. Catholics) and in 1977 (of Catholics in the archdiocese of Chicago), consistently high percentages of self-described "practicing Catholics" approved of Catholic couples using birth control. When age was factored in, the percentages became even more dramatic: 76 percent of Catholics polled approved of birth control when "a married couple feel they have as many children as they want"; 92 percent of Catholics under the age of thirty approved of the statement. Thus Greeley observed about the Chicago data that

> the most devout young people in a particularly devout diocese reject the Church's sexual teaching in a ratio of approximately two to one. They may be materialists, pagans, secularists, selfish [or] pawns of the mass media . . . but their devotional behavior suggests that they consider themselves dedicated Catholics and are able at the same time to be devout and reject the Church's sexual teaching. . . . Most bishops would admit this.[39]

Greeley's larger sociological interpretation of the monolithic direction of the data he gathered for four decades posits the same level of contraceptive practice among American Catholics for four decades after 1968—this despite the efforts of Paul VI's successor, John Paul II, to "explain more clearly" the meaning of *Humanae Vitae* in two successive follow-up encyclicals, *Donum Vitae* and *Evangelium Vitae*.

It is therefore difficult not to consider seriously Greeley's interpretation of the whole affair. As he saw it, many (most?) American Catholics saw the very possibility that Popes John XXIII and Paul VI could even *consider* changing the Church's position on the issue as meaning that the Church's condemnation of contraception was not unchangeable and immutable. Thus, in Greeley's estimation, the very issuing of the encyclical in July 1968 was tragic: "[Paul VI] locked the barn door after the horse had escaped." The effect of the encyclical, in this retelling of the story, was not to "form" the consciences of the faithful, but to bring discredit to Church teaching itself:

> If the pope had intended no change, he should never have assembled the commission. . . . The encyclical's only practical effect was to confirm and indeed increase opposition to birth-control teaching, and it led to a sharp and sudden decline in Catholic practices. . . . The laity had already made up their minds that the pill and later all forms of birth control were morally acceptable. They were not going to change their minds because a celibate in Rome told them to do so. Some of them in anger diminished their church attendance and their Sunday contribution. Hardly any left the Church.[40]

Greeley's terse and convincing interpretation of the reception of the birth control encyclical among American Catholics helps us to understand and contextualize the larger meaning of the Curran Affair. Charles Curran and his colleagues offered a telling and, for many fellow theologians and lay Catholics convincing, critique of Church sexual teaching that was based on the older classicist model of natural law just when increasing numbers of rank-and-file Catholics felt empowered by the Church itself. Not least among the factors fueling this sense of empowerment was Vatican II's favored description of the Church as the entire "People of God"—laity as well as clergy, priests as well as bishops and popes. The new, dynamic metaphor of the Church as a people on pilgrimage in history made the older metaphor of the Church as a *societas perfecta*—a static, timeless, and hierarchical institution in, but not of, history—more than simply problematic or strangely dated. The new metaphor announced, finally, the fact that historical consciousness was now part of the way Catholics understood the Church itself, as they had long since come to see and interpret the world outside the doors of the Church. And if the Church changes and adapts, so does its teaching—on contraception and a host of other things as well. Once the Church had embarked on a pilgrimage, there was no turning back. And that fact was being played out on another coast, not among clerical theologians but among religious women who rediscovered a surprising identity in returning *ad fontes,* to their historical sources, precisely in obedience to the call of the Second Vatican Council.

American bishop Albert Fletcher from Little Rock, Arkansas (center), sitting in the nave of St. Peter's Basilica during the Second Vatican Council. Arkansas Catholic file photo, Diocese of Little Rock. Reprinted with permission.

The Reverend Bernard Lonergan, S.J., Canadian Jesuit theologian, speaking at an academic conference. Reprinted with permission of Aquinas College.

The student sodality during a service in the Fordham University Church, 1950s. Reprinted with permission of Fordham University.

Post–Vatican II liturgy, with the priest and altar facing the people and with the altar rails removed. Reprinted with permission of Fordham University.

Catholic University of America's student newspaper, *The Tower*, covering the battle of the board of trustees with Professor Charles Curran. Reprinted with permission of *The Tower*, Catholic University of America.

The May Day celebration at IHM College in Los Angeles transformed from a crowning of the statue of the Virgin into a Happening in the 1960s. Reprinted with permission of the Corita Art Center.

One of Corita Kent's most famous lithographs, showing the profile of Pope John XXIII with lyrics from the Broadway musical *Hair*. Reprinted with permission of the Corita Art Center.

Selective Service office in Catonsville, Maryland, immediately after the burning of draft files by Daniel Berrigan, S.J., and other members of the Catonsville Nine. Reprinted with permission of the Baltimore County Public Library.

Charred papers and ashes remain in the wire baskets that were set on fire in the parking lot by war protesters who invaded the local draft board in the Knights of Columbus building in Catonsville, Maryland. Reprinted with permission of the Baltimore County Public Library.

Avery Cardinal Dulles, S.J., delivering a paper at the Acton Institute in Michigan. Reprinted with permission of the Acton Institute.

The Dangers of History

In his own diocese a bishop (or ordinary, as he is called in canon law), has virtual Caligulan powers; his word is law, and if, unlike Caligula, he cannot ordain a horse, there is little else not within his power and the reach of his discipline.
—John Gregory Dunne, "Angels of L.A."

THE ANGELS AND CALIGULA

While the seemingly more newsworthy Charles Curran Affair was not yet national front-page news, what some took as a puff piece appeared in the *Los Angeles Times.* On October 18, 1967, Dan Thrapp published a human interest story about the General Chapter meeting of Los Angeles's Immaculate Heart of Mary sisters, the "IHMs" to those who inhabited the Catholic universe. The 119-year-old teaching order of 560 religious women was already famous among Angelinos, both for the academic excellence of the schools they staffed and, by the mid-1960s, for the presence among them of Sister Corita Kent, a nun-artist whom the theologian Harvey Cox would later call "an important contribution to the whole church and to the whole of life."[1]

The IHMs' superior, the Reverend Mother Mary Humiliata Caspary, explained to Thrapp that the Ninth General Chapter had voted to begin a several-years-long process of changes to their rule and lifestyle, changes undertaken so that the order could become "more open to the world, reaching out into fresh fields, more part of the world, and more responsive and involved in it." Among the changes were several that would very quickly elicit the ire of the archbishop of Los Angeles, Francis Cardinal McIntyre, as well as of pastors whose parish schools were staffed by the order's famed teaching sisters. IHM sisters who felt called to another kind of work would now be allowed by their order to choose new careers outside of the classroom. Further, the sisters' concern for the quality of education they were offering Catholic schoolchildren led to a demand by the chapter that maximum classroom size in the schools they staffed be lowered from forty to thirty-five students. But other changes—more symbolic and less immediately practical in terms of their effect on how parishes ran—would actually prove to be even more controversial in the long run. The sisters would now have "options" as to their dress. The members of the order could wear traditional veils over their hair, or they could wear abbreviated veils— or they could wear no veils at all. They could likewise choose to retain their traditional habit (ankle-length dresses) or wear a modified (knee-length) habit, or merely dress simply and modestly in street clothes. Even more, each convent would develop its own lifestyle; in place of their regimented past in which "each convent had a superior who was in charge, and community prayers were set out in detail by the order's constitution, members of each local convent will decide what kind of government they want, and then set it up, and when and how they will say their community prayers."[2]

Mother Caspary was quoted in the article as observing (in what we might now see as something of a prophetic utterance) that the reforms being undertaken by the IHMs were "more profound than any thus far announced by any American religious society of Catholic women." Likewise an unidentified sister was quoted as saying that the experimentation proposed by the order's General Chapter represented a "major breakthrough for Roman Catholic nuns in America."[3]

Many who have examined the experimentation undertaken by the IHMs have attempted to cast the narrative as a battle royal between the liberal sisters, who consistently viewed their efforts as a "major breakthrough" both for themselves and for other religious women in the United States, and conservative members of the hierarchy such as Cardinal James Francis McIntyre, who consistently viewed the order's various experimentations as the slow-motion stages of a train wreck. Such a view has in its favor an easily understandable "good guys versus bad guys" (or girls) quality, but it fails to duly appreciate that the entire process of experimental change envisioned by the order's General Chapter was rooted in a mandate of the hierarchical Church itself. More specifically the reforms undertaken by the IHMs were rooted in the call of the bishops of the Second Vatican Council to religious men and women to discern "the signs of the times" in order to serve the present age more effectively.[4]

The call issued by the bishops of the universal Church in 1965, to which the Los Angeles IHMs were dutifully responding, fell on ready and open ears. Like many other orders of sisters whose founding purpose was largely ignored by personnel-strapped American bishops who placed them in positions of institutional "usefulness" (running schools, staffing hospitals, etc.), the IHMs heard the call of Vatican II to uncover the original—and, as it would turn out, often quite radical—vision of their founding mothers as something close to the action of the Holy Spirit Herself. But the "opening of the windows" envisioned by Good Pope John was experienced as something closer to a cyclone than to the gentle breeze described in scripture. Renewal "along the lines envisioned by their founders," which was exactly what the Vatican II document *Perfectae Caritatis* mandated, in fact involved the replacement of unquestioning obedience to local church officials with a newly won corporate responsibility for defining and implementing a recovered sense of the order's corporate mission and identity.[5]

The Council's call for a reform of the work and lifestyle of religious women that had appeared both moderate and salutary in Rome took on a life of its own in the North American context. Thus paragraph 17 of the Council's "Decree on the Appropriate Renewal of Religious Life" had appeared to be unexceptional when passed almost unanimously by Vatican II's bishops:

> Since they are signs of a consecrated life, religious habits should be simple and modest, at once poor and becoming. They should meet the requirements of health and be suited to the circumstances of time and place as well as to the services required by those who wear them. *Habits of men and women which do not correspond to these norms should be changed.*[6]

Likewise, paragraph 20—on the "adjustment" in lifestyle and apostolic work that missionary communities should undertake in fulfilling the Council's call for reform—had urged groups like the IHMs to "resort to suitable techniques, including modern ones," in preaching the gospel in the modern world, adding that such groups should "abandon whatever activities [that] are today less in keeping with the spirit of the community and its authentic character." Further (and even more pointedly), the "Norms for Implementing the Decree on the Up-to-Date Renewal of Religious Life," issued by no less an authority than Pope Paul VI himself a year after the close of Vatican II, actively encouraged communities of religious women like the IHMs to experiment with dress, lifestyle, and apostolic work *precisely* along the lines that the Ninth General Chapter proposed, provided only that the experimentation undertaken be based on a "return to the Gospel as a source for living religious life," and that the reforms reflect the "original inspiration of [their] founders."[7]

The good religious women of the Immaculate Heart of Mary acted on these calls with alacrity. The Ninth General Chapter decided to extend an invitation to the order's sisters for a "period of experimentation" with dress, lifestyle, and apostolic works, which would continue for eight years, until 1975, when the next general chapter of the order was to meet. But the specific changes implemented would be evaluated annually. One of these specific changes was that sisters were now given the opportunity of retaining their "names in religion" (saints' names given at the time of vows) or returning to their given names. Yet another of the specific changes touched on where the sisters worked:

> "We won't abandon our traditional works," said reverend mother [Caspary], "but we also say that diversity in works is not to be discouraged, but encouraged. Thus we may assume social service, or work with economic opportunity projects, or such specialized tasks as [work] with the mentally retarded, or with young people. If one of our sisters has a special talent or interest, we will encourage her to pursue it. She might be a commercial artist, or a newspaper woman, or a musician, or almost anything else."[8]

Whatever the commitment of the archdiocese of Los Angeles to the reforms mandated by the Second Vatican Council—and it would be understating the situation by half to observe that its cardinal archbishop was less than completely enamored by the vision of a "modernized Catholicism"—Church bureaucrats immediately recognized the institutional threat posed by the decisions of the IHMs' General Chapter. The network of Catholic grade and high schools was one of the jewels in the crown of the Catholic empire in Los Angeles, and the IHM sisters ranked near the top of the list of valued parochial schoolteachers. Mother Caspary's happy vision of a "diversity of works" staffed by her sisters looked like institutional chaos to Cardinal McIntyre and the superintendent of the archdiocesan school system. A "return to the original inspiration of their founder" looked fine as a phrase in a Roman document; it was quite another matter for such a phrase to actually impact running the immense and complex system that the Los Angeles archdiocese had to oversee every day of the school year.

Shortly after the promulgation of the chapter meeting's proposed reforms on October 24 Monsignor Donald Montrose, the superintendent of the Los Angeles archdiocesan school system, forwarded a letter to the sisters from the cardinal, asking them to "determine promptly how many of the sisters will wish to retain their teaching capacity in our schools as religious":

> It would appear that the action of the chapter presents to the archdiocese of Los Angeles an ultimatum that does not even admit of discussion or negotiation. This ultimatum, with its elements, is not acceptable to the archdiocese of Los Angeles and its ordinary. Consequently, there is no alternative than to accept the threat of the community that they withdraw from the teaching staffs of our parochial schools in the archdiocese.[9]

The IHMs, stunned by the archdiocese's reading of their earlier announcement as actually constituting a "threat," announced to reporters that they could not respond to questions about the October 24 letter, as the entire matter had been remanded to the pope's representative in the United States, the apostolic delegate Archbishop Luigi Raimondi. This was a correct canonical action for a pontifical order answerable to Rome (and not the archbishop) in any case. But this handoff to the apostolic delegate likewise contributed immediately to both the animosity and the newsworthiness of an exchange that would rival the Curran Affair for newspaper space on the West Coast. And the newspapers ate up the events that would shortly follow: the IHMs sent out a letter to the parents of the 7,500 students in the diocese of Los Angeles taught by their sisters, stating that they were "being asked to stop teaching [the] children in the parochial schools of the archdiocese." In response to this the eighty-one-year-old cardinal immediately informed the papers that the archdiocese had not dismissed a single sister of the order from a teaching post, but rather that "the community has simply been asked to determine promptly how many of the sisters will wish to retain their teaching capacity in our schools as religious."[10]

In January 1968 a new Catholic organization was formed in the archdiocese, the Los Angeles Association of Laymen, which quickly jumped into the fray on the side of the sisters, releasing to the press a strongly worded statement that read, in part, "For the Immaculate Heart Sisters, the leaders of all the religious in this country, to be refused the right to experiment and make their own rules leads to the decline of not only the religious orders, but to the quality of Catholic education."[11]

Support for the sisters' stance quickly spread well beyond the archdiocese. The February 3, 1968, issue of *Ave Maria*, a popular Catholic magazine published out of the University of Notre Dame, carried a letter of support signed by thirteen Jesuit seminary professors praising the reforms undertaken by the IHMs. The Jesuits, all professors at their order's seminary at Alma College in Los Gatos, California, called the experiments envisioned by the sisters' General Chapter "a splendid response to the call for renewal and adaptation of religious life." Addressing the nuns directly, and despite the sure disapproval of Cardinal McIntyre, the professors wrote:

> [You] made a notable contribution to a restored understanding of authority in religious life. You have taken seriously the principle of subsidiarity commended by both the [Vatican] council and the pope, according to which no task or problem should be referred to a larger group or to a more general authority if it can be handled by a smaller subsidiary group.[12]

By March 8, 1968, the fracas between the sisters and their ordinary had reached an unsettling level of unpleasantness. The Los Angeles TV station KNBC reported on its evening news program that the IHMs were now prepared to resign from all of their teaching positions in the Catholic schools of the diocese rather than comply with the demands of Cardinal McIntyre. Four days later the *New York Times* wrote that the order would appeal its case directly to Pope Paul VI himself. Slightly over a month later, on April 16, the Vatican's Sacred Congregation of Religious and Secular Institutes, the Roman office assigned to deal with issues relating to groups of religious women like the IHMs, appointed a four-member committee of American bishops to investigate the entire affair and make recommendations for its resolution. Presided over by James Casey, the archbishop of Denver, the committee included Joseph Breitenbeck, auxiliary bishop of Detroit; Thomas Donnellan, bishop of Ogdensburg, New York; and Monsignor Thomas Gallagher, who represented the apostolic delegate in Washington.[13]

Only later would it be revealed that over a month before the naming of the investigating committee, the sisters had received a four-point *responsum* from the Sacred Congregation of Religious. The ruling was in fact a response to Cardinal McIntyre's own (separate) appeal to Rome regarding the controversy and represented what the *National Catholic Reporter* later termed a "crushing defeat for the sisters." The Roman congregation decreed that the sisters (in compliance with McIntyre's wishes) must adopt some kind of uniform habit; it decreed that the sisters were "obliged" to retain the apostolic commitments they had agreed to in the archdiocese (meaning, for most of them, teaching in the parochial schools) rather than "branching out into a variety of work"; it mandated that they must maintain some form of daily prayer in common (including Mass); and, most important for shaping subsequent events, even though they were subject to the Sacred Congregation for Religious in Rome, they were nonetheless answerable to the archbishop of Los Angeles.[14]

Not surprisingly, all of this became grist for the mills of the media, in both Los Angeles and the national Catholic press. But all of this paled in comparison to the sisters' next move. The IHMs announced publicly that a majority of their order had decided to "put off compliance" with the four-point Roman directive. This dramatic stand was immediately supported by a national write-in campaign in which three thousand women religious in the United States, as well as assorted Protestant denominational leaders and Catholic political figures, sent their signatures to Rome in support of the sisters. What Vatican bureaucrats, accustomed to hierarchical-style interactions with religious, especially women religious, made of such a democratic display one can only imagine.[15]

An extraordinarily public tripartite standoff now existed among the sisters, Cardinal McIntyre, and the Roman Congregation of Religious—an unprecedented airing of Catholic dirty laundry in a Church whose leaders were more accustomed to dealing with conflict behind closed doors. It was Archbishop James Casey, the head of the investigating committee appointed by Rome, who announced a resolution to this ecclesial mess. In the estimation of the committee, the 560-member order of the Immaculate Heart of Mary *already* constituted two separate communities: a progressive faction that claimed the loyalty of the vast majority of members of the order who would follow the lead of Mother Caspary and Corita Kent, and a smaller (and generationally older) faction, hoping to hold on to the old habit, lifestyle, and traditional apostolic commitments. Thus the investigating committee recommended that the IHMs should be left free to determine their own future, offering a Solomonic resolution to the messy affair. Cardinal McIntyre and his school superintendent would inherit the "no-nos" (as the press quickly dubbed the smaller conservative group), and Rome would be free of the ruckus created by the "go-gos" (progressives like Caspary and Kent) while affirming their right to determine the nuns' future. Roman authority, diocesan institutional needs, and American democratic ideals would thus all be (more or less) affirmed and all sides placated. Casey announced to the press in June, "For practical purposes, while a decision by the Holy See is pending, two groups are recognized, and each is authorized to act separately."[16]

About fifty sisters voted against the reforms planned by the General Chapter and found a peaceful resolution to the unpleasantness under the leadership of Sister Eileen MacDonald as superior. These sisters, retaining the original name of the order, the California Institute of the Sisters of the Most Holy and Immaculate Heart of Mary, adopted modified habits, retained common prayer as the organizing principle of their day, and committed themselves to remain teaching in nine parochial schools in the archdiocese. The great majority of women in the order, however, decided to fight rather than switch: close to 150 members chose to leave religious life altogether, following God's call out of the order. The remaining sisters organized themselves into the Immaculate Heart Community under the leadership of Mother (now Ms. Anita) Caspary, now president of an intentional community of laywomen committed to living the Christian life in the world. In 1970 this community became the single largest group of religious women in the history of the American Catholic Church to become exclaustrated, that is, formally released from their vows by the Vatican. Though not strictly religious sisters according to the Church's canon law, the community nonetheless retained a communal and distinct identity focused on apostolic work in the world. Each group received an undisclosed financial settlement, but the larger intentional community retained the right to administer Immaculate Heart College, Queen of the Valley Hospital, and the order's retreat center overlooking the Pacific near Santa Barbara.[17]

RETURNING TO THE ORIGINAL INSPIRATION OF THEIR FOUNDER

Until Rome issued something of a delayed recognition of what had actually been taking place among Catholic women in religious life in the 1900 bull *Conditae a Christo*, groups like the IHMs of Los Angeles were in an anomalous position with regard to official Church status. Orders of active religious women founded in the United States—groups like the Sisters of Charity founded by Elizabeth Ann Seton in 1809 in Emmitsburg, Maryland,

and the Dominican sisterhood founded in Kentucky in 1822 by the Dominican priest Samuel Wilson—were not nuns at all in the eyes of the Church, by which canon law referred to as only "second orders" of contemplative, cloistered women. Groups of women active in the works of charity and bound together by simple vows were (technically speaking) "third orders" of pious lay people living a common life of simplicity and good works. They were, in the exceedingly exact terminology of canon law, "lay sisters," *not* nuns. It was only in the year 1900—that is, over a thousand years after the first communities of religious women were organized in Europe—that Rome recognized active communities of women who taught, nursed, and helped the needy as authentic women religious, that is, as nuns.[18]

In the context of the New World, however, it was the third order of women religious that flourished and indeed became the pillars of the young American Church. Twelve different groups of religious women attempted to establish orders in the United States between 1790 and 1830; six were founded along American activist lines (like the Sisters of Charity), and six were modeled on the cloistered, European model of second orders. By the twenty-first century all six American groups but only one of the European cloistered groups still existed.[19]

What *Conditae a Christo*, the papal bull of 1900, thus represented was a delayed recognition that the vast majority of these religious women, whom American Catholics and others had always called nuns in any case, were, canonically speaking, just what others took them to be. But part of the conditions for receiving such Roman recognition involved giving up the original apostolic vision of their oftentimes quite radical or free-spirited founders. In place of an active life of service among the poor, groups of religious women were now expected to construct something of a wall (sometimes literally) between their common life and the outside world. In place of an apostolic presence moving freely among those they served, orders of nuns were now told that they could leave the convent only in pairs, both for safety's sake and for the sake of "propriety" (at least as that word was defined by Vatican bureaucrats). In place of lives centered on the needs of those around them, the nuns' communal lives had to be organized by regular hours of common prayer, sometimes up to five times daily. Thus, with their newfound canonical status as nuns, groups like the IHMs found their lives to be increasingly circumscribed by concerns that were, at best, extraneous to the original visions of their founders. The promulgation of the New Code of Canon Law in 1917 made the cloister mentality even more pronounced, and by the 1920s all American women religious were being warned by both Rome and their local, bishops to restrict their contact with the outside world as much as possible. Thus the trajectory of religious life for women in the opening decades of the twentieth century—at least as religious life was understood by Rome and the majority of American bishops—appeared to be shifting away from activist impulses and inexorably toward a more traditional, cloistered (European) definition of nuns.[20]

The decree on religious life issued by the Second Vatican Council, followed by Paul VI's norms for implementing that decree in 1966, thus represented a dramatic recharting. Suddenly groups of religious women were not only allowed, but expected to reexamine the historical visions of their founders and to reorder their common lives and apostolic commitments as closely along the lines of these visions as they could. Decades of movement toward ever-stricter standards of cloistering were halted, and then seemingly reversed by two directives issued by the highest authorities in the Church: first by an ecumenical council, and then forcefully by the pope himself! What the IHMs of Los Angeles found when they returned to the "original vision of their founder" would not bring joy to those (like their cardinal archbishop) who had come to rely on them to live lives of cloistered submission to Church leaders and who needed nuns to staff the growing institutional commitments of a complex religious organization.

The IHMs were founded as a semicloistered community of women in Gerona, Spain, in 1848 by a Spanish diocesan priest, Joaquin Masmitja de Puig. But Masmitja de Puig's emphasis in their founding had been on the *mission* part of their identity, which was to be active among the poor, with the semicloistered part added in order to meet the accepted notion of the time as to how groups of religious women should organize their communal lives. From their founding, then, the sisters of the Immaculate Heart of Mary had a spirituality focused on active service to those on the socioeconomic edges of society. Their habits (like the clothing of many other such groups) were simple renditions of the common dress of sober and pious laywomen, mandated not to set them off from those they served, but to provide no-fuss clothing that was durable and practical for service among the poor. Their clothing was to be simple, not special; it was to make them invisible, not obvious; it was to mark them as members of the working poor, not a caste apart. Likewise their common life of prayer was to be balanced by their apostolic work; they were not meant to be cloistered women who broke up their real lifestyle with active ministry among the poor, but women who actively brought the fruit of their prayer to apostolic activity that was intrinsic, indeed central to their communal identity.[21]

Within ten years of its founding the order had attracted a growing number of young women interested in the demanding work of running orphanages and schools for those who had no social safety net at all—a network of good works that by 1858 had grown to apostolic works in seven cities of Spain. Their reputation as selfless and highly effective catechists and teachers was such that, by 1871, the bishop of Monterey-Los Angeles, Fray Francisco Mora, invited the order to send missionaries to a vast Spanish-speaking diocese on the rough-and-tumble California frontier of the New World. Ten of the sisters volunteered for the harrowing voyage to the semibarbarous West Coast of the United States. But once there, their mission subtly began to change in ways their Spanish founder might not have recognized (or approved). Still learning to speak English, the sisters began teaching music, art, and embroidery to the wealthy Catholic families of the Spanish landholding aristocracy in order to make ends meet. After they mastered the new language, the schools they opened—like that on the grounds of St. Vibiana's Cathedral in Los Angeles in 1886—attracted the children of the first families of the city as well as the children of the less well-off. The very success of the order in meeting the demand of Bishop Mora—that "only the finest teachers of the community be entrusted with this important project"—made their school a magnet for the children of the powerful in a culture where good schools were at a premium.[22]

Soon American-born young women were attracted as well by the educational zeal and success of the sisters—not surprising in a culture where the options for talented young women were few and far between. In 1905 their first American-born provincial, Mother Magdalen Murphy, purchased fourteen acres in Hollywood (then more notable for its orange tress than for its starlets), where the sisters built a large and handsome motherhouse as well as Immaculate Heart College, the first standard college for women in southern California, which would soon become known for its academic rigor and its student body of talented young women.[23]

But the California-based sisters also realized that the six thousand miles that now separated them from Spain might serve as an apt metaphor for other strains between them and the progressively more cloistered lives of their Spanish sisters. Over against a life focused on common prayer and a cloistered lifestyle, which Spanish bishops successfully imposed on their sisters in Gerona, the California sisters increasingly came to see the wisdom of the more flexible rule originally designed for them by their founder.

Indeed the growing demand that the American sisters conform themselves to the increasingly cloistered identity accepted by their Spanish sisters reached boiling point in 1921, when the superiors of the order in Gerona sent a "special visitor" to the California province, Mother Augustana Coromina, to investigate why the American sisters seemed so recalcitrant in implementing the cloistered practices being pressed by Rome. The visitor, who stayed for two years, was not amused (or impressed) by the "free-spirited" comings and goings she found in California houses and let that be known both locally and to her superiors in Spain. By 1923 everyone on the American side of the visitation—the sisters, their ordinary Bishop John Cantwell, and American superior of the California houses—had decided that Mother Coromina had overstayed her welcome and cordially invited her to return to Spain. This she did, but not before penning a very critical report of her findings for her superiors in Gerona.[24]

The presence of the Spanish visitor had other, unintended consequences as well. The California sisters recognized that the restrictions being accepted by their European counterparts were so far removed from the realities of their American context that they had progressively fewer things in common with what they had always thought of as their "spiritual motherhouse," if only in a sentimental sense. They approached the bishop of Los Angeles to petition for a formal separation from their Spanish sisters, a separation that was granted by the Vatican on April 18, 1924. But the Roman document granting the nuns' request also declined Bishop Cantwell's request to make the Los Angeles IHMs a diocesan foundation (i.e., sisters under the control of him and his successors in Los Angeles). Instead it gave them a new pontifical status: they were now to be a new institute separate from the Spanish IHMs, called the *California* Institute of the Sisters of the Most Holy and Immaculate Heart of the Blessed Virgin Mary. And the new institute was to be under the care of a cardinal protector in Rome, whose duty it was to protect their works and lifestyle from any possible future encroachments of the local hierarchy—a canonical status that would greatly complicate events in 1967 and 1968.[25]

Their newfound independent status as a Roman-recognized American institute of "progressive sisters," or at least progressive by the Catholic standards of the time, allowed them to flourish. In the Los Angeles diocese alone, the IHMs had 125 sisters teaching in elementary schools and seventy-two sisters teaching in parochial high schools. Part of their success in attracting talented and effective women to their order was a succession of charismatic leaders, such as Mother Eucharia Harney—"Mother E." as she was known by her sisters—who served as superior from 1939 to 1951. Harney gained a reputation both in the diocese and well beyond it for inviting high-powered (and not always docile) Catholic women to the order's college, "independent spirits" like Dorothy Day, Madeleva Wolff, Maisie Ward, and Claire Booth Luce, well before the Second Vatican Council began its epochal reforms. Decades before the revolution of the Catholic sixties erupted, the IHMs of Los Angeles were already well-known as educated, independent-minded, and highly effective teachers and catechists who hardly fit the caricature of submissive, naïve, and otherworldly nuns to be found in films like *Going My Way* and *The Bells of St. Mary's.* What made all of Mother Harney's apostolic outreach work so well for the IHMs in the decades before Vatican II was that her sense of their communal identity remained close to that of their Spanish founder, who had no desire to establish yet another order of nuns shut off from the world:

> Mother E. took an intuitive delight in the Christian intellectual tradition, with a fine disregard for the minute details of the Rule. She brought to all with whom she came in contact a reminder of the essential spirit of Christian love and of the perfection of charity rather than the letter of the law. It is perhaps in this characterization that is rooted the spirit of the IHM sisters' 1967 renewal decrees.[26]

For a group of talented and well-educated religious women like the IHMs of Los Angeles, the call of Vatican II's "Decree on the Up-to-Date Renewal of Religious Life" (*Perfectae Caritatis*) appeared like water in the desert. First of all, the decree announced that the ultimate authority for the renewal of religious life rested within the religious communities themselves, and not with bishops. This alone made the document noteworthy and beloved among religious women. The famous fourth paragraph announced in simple declarative prose, belying its overturning of more than a century of centralizing control of the lives of groups like the IHMs, that

> it is for the competent authorities [of religious communities] alone, and especially for general chapters, to establish the norms for appropriate renewal and to legislate for it, and also to provide for sufficient prudent experimentation. . . . Superiors, however, in matters which concern the destiny of the entire institute, should find appropriate means of consulting their subjects, *and should listen to them.*[27]

The bishops of the Universal Church had actually mandated that experimentation in both lifestyle and apostolic work must now be undertaken by religious communities, and that the assent of the members of those communities was essential to genuine reform. This was precisely what prophetic voices within the order (like Mother E.) had been saying for decades. Further, Paul VI's norms, published a year after the close of the Council, called for a much more clearly defined definition of communal identity than was to be found in many communities of religious women in the Church. This, as both the pope and the IHMs clearly recognized, was due to centuries of cloistered traditions imposed (inappropriately) onto active orders, orders that had been founded to work and pray in the world, not be shut off from it. The IHMs of Los Angeles lost no time in organizing study commissions to report back to the order on how best to reform their current identity much more closely to the original vision of Joaquin Masmitja de Puig, and elected delegates to what was hopefully being called the "Chapter of Renewal." But the chief pastor of their local church would have other ideas about all of this liberalizing nonsense and would not have to overcome any native shyness to make his position known.[28]

HIS EMINENCE OF LOS ANGELES

James Francis McIntyre entered St. Joseph's ("Dunwoodie") Seminary in Yonkers, New York, in 1916. Dunwoodie was then considered a showplace of the American seminary system of priestly formation. In interviews with fifty priests who had passed through its doors between 1915 and 1929, Philip Murnion found that almost all felt they had completed "a superior regimen of intellectual formation." But superiority in seminary formation, as in so much else, lies in the eye of the beholder. Michael Gannon, studying the Yonkers seminary in those very years, came to a somewhat different conclusion than the alumni. Gannon offered a bleaker picture of the intellectual world encountered by the young McIntyre: "The course work required little or no reading outside the textbooks and some notes; no papers to do; a library open to students only two hours on Sunday and Wednesday mornings; and an institutionalized four hours and forty minutes of study."[29]

But whatever intellectual shortchanging occurred at St. Joseph's Seminary did not slow McIntyre's rise into the upper reaches of the American hierarchy. Ordained as a priest in 1921 at the age of thirty-five, he was quickly appointed assistant to the chancellor of the archdiocese of New York, and was named chancellor himself in 1934. His preeminence in that position—running the vast network of parishes, schools, hospitals, and orphanages on a day-to-day basis—brought him national visibility. McIntyre managed to refinance dozens of debt-ridden parishes under his care during the Great Depression, making him indispensable to his ecclesiastical mentor, Francis Cardinal Spellman. But Chancellor McIntyre's relations with the priests of New York, who actually ran the operation on the parish level, reflected the theological poverty that was his inheritance from Dunwoodie Seminary. Things in the Church didn't (or couldn't) change, so that the duty of his underlings was to learn *the* correct answer, and simply apply it. Usually this meant McIntyre's answers. Thus many of the clergy who reported to McIntyre in these years found him to be authoritarian, even harsh, in dealing with subordinates. He was respected for his business acuity and for his economic abilities, but this prominent alumnus of St. Joseph's Seminary was also "a pragmatic man not noted for the range of his intellectual interests or sympathies."[30]

As chancellor, McIntyre viewed with suspicion, or even outright hostility, priests who evinced anything like progressive sympathies. Any cleric who publicly voiced prolabor or pro-union sentiments; who supported ecumenical or interdenominational programs, or who had close friendships with Protestant ministers; any official of the diocese (nuns included) who supported modern artistic or musical activities or who evinced "progressive" ideas about education or classroom style—all such "liberals" quickly received disapproving letters with more than a subtle hint of threat. Perhaps the most famous victim of McIntyre's tenure as chancellor was George Ford, the charismatic pastor of Corpus Christi Church on the Upper West Side of Manhattan and spiritual mentor to generations of students at Columbia University next door. When the university's Newman Club sponsored a weekend conference in Ford's parish, McIntyre sent a strongly worded letter to Ford protesting the presence of Frances Perkins, secretary of labor under Franklin Roosevelt, among the speakers. The chancellor was especially disturbed "not so much because she was Episcopalian as because of the liberality of her views," which, to him, meant that she must be a communist. Contact with communists, like contact with Jews and African Americans, was to be eschewed by all who answered to him. Indeed McIntyre's prejudice against the latter two groups was never hidden, so that "priests asked him in private not to make racial slurs." It was thus Ford's invitation to join the National Committee to Combat

Anti-Semitism that drew McIntyre's strongest wrath. On September 8 and then again on September 16, 1944, McIntyre wrote to Ford on Chancery stationery, demanding that he withdraw from membership in such an extreme organization. Ford's reply to these letters was both measured and poignant, expressing his strong regret that such an action would seem to confirm the impression of many (both inside and outside the Church) that Catholicism left the fight for social justice to others. This letter was followed shortly thereafter by a letter from Ford resigning both as pastor of Corpus Christi parish and as Catholic chaplain to Columbia University. To McIntyre's undoubted fury, Cardinal Spellman refused to accept either resignation, and Ford was allowed to remain on the committee.[31]

McIntyre carried his dismissive attitude toward liberals, and, indeed toward anyone who sought to change what he took to be the changeless truths of a Catholicism he learned in seminary, to the other side of the continent, when he was named archbishop of Los Angeles in March 1949. The death of his predecessor, the much-respected John Cantwell, opened up what had been the See of a desert city known more for its battles over water rights than its Catholic identity. But that had changed quickly after the Great Depression. A million new parishioners had swelled the ranks of the faithful during the 1930s and 1940s, so that what had been a largely sleepy diocese now needed a bricks-and-mortar leader, someone who could oversee a massive expansion of parishes, schools, and Catholic social services. McIntyre's boss, Cardinal Spellman, informed Rome that he had just the man for the job in the person of his chancellor, and (not surprisingly, given Spellman's powerful influence at the Vatican) McIntyre got the job. He oversaw an impressive institutional expansion: the number of parishes grew from 221 to 318 during his years there, and the number of Catholic schools doubled, from 159 to 351. McIntyre, who had been a Wall Street investor before heeding the call to the seminary, was a master money man and was widely praised for his creation of an entirely new ecclesiastical fund, the X Account. He decreed that wealthier parishes in the L.A. diocese would contribute to this account, which would in turn provide resources to pay for the mortgages of poorer parishes. The contribution from the wealthier parishes was hardly voluntary, as the new archbishop simply decreed that this was the way things would now run. Run they did, and to McIntyre's stopwatch.[32]

Although McIntyre had a creative approach to Church bookkeeping, he did not tolerate creativity in Church belief or practice. Indeed his devotion to a timeless and decidedly noncreative understanding of Catholic

Christianity was played out (if not to respectful reception, then at least to humor) on the floor of St. Peter's Basilica itself. It was here, in the heart of the Catholic world, under the confused gaze of the pope and a great many of the bishops gathered, that McIntyre offered what many thought of as his most famous (or infamous) public performance. During the discussions leading up to the vote on the council's "Constitution on the Sacred Liturgy," McIntyre—something of a butt of episcopal humor because of his well-known inability to speak or translate all but the most rudimentary Latin phrases—stood up and offered an impassioned intervention against changing the language of the Mass from Latin into the spoken language of local cultures. The long Latin discussion, which he had been following secondhand through willing or unwilling translators, about the need for more active lay participation in the celebration of Mass was, he announced, "receiving more attention than needed." Such excessive concern for those whose "whole intellectual capacity was not great" was taking up far too much of the bishops' time, and "furthermore, active participation was frequently a distraction." McIntyre's fellow American cardinal, Archbishop Paul Hallinan of Atlanta, himself a member of the council's liturgical commission presenting the case for changing liturgical language from Latin to the vernacular, described both McIntyre and his performance in his diary in just two words: "absolutely stupid." But the bright side was that McIntyre had provided bishops like Hallinan with jokes about "His Eminence of Los Angeles" (and his Latin) for years after the council.[33]

McIntyre also found himself in the small but exceedingly vocal minority in the council sessions on ecumenism. There was widespread support among the council's bishops for changing the Church's centuries-long distrust of engaging Protestant and Jewish believers in discussion about faith and service to the poor. But in McIntyre's estimation Protestant Christians were not "separated brethren"; they were simply wrong, or worse. When the third session of Vatican II opened in September 1964, during which the famous schema on ecumenism was to be voted on, McIntyre collapsed at the opening Mass and had to be carried out of the church. His auxiliary bishop of Los Angeles, John Ward, blamed the long nonstop flight from Los Angeles, as well as the heat. But others, less charitably, opined that the cause was more likely McIntyre's anxiety about the direction the entire council was taking.[34]

McIntyre's dramatic performances at the council could not stifle the excitement of the IHM sisters about what was happening in Rome. The 1963 General Chapter of the order, which convened after the opening of

the council, had offered some "minor but significant" long-range directives. Not least among them was the suggestion of a five-year period of
study of both their constitution and their book of customs, in order to
bring their current communal lifestyle and apostolic spirit more into line
with the original spirit of their order, "guided by the spirit and decisions of
the Second Vatican Council, and by the lived reality of the Institute." The
five-year plan promulgated by the chapter in 1963, itself far less radical
than the document eventually published by the Council two years later as
Perfectae Caritatis, called for all the sisters of the community to consider
how they might need more education (even at secular institutions) to meet
the needs of their times in light of the intentions of their founder—that
they be active apostles in the world on behalf of the gospel. The completion
of (appropriate) degrees and credential programs for sister-teachers
currently in service, on all levels of their apostolic work, was now deemed
a basic requirement by the community. Sisters might thus have to be given
reduced teaching schedules, or even time away from their classroom duties,
in order to pursue degrees in social science, communication, and modern
pedagogical methods to help them answer the demands of a culture far
removed from that of their institutional origins, and of their 1924 refound-
ing in the United States.[35]

By November 1965 the order's General Council decided that they
needed to send one of their own to the Eternal City to report back, firsthand, on what the Universal Church was legislating regarding the reform
of women's religious orders. Mother Caspary was duly selected to make
the trip and provide personal commentary on the council's documents
when those decrees were finally promulgated. But Caspary only just arrived
in Rome when she received a disturbing phone call from the vicar-general,
Sister Elizabeth Ann Flynn, who was overseeing the day-to-day affairs of
the community in her absence. Flynn informed the nonplussed Caspary
that Cardinal McIntyre had decided, without previous warning, that the
order was to undergo an "official visitation" from priests of the archdiocese. Theirs, moreover, was to be the only community of women in the
archdiocese to be so visited.[36]

Caspary immediately intuited that something other than concern for the
spiritual well-being of her sisters had motivated such a surprise visitation,
especially given its irregularity in Church law. Church tradition called for
the regular visitation of religious orders at five-year intervals, usually undertaken by a single priest appointed by the local bishop. McIntyre himself
had undertaken a special canonical visitation of the order just six months

before Caspary left for Rome. But the vicar-general informed an astonished Caspary that the cardinal had appointed not one, but a team of priests
from the diocese to conduct the visitation, and this less than a year after the
previous one. Flynn had protested to the chancery that such a visitation
would be most inconvenient, given Caspary's absence in Rome. But
McIntyre would not be put off: the visitation would take place, and the
cardinal fully expected Mother Caspary to be present for it. Caspary later
reported that many in the archdiocesan chancery interpreted the visitation
as a "form of persecution of the community." What she found when she
arrived back in Los Angeles confirmed her fears:

> Once home, with a sense of helplessness I heard from the sisters of
> the humiliating interrogations by the visiting priests. The fear the
> sisters felt soon gave way to honest indignation as each one faced
> questions designed, it would appear, to undermine their faith in the
> renewal process. . . . "Do you think it would take too much time to fix
> your hair if you were to change your habit?" "Do you have any books
> by non-Catholics in your library?" "Do you want to look like a floozie
> on Hollywood Boulevard?" "Do you have hootenanny masses?" "Do
> you read and approve of the diocesan newspaper?"[37]

On December 27 Caspary and Flynn were summoned to a meeting with
McIntyre and his staff: Bishop Timothy Manning, Bishop John Ward, and
Monsignor Edward Wade (who as vicar for religious in the archdiocese
was presumably responsible for the surprise visitation). Based on the statements of a few sisters during the investigation, McIntyre accused Caspary
of "disobedience to the Ordinary [namely McIntyre himself], failure to
cooperate with the archdiocese, and of the adoption of regulations and
customs at variance with the views of the archdiocese on what was proper
for religious communities." Although certain practices experimenting in
flexibility (e.g., ending the requirement of attending morning celebration
of the eucharist, at which no nun, regardless of apostolic commitment,
could be exempted) were offered as examples of such disobedience, it is
difficult not to reach the conclusion that other issues rankled McIntyre at
least as much—such as the prospect of the good sisters taking time away
from their classroom duties in *his* schools for further education. It was
equally clear that McIntyre cared not a whit if such disobedience was a
result of the directives of a duly constituted General Chapter of the order.
He further announced that the sisters would have sixty days to respond to

his accusations. If the community failed to conform to his views, which amounted, more or less, to the abrogation of the five-year plan promulgated by the 1963 General Chapter, "all moral support and help of the archdiocese would be withdrawn."[38]

All of this, in terms of the excruciatingly exact statues of canon law, was more than just irregular. As a pontifical order of religious women, the Los Angeles IHMs were not under the jurisdiction of the local bishop at all regarding changes in their rule or lifestyle. The sisters answered directly to the Sacred Congregation of Religious in Rome, and the internal governance of the order was, according to their Roman-approved rule, determined by duly elected chapters of sisters, which the 1963 General Chapter had been. There was no basis at all in canon law for the kind of threats McIntyre now issued. But as Caspary later confessed, a number of questions—both during the tense meeting at the chancery and later—crossed her mind: What kind of "moral support" did the cardinal believe he offered the sisters? Was there an implied threat that the chancery would reduce or even suspend the monthly stipends (well below the salary level of lay teachers in any case) of the sisters if they failed to comply with his demands? But even before she left the meeting, Caspary, an expert in navigating the waters of Church politics and never one to bow to bullies, ecclesiastical or otherwise, made it quite clear what she thought of the cardinal's demands:

> [In all that concerns public worship or the works of the archdiocese we will] submit in loyalty and obedience to the Ordinary and consult with him. However, in those things which have to do with the internal life of the community, especially the decrees of the general chapters, we do not feel that we must consult the Ordinary. By rule and according to canon law, we do not believe that we should submit these matters to the direct authority and approbation of the Ordinary.[39]

Caspary immediately appealed the situation to Cardinal Hildebrand Antoniutti in Rome, who as prefect of the Sacred Congregation for Religious was in charge of orders like the IHMs. The delicious irony of such an appeal was not lost on Mother Superior: McIntyre the hierarch, always deeply suspicious of anyone in his diocese who appeared to question centralized authority, was insisting on local control of the sisters in the face of the community's insistence on its pontifical status. As Caspary correctly recognized, McIntyre sought "absolute fidelity to the past and unquestioning obedience to the [local] hierarchy—this in spite of the fact that the community as a pontifical institute was exempt from the local hierarchy's special directives except in public matters that might prove scandalous."[40]

Caspary and her vicar-general Flynn duly traveled to Rome in early January 1966 to meet with Cardinal Antoniutti, who informed them that they had not in fact violated any protocols or Church laws in the recommendations of the 1963 General Chapter, and even made helpful suggestions on how to word their response letter to Cardinal McIntyre. Antoniutti further suggested that the sisters "gently remind" their Los Angeles archbishop that they were directly responsible to the Holy See as a pontifical institute. On February 7, 1966, Caspary sent to McIntyre the official response he had demanded in December, incorporating some of Antoniutti's recommendations. Their letter was a polite affair, assuring McIntyre of their continued cooperation in the work of the archdiocese but sagely omitting any specifics as to the terms of the sisters' presence in the classroom or of the numbers of students that they would teach.[41]

The IHMs continued both their discernment process and their examination of their founding vision in preparation for the Chapter of Renewal, which was scheduled to take place at their Los Angeles motherhouse the next summer. Thus it was extraordinarily annoying, but not surprising, that they received notification from the cardinal in March 1967 of yet another canonical visitation (the third in two years), which was now to include interviews not only in the motherhouse, but in their college and novitiate as well. Regarding this third visit, Caspary observed (with commendable restraint), "As might be supposed, by this time the patience of the majority of sisters had worn thin." Yet again the sisters answered the negatively cast questions as best they could. But perhaps the real animus driving these constant visitations was overheard by one of the sisters showing the visitors out of the motherhouse: "The trouble with the Immaculate Heart Sisters is they're all hung up on Vatican II."[42]

Two months later, on May 15, 1967, Caspary received the official report of that third visitation from the chancery, which included the comment that a "fair segment of those interviewed [were] quite willing for change but did not wish it to be so rapid or radical." This was news to Mother Caspary, as it was to most of the sisters in the community, who now resolved not to receive the report (which would eventually be forwarded to Rome) in silence. Without Caspary's knowledge, more than a hundred of the sisters responded in a letter to the cardinal, protesting the findings and declaring that their process of renewal was not a hindrance but a help in living lives of service:

> For many years now, our community has been doing what the Decree on Renewal points out as being of the utmost importance, that "religious should be properly instructed, according to the intellectual gifts and personal endowments of each, concerning the prevailing manners of contemporary social life and in its characteristic ways of thinking and feeling" (*Perfectae Caritatis*, No. 18). It is by doing this, we are convinced, that we have been able in the past and are able at the present time to make our contribution to the various aspects of the apostolate in which you are so vitally interested.[43]

In the wake of that private missive to their bishop the IHMs convened their much-anticipated chapter on renewal. After the opening Mass on June 26, 1967, the delegates to the chapter debated for six weeks, in the course of which they gradually came to the conclusion that the kind of change called for by both Vatican II and the letter of Pope Paul VI could not be accomplished in small units. On the contrary, they believed that a completely new theology for their common life had to be developed, out of which discreet changes in lifestyle and apostolic work would develop. Thus it was on Independence Day (a correlation not lost on them) that the General Chapter decided that they had a duty to face Cardinal McIntyre's strong disapproval of their experimentation head-on. The drama of that moment can be appreciated even from a historical distance. The cardinal would certainly not be happy if the chapter recommended the kinds of experimentation being contemplated: "the possibilities of recrimination that the entire community might suffer from [their] actions had to be honestly examined" before discussion could continue. An emergency meeting of the chapter was therefore called on the evening of Independence Day. Mother Mary Humiliata later recalled that tense meeting:

> The faces of the chapter members reflected the grave concern and worry we had passed on to them. Suppose the chapter were to make superficial changes and close, awaiting a more favorable time, we asked. There was an almost unanimous "No" from the chapter members, for they were full of hopeful joy that their ideal community, formed from their dreams, might at least be given a foundation at this chapter.[44]

But the members of the renewal chapter knew that their cardinal protector in Rome, nominally in charge of looking after their concerns, was quite elderly and probably out of touch with a "conflict that promised to be of such magnitude" if they proceeded on the course that seemed to be before them. They also knew of a small but highly vocal group of sisters in their order who were opposed to the experimentation they were considering. Thus well before the fireworks that their deliberations would ignite they wondered (prophetically, it would turn out) whether that small band opposed to their reforms would become the "real" sisters of the Immaculate Heart.[45]

It was decided at that point in the evening's deliberation that everyone was too exhausted to continue, and the vote about proceeding with the changes was postponed until the next morning. After the roll call the following morning Mother Humiliata simply called for a vote: Should the chapter attempt only preliminary changes and put off substantive reforms until later? "A firm 'No' was the response. Should we continue to restructure, rebuild, renew the community? A clear 'Yes' was heard as the roll call revealed unanimous agreement for immediate and complete renewal." Thus the renewal chapter continued to meet, drawing up plans for a reformed and up-to-date community more in touch both with its founding vision and with the modern world outside its doors.[46]

"Promulgation Day," the date on which the decisions of chapter were to be made public, was October 14, 1967, a Saturday, on which every sister who could gathered at the motherhouse to hear Mother Caspary thank the members of the chapter for their selfless and exhausting work during the six weeks of their deliberations, and to hear the specifics of the experimentation being proposed for the IHMs. Caspary observed that none of the reforms proceeded from a desire for change for change's sake, but rather from an apostolic desire to answer the real needs of their fast-changing world. But among the implications of that apostolic desire would be a "constant review of [their] ability to continue in certain works as well as attention to the gifts of individuals." Thus sisters would no longer be assigned their apostolic work by the superior or her council, but would be free to choose their own apostolic endeavor. Further—and much more dramatically to the point—each sister might decide to "serve in a Church-related institution, in one not so related, or in one without specific institutional commitment." It would be that last area of experimentation that would prove to be too much for Cardinal McIntyre.[47]

The storm would come sooner rather than later. On Monday, October 16, the five members of the order's General Council (Caspary included) were ordered to the chancery, yet again, to hear McIntyre's response to the renewal decrees outlined just two days before. As Caspary later set the scene, "[All the sisters were] praying silently as we ascended the marble staircase to the conference room of the Los Angeles Archdiocese chancery office, prepared to meet the criticism that was inevitable." Sure enough, the inevitable criticism was there to meet them. McIntyre professed to be "shocked" and angered at the possibility that the sisters might actually teach in "street clothes" in archdiocesan classrooms the following September. He therewith reminded the council members of the position of canon law on compulsory habits for all religious women. Caspary began to respond to this challenge—that such experimentation in clothing was being undertaken in response to the call of both Vatican II and the letter of the pope—but the cardinal interrupted her in midsentence by standing up and announcing that the meeting was over. He declared that he would not allow any IHM sister who was not wearing a religious habit in the classroom of a Catholic school, and further announced that the Immaculate Heart Sisters would not be teaching in *any* archdiocesan school the following fall.[48]

As Caspary later remembered, the sisters had correctly anticipated McIntyre's reaction to the General Chapter's most institutionally sensitive issue—requiring professional standards for teacher preparation—"because it would directly affect staffing and budgeting in the archdiocesan schools." Even so, she arrived at the tense meeting that Monday with the intention of presenting to the cardinal the clear directive laid down by their reforming chapter, that the order would assign to the schools "only those members of the community who are duly qualified to engage in such an important work for the Church." "You dare to threaten me with withdrawal from my schools unless I agree to your conditions?" McIntyre thundered in response. "You want an ultimatum? Very well, I accept your threat to withdraw from our schools. The date for your withdrawal is then June 1968!" Thus it was that the grand experiment undertaken by the Los Angeles IHMs, seen as a "major breakthrough for Roman Catholic nuns in America" only days before, began a downward spiral that would lead many of them out of formal religious life altogether by 1970.[49]

A MORE ACCEPTABLE TIME

Much has been written about the meaning of the dramatic events surrounding the Los Angeles Sisters of the Immaculate Heart and their relations with

Francis Cardinal McIntyre. Most of these accounts have emphasized the good faith of the sisters in their efforts of communal reform; most likewise have underscored McIntyre's difficult personality and (even apart from considerations of his Latin grammar) his tenuous hold on the finer points of theology and canon law, which made the sisters' interaction with their ordinary more difficult than might have been the case in another diocese. There is no need to rehearse those accounts again. But let it suffice here to make three points about the history of the order that ensued.[50]

First, the bishops who so strongly endorsed Vatican II's vision of inviting groups of religious like the Los Angeles IHMs to return to the "original inspiration" of their founding believed that this goal could be tidily accomplished without much conflict in the Church. In this vision (and version) of *aggiornamento*, tinkering with the details of religious identity could be effected without fuss and without drama. There would be no *discontinuity* between past and present identity at all: just the silent, *continuous* hum of communal structures running as they should, at the behest of duly appointed Church leaders, with religious women doing what they were told to do, such as staffing the overcrowded parochial schools of growing dioceses.

This did not turn out to be the case. What the good fathers at Vatican II were quite blithely undertaking in promulgating their famous documents now appears more like placing sticks of dynamite into the foundations of Tridentine Catholicism than simply "opening the windows" of the church to the world outside. What the bishops at the council had failed to include in their equation was, quite simply, the potential of the radical lessons of history to challenge the supposedly secure (and supposedly continuous) commitments of the institutional Church. Thus it was that the sisters of the Immaculate Heart who took both the council and Pope Paul VI at their word, and undertook a long and arduous recovery of their history and founding vision, found a very different identity as sisters of the Immaculate Heart than the one they had accepted from the hands of Church leaders like the archbishop of Los Angeles.

In the years after 1963 they found a vision of apostolic life and mission very different from the institutionally defined vision in Los Angeles. What marked their founding and distinctive identity represented something different, perhaps even radically different, than staffing schools for middle class students in greater Los Angeles, which itself began as an accident, a way of making ends meet when their Spanish forebears first arrived in the New World. With the kind of shock of recognition that history sometimes allows its most devoted students, they saw that they were called to work in the world among those who otherwise might not hear the Word preached at all, who might not fit neatly into a diocesan grid of institutional coverage, indeed, among those whom the Church might classify as "bad Catholics" because of their refusal (or inability) to support parochial schools like the ones the sisters staffed. They came increasingly to question, especially in light of their community discernment, precisely those "settled" commitments. Was it for *this* purpose that Joaquin Masmitja de Puig had founded his order of poor working sisters in Spain in 1848? Was this the "catechetical mission" he had envisioned for those whose duty it was to spread the good news among the poor?

Second, the deep anger of Cardinal McIntyre toward their proposed reforms, initially the reform of their habits ("nuns in *street clothes* teaching in his classrooms!" as he so colorfully, and naïvely, put it), demonstrated the vast gulf that separated the concerns of a settled institutional Church from those of the IHMs. As a result of taking magisterial documents seriously, the sisters realized that this emphasis on clothing that "set them apart" was not only irrelevant to their true identity, but even came close to betraying that identity. "Being true to their mission in the Church," from the sisters' point of view, meant precisely *not* being a caste apart from those with whom they worked. On the contrary, it meant living and dressing simply, like the poor, who had a limited range of options regarding clothing (and everything else). But it also meant changing the focus of their apostolic priorities, and it was this realization that caused the real sparks to fly.

The sisters of the Immaculate Heart in Los Angeles realized, precisely as a result of their engagement with the vagaries of history, that staffing classrooms for affluent white children was, at best, extraneous to the kind of apostolic endeavors they had been founded to undertake. Whatever the personnel needs of the cardinal (and none of the sisters, even after being bullied by Francis McIntyre, ever belittled the importance of such classroom needs), they were now called on by the council and the pope to recover an identity that, by definition, was noninstitutional. They had not been founded (as so many other orders of religious women had been) to be "school sisters," but to be catechists to those who did not have the opportunity to encounter the message of the Church in other ways. The IHMs also realized (in good historical critical fashion) that what history gave, history could take away. An accident of history had demanded that the sisters who had originally arrived from Spain had to tutor the daughters of the Spanish aristocracy in order to make ends meet. Things had changed, and they were now offered the opportunity to right that accident of history and reclaim an identity closer to their original vision.

Cardinal McIntyre would have none of this. He viewed their presence and purpose in *his* diocese as a settled question. Much like his view of the Latin Mass (indeed like his view of the Church itself), Catholicism and its institutional commitments did not change because they could not change. The sisters of the Immaculate Heart already had an identity when he arrived as the new bishop, and that identity was to help staff the growing schools packed with students in the decades after the Second World War. Their identity was thus both given and settled: they were in his diocese to teach, and they were to do so dressed like nuns as he understood nuns should dress.

McIntyre's theological education failed him at a number of important points during his long career, perhaps most famously on the floor of St. Peter's itself, but no less certainly in his relations with the IHMs. It appears as though the very possibility that the sisters *might* be correct in the direction of their reforms never occurred to His Eminence; apparently the "grace of self-doubt" was not a grace vouchsafed to him. The very same seminary education that had allowed him to believe that the Church never changed failed him in dealing with the changes mandated by an ecumenical council of that same Church. The law of unintended consequences had created a difficult situation in which it never occurred to him that he might be in the wrong and the sisters in the right and that customs in the Church do change, and sometimes change radically.

Whatever the intentions of the bishops of the Second Vatican Council—and the debate over those intentions is a heated one—historical events have a life, and a logic, of their own, and even ecumenical councils cannot control them. That is part of the messiness of history. Believers are not promised exemption from such messiness.

Third, and perhaps most important, the treatment accorded the sisters of the Immaculate Heart by their own bishop (and eventually by curial officials in Rome) might very well stand as a powerful metaphor for other individuals and groups in the Church who read the signs of the times too radically and found themselves in ecclesiastical hot water for attempting to do precisely what they thought they were bidden to do by the Church itself. While the Los Angeles IHMs represent the most dramatic instance of what happened to other women religious in the American Church who sought to reform their identity and apostolic work along the lines of their original founding vision, they were certainly not alone. Nor were they alone in the sometimes rough treatment such women received from Church officials. What their example does offer, however, is a dramatic instance of the unintended conflict generated by Church officials who call for reform but believe that such reform can be accomplished without mess and without changing current Church structures.

Perhaps chief among the ironies of the IHM story is that they (and many others since) believed that the real force guiding them in their efforts at communal reform was none other than the Holy Spirit. Such an idea would have scandalized Cardinal McIntyre, as it has scandalized others since. The possibility of such a theological reading of the Los Angeles IHM affair discomfits those who believe that religious faith offers the antidote to historical messiness, who believe that religious faith cannot exist in or alongside such messiness. The IHM affair allows us to see the possibility that Mother Humiliata and her sisters had a better grasp than their archbishop of the unintended consequences of Church decisions.

But what appeared to be such radical behavior to the cardinal archbishop of Los Angeles would pale in comparison to events that unfolded in a quiet suburb of Baltimore, Maryland—events with more overtly political overtones.

6

"Death Shall Have No Dominion!"

At 12:30 on the afternoon of May 17, 1968, an unlikely crew of seven men and two women arrived at the Knights of Columbus Hall in Catonsville, Maryland, a tidy suburb of Baltimore. Their appearance at 1010 Frederick Road, however, was only tangentially related to the Knights. The target of their pilgrimage was Selective Service Board 33, housed on the second floor of the K. of C. Hall. The nondescript parcel they carried with them contained ten pounds of homemade napalm, whipped up several evenings before by Dean Pappas, a local physics teacher who had discovered the recipe in a booklet published by the U.S. Special Forces (two parts gasoline, one part Ivory Flakes). On entering the office, one of them explained calmly to the three surprised women typing and filing what was going to happen next. But either out of shock or because they hadn't heard the announcement clearly, the women continued about their business until the strangers began snatching up 1-A files, records of young men whose draft lottery numbers made them most likely to be drafted to fight in Vietnam. At that point one of the women working in the office began to scream.[1]

The raiders began stuffing the 1-A files (and as many 2-As and 1-Ys as they could grab) into wire trash baskets they had brought for the purpose. When one of the office workers tried dialing the police, Mary Moylan, one of the nine intruders, put her finger on the receiver button, calmly advising the distraught worker to wait until the visitors were finished. The burning of the draft records was intended to be entirely nonviolent, although one of the office workers had to be physically restrained from stopping the protesters, in the course of which she suffered some scratches on her leg. With that one exception, the raid went according to plan. Indeed, as Daniel Berrigan, S.J., one of the leaders of the event, later remembered it,

> We took the A-1 [sic] files, which of course were the most endangered of those being shipped off. And we got about 150 of those in

our arms and went down the staircase to the parking lot. And they
burned very smartly, having been doused in this horrible material.
And it was all over in 10 or 15 minutes.[2]

Once Berrigan and the others left the office, Moylan said to the office
worker with the phone, "Now you can call whoever you wish." But instead
of calling the police she hurled it through the window, hoping to get the
attention of workmen outside the building, which she did: one of the
workmen quickly rushed up to the office to see what the ruckus was. But
his arrival on the scene came too late to interrupt the protest. A small group
of reporters and photographers, as well as a TV crew, had already gathered,
having been tipped off by a member of the Baltimore Interfaith Peace Mission that an "action" would be taking place in Catonsville that afternoon.
While these members of the Fourth Estate watched in silence, the protesters recited the Lord's Prayer while adding files to the napalm-fueled
fire. In all they managed to burn 378 files, more than Berrigan initially
realized. In short order police cars began to arrive, and out of the first of
them an officer strode over to the group around the still-smoldering fire,
calling out, "Who is responsible for this?" David Darst, one of the nine,
answered, "I wanted to make it more difficult for men to kill each other."
But this seemed to confuse the police officer, so another member of the
group called out, "We speak in the name of Catholicism and Christianity."
Finally the frustrated cop turned to one of the nine who looked like the
leader and asked, "Your name please?" "Father Daniel Berrigan, S.J.," was
the response. "Thank you, Father," the policeman responded respectfully,
writing down Berrigan's as the first name on his list. In due course other
officials arrived, including federal agents as well as local police, since tam-
pering with Selective Service files was a federal offense. An FBI agent, spot-
ting Dan Berrigan's brother, Phil, also a Catholic priest, exclaimed, "Him
again. Good God, I'm changing my religion!" Thus began, in the light of
fading embers, a defining event of the American Catholic revolution
known as the Trial of the Catonsville Nine.[3]

Only two things united the group of nine individuals who had planned
and carried out the raid on Selective Service Board 33: all were activists
opposed to America's war in Vietnam, and all were Catholics who viewed
the silence of their fellow believers generally, and the silence of their bishops
specifically, as complicity in moral evil that required an extreme response.
As one of them informed the police who arrived at the site of their protest,
"We do this because everything else has failed." Indeed all the members of

the group believed that their action was a profoundly and explicitly *religious* act, as Dan Berrigan testified in a powerful statement written several days before their appearance in Catonsville:

> Our apologies, good friends, for the fracture of good order—the burning of paper instead of children, the angering of the orderlies in the front parlor of the charnel house. We could not, so help us God, do otherwise. For we are sick of heart, our hearts give us no rest for thinking of the Land of Burning Children. And for thinking of that Other Child, of whom the poet Luke speaks, small consolation; a child born to make trouble, and to die for it.[4]

The group, which succeeded in capturing the attention of America, Catholic and otherwise, with such arresting rhetoric during that especially troubled spring of the sixties represented well the variegated nature of the Catholic Left of the time. The Berrigan brothers were both Catholic priests: Dan a Jesuit poet deeply influenced by Dorothy Day and the Catholic Worker Movement, Phil a member of the Josephite order (originally founded to minister to freed slaves) and the founder of the Baltimore Interfaith Peace Mission. David Darst was a Christian Brother who had lost his clerical draft deferment in 1967 by sending back his draft card, and John Hogan had worked for a number of years in Guatemala as a Maryknoll Brother and had been recalled to the United States by his order because of his support for the Christian Guerrilla Movement there. Marjorie Melville had likewise worked in Guatemala before being expelled for involvement in the internal politics of that country, and her husband, Thomas Melville (a former Maryknoll priest) had been expelled from Guatemala for organizing peasants against government economic policies there. Mary Moylan, she of the finger on the telephone in the Selective Service office, was a registered nurse and certified midwife who had worked for many years in Uganda. She later said that she had joined the others because she wanted to be part of a "celebration of life, not a dance of death." Tom Lewis, who had close ties to the Catholic Worker Movement, had done much of the upfront preparation for the event in Catonsville by scouting the location of the 1-A files and by checking out routes in and out of the building on the pretext of wishing to rent space for a wedding. George Mische had worked for several years with teenage offenders and had worked for several years in Mexico with Maryknoll Missionaries. These were the nine legionaries of the Lamb in the front parlor of the charnel house.[5]

But the events of May 17, 1968, were hardly the first instance of radical Catholic activism in the late sixties, as the "You again!" exclaimed by the FBI agent at Catonsville testified. A year earlier Dan Berrigan had called what turned out to be a protracted meeting at the Baltimore Peace Mission to craft reasonable protest strategies against the escalating U.S. military involvement in Southeast Asia. Rejecting a plan to blow up the Baltimore Customs House (where thousands of military draft files were stored by the federal government) as a violation of Christian principles, the group decided to pour human blood directly on the files. The three other men who would join him in this action, David Eberhardt, James Mengel, and Tom Lewis (soon collectively to be known as the "Baltimore Four"), pledged their involvement in order to accomplish four ends. First, all four sought to stall the Pentagon's induction machinery, in the process possibly sparing a few young lives. Second, they sought to stimulate a much broader national debate about the morality of the draft, especially among religious people across the denominational spectrum who were just then becoming increasingly uncomfortable about Vietnam as a moral issue. Third, they wanted to inspire others to assume greater personal risks in acting against the war, therewith producing legions of martyrs who would discredit (and clog) the legal machinery used to prosecute offenders. Fourth, they sought eventually to use courtrooms as venues in which to denounce the war and the injustice of a conscription system in which the poor (which in the 1960s usually meant young men of color) bore an unfairly high burden of the fighting.[6]

Thus it was that eight months before the Catonsville raid, Eberhardt, Lewis, and Mengel picked up Phil Berrigan at the St. Peter Claver rectory in Baltimore and, with several reporters who had been invited as witnesses to observe firsthand "an unusual act of protest against the Vietnam War," drove to the Customs House in downtown Baltimore. The day before, a nurse from the Johns Hopkins University Hospital had attempted to draw blood from the group, but Mengel had fainted and Berrigan had stabbed his arm so many times in order to hasten the suction of the syringe that the others begged him to stop. In lieu of having the nurse mount yet another effort, duck blood bought at a local poultry market had been mixed with some calves' liver juice and a small amount of human blood (mostly Phil Berrigan's) and poured into four emptied Mr. Clean bottles. Then, to officially ritualize preparations for an act that the Baltimore Four saw as religious as well as political, Phil Berrigan had performed the Catholic rite of marriage for Eberhardt and his fiancée, Louise Yolton.[7]

The next day, armed with the four containers of blood, Berrigan, Eberhardt, and Lewis entered the ground-floor Selective Service office in the Customs House at 12:10, when most of the workers would be at lunch. With Mengel posted at the door as a sentinel, Phil (wearing a Roman collar) told the clerk on duty that he needed to consult the records of a member of his parish, while Lewis and Eberhardt (wearing ties) said that they had problems with some of the details on their draft cards. When the clerk went off to look up the requested information, the three men ran to the cabinets, pulled out a number of drawers, and poured the bloody cocktail onto as many files as they could. At that point (and on cue) the press appeared in the Selective Service office with cameras rolling, capturing for the news that night—and for the court trial somewhat later—the actions of the four and the horrified reactions of the office workers. One of the most mesmerizing images caught on camera was the failed attempt of one woman employee to restrain Berrigan from moving "quite methodically, back and forth" (in the words of the later trial testimony) over the files, emptying as much blood as possible on as many files as he could reach. In the thirty tumultuous seconds during which all of this was occurring, Tom Lewis read aloud from the Bible to the stunned office workers and reporters present. Their prophetic action carried out, the Baltimore Four sat down on the wooden bench in the waiting area, waiting for the police to arrive. When they (and the FBI) duly appeared, the four culprits offered them free Bibles and antiwar tracts. While this unusual gift exchange was enacted, the reporters tore open the sealed envelopes they had been given that morning at St. Peter Claver's rectory. Inside they found the group's statement of purpose, written largely by Phil Berrigan:

> We shed our blood willingly and gratefully in what we hope is a sacrificial and constructive act. We pour it upon these files to illustrate that with them and with these offices begins the pitiful waste of American and Vietnamese blood 10,000 miles away. . . . We invite friends in the peace and freedom movements to continue moving with us from dissent to resistance. We ask God to be merciful and patient with us and with all men. We hope he will use our witness for his blessed designs.[8]

As the police led the four out of the office in handcuffs, Mengel handed one of the office workers a Bible brought for the purpose; she duly took it and hit Eberhardt over the head with it: "Maybe it gave her a Christian feeling," he later opined. At FBI headquarters a few blocks away the four were charged with the mutilation of government property and interference in the working of the Selective Service system. Eberhardt and Mengel were freed after signing a promissory note to appear in court, but Berrigan and Lewis refused to sign any such agreement and were carted off to the Baltimore City Jail, where they commenced a fast that lasted until their court hearing a week later.[9]

Dan Berrigan knew nothing of the actions of the Baltimore Four beforehand; he learned of it while watching TV in a Washington, D.C., jail, following his own arrest as part of the massive October 22 March against the Pentagon that had taken place the week before. But even before learning of his brother's arrest and imprisonment, Dan had written in his prison diary, "Oremus pro fratribus in periculo" ("Let us pray for our brothers in trouble"). He had then added a line from the prophet Isaiah: "Give honor to the Lord of Hosts, to Him only. Let Him be your only fear, let Him be your only dread."[10]

Thus considerably before May 1968 a number of those involved in the Catonsville raid had already been arrested for acts of civil disobedience. Indeed just seven days after the Catonsville event the Baltimore Four came before Judge Edward Northrop for their actions at the Customs House. The local press recorded upwards of 180 people crammed into the courtroom on May 24, 1968, many of them, to the consternation of some American Catholics, priests and nuns wearing clerical or religious garb. William Carter, a local African American civil rights figure testifying on behalf of the Four at the behest of their defense attorney, Fred Weisgal, compared them to Jesus; other witnesses for the defense spoke movingly of their explicitly Christian motivations for their actions. But U.S. Attorney Stephen Sachs, charged with presenting the case against the Four, reminded the court that the defendants had committed a similar crime against government property just seven days before.[11]

Carter's comparison of the four with Jesus stood in marked contrast to the response of Phil Berrigan's own local bishop, Lawrence Cardinal Shehan of Baltimore, who, following the events at the Baltimore Customs House, censured the priest and denied him the right to publicly celebrate the eucharist or preach. Cardinal Shehan had publicly declared that everyone had the right to freedom of speech, but that he could not "condone the damaging of property or the intimidation of government employees."[12]

The Baltimore Four, notwithstanding any potential similarities to Jesus, were all sentenced to prison time by Judge Northrop. As they were led out of the courtroom handcuffed and surrounded by state marshals, a roar erupted from spectators, all of whom stood in respect for them and their courageous action against the "death machine" that sent young men off to shed blood half a world away. That roar betokened widespread support among Catholic young people for their protest, to the undoubted fury of Cardinal Shehan. The actions of both the Baltimore Four and the Catonsville Nine set off a wave of other Catholic protests against the Vietnam War around the country, so that soon the papers were flooded with accounts of the Boston 8, the D.C. 9, the Milwaukee 14, the Chicago 15, the "East Coast Conspiracy to Save Lives," and the "Flower City Conspiracy" in Rochester, New York. In all of these events inspired by the Baltimore and Catonsville actions, most of the participants were Catholics (including former seminarians and nuns), and, just like the Berrigan group, all invariably waited at the scene of their protest for the police to arrest them and issued public statements taking responsibility for their acts. For the first time in living memory American Catholics were actually out in front of a broader progressive movement, rather than bringing up the rear with hierarchically approved activities. The Church had produced countercultural radicals as well as flag-waving patriots. American Catholic "lefties" proudly claimed to be among the arrested rather than the arresting officers. In a reversal of what occurred in the civil rights movement, American Catholic clergy instructed their Protestant ministerial colleagues on strategies of civil disobedience.[13]

Five months later, on October 7, 1968, when it was the Catonsville Nine's turn to appear in court, the national news media descended on Baltimore as the epicenter of a movement that spread from coast to coast. Outside the Federal Courthouse on Calvert Street in Baltimore (a street and a city named after Maryland's Catholic founder, George Calvert, Lord Baltimore), two hundred helmeted police officers armed in riot gear kept tense watch on the several thousand people gathered for the event, many of whom had arrived at the courthouse after marching through the streets of downtown Baltimore with linked arms chanting "Free the Nine!" Among the thousands were six hundred students who had driven overnight from Cornell University in upstate New York to support Dan Berrigan, who served as one of the Catholic chaplains there.[14]

The federal judge appointed to hear the case, Roszel Thomsen, was himself a hero among civil rights advocates in the state. As a member of the Baltimore School Board in 1952, two years before the landmark *Brown v. Board of Education* ruling of the U.S. Supreme Court ended school segregation nationally, Thomsen had played a major role in ending the racial segregation of the city's public schools, and from the bench he had demanded reforms in both the police department and the state prison system. Thus representing what might be termed a center-left position in the Baltimore Bar, Thomsen ruled out the possibility of the nine defendants offering a "justification" defense (that is, offering explanations justifying their willful destruction of government property, which they all admitted to in any case) as soon as the case opened. But he did allow them to talk to the jury about their lives. Phil Berrigan explained his actions in Catonsville as a way of anointing the draft files with Christian symbols of blood and fire. "As a Christian," he announced, "I must start from the basic assumption that the war is immoral." When his brother, Dan, took the witness stand he asked Judge Thomsen for permission to recite the Lord's Prayer. To the astonishment of almost everyone present, both the judge and the prosecutor agreed. What followed was described by Harvey Cox, a supporter of the Berrigans and a Harvard Divinity School professor present in the courtroom, as a "Pentecostal Moment." As the prayer was recited by almost everyone present,

> women sobbed, United States marshals bowed their heads and wiped their eyes, jurors and prosecuting attorneys mumbled "forgive us our trespasses as we forgive those who trespass against us." City police, bearded peace workers, nuns and court stenographers prayed together: "For Thine is the Kingdom and the Power and the Glory."[15]

While these events were enacted on the streets and in the courtrooms of Baltimore, an equally dramatic religious ritual of "witnessing" was being celebrated in the parish hall of St. Ignatius Church, the old Jesuit parish in the heart of the city. J. William Michelman, the church's pastor, had opened up the hall for the hundreds of people who had flooded into Baltimore to support the actions of the Catonsville Nine, which of course included one of his brother Jesuits, Dan Berrigan. Protesters from all over the East Coast and beyond flocked to the vast parish hall to hear rousing speeches from the leaders of the antiwar movement: Dorothy Day of the Catholic Worker Movement, Noam Chomsky, Abraham Joshua Heschel, Robert Bly, and dozens of others who had already made (or would soon make) a name for themselves in the far-flung coalition of antiwar groups. It was there that Richard John Neuhaus, then a Lutheran pastor of a parish located among the Bedford-Stuyvesant projects in Brooklyn but fated to become the most respected voice of the Catholic neoconservative movement several decades later, denounced the Johnson administration for "selling out the American dream of liberty for the mailed fist of repression." And it was in that parish hall, at the end of a fiery succession of prophetic speakers denouncing U.S. military policy in Southeast Asia, that William Stringfellow hobbled to the microphone. Stringfellow, a lawyer by trade but social prophet by inclination, who worked among the poor of Harlem out of deep religious (Episcopalian) principles, moved to the microphone with a cane ("an elegant skeleton") because of his physical disabilities. But once there he shouted to the packed and astonished hall with an astounding inner strength. "Death shall have no dominion!" he proclaimed over the astonished throng. Having thus pronounced an apocalyptic judgment on U.S. foreign policy from that most apocalyptic book of the New Testament, the Book of Revelation, Stringfellow mysteriously disappeared, as though taken from their midst like the prophet Elijah, carried into heaven on a chariot of fire.[16]

THE PAST WASN'T WHAT IT USED TO BE

The events surrounding the protest and trial of the Catonsville Nine was only one episode, if an admittedly gripping one, in a series of dramatic political and social protests during 1968, arguably the most contentious and militant year of that cultural construct known as the sixties in the United States. The assassinations of both Martin Luther King Jr. and Robert Kennedy in the spring of that year; the massive student strike at Columbia University that same month led by the Students for a Democratic Society (the SDS); the battles (literally) on the streets of Chicago (also literally) between the Yippies and the police ordered out by Richard Daley during the Democratic National Convention in August; the announcement of Georgia governor George Wallace that he would be running for the highest office in the land in the next presidential election on the (largely racist-supported) American Independence Party ticket; the long-expected and equally long-feared announcement of the Selective Service office that its December quota for the draft would be the highest set thus far (17,500 men) to fight in Southeast Asia—all contributed in important ways to a political and social militancy that no one living at the end of the 1950s could have foreseen. These and a host of other events elicited organized (and disorganized) protests from civil rights and peace activists, proto-feminists and hippies, SDS radicals and pacifists, and a more amorphous (but also much larger) network of young people who took the proclamation of a "Summer of Love" (centered on the Haight-Ashbury neighborhood of San Francisco) to be the dawning of the Age of Aquarius, or at least a reasonable facsimile thereof.[17]

But even granted that 1968 was arguably the most tumultuous year of political, social, and educational unrest in the United States in the second half of the twentieth century, the protest and subsequent trial of the Catonsville Nine were events of singular importance for Catholics in the United States. Indeed the Pentecostal metaphors used to described the burning of the draft files in the sleepy town of Catonsville and the events that followed it seem more than warranted in light of Catonsville's import for American Catholicism.

Catonsville announced that an older American Catholic identity, built on the presupposition that it was something like a moral duty for Catholics to accept mainstream American cultural values (chief among which was the duty of serving in the armed forces) was now challenged by another cultural identity altogether. Catholics in the United States had always been taught, or at least been taught since the massive waves of Catholic immigration began in the mid-nineteenth century, that being American and Catholic were balanced and complementary value systems: to be a good (practicing) Catholic was also to be a faithful (law-abiding) citizen. American flags and statues of the Virgin Mary appeared side by side on the front lawns of Catholics in Brooklyn and Parma, Ohio, in New Orleans's Irish Channel, and in Southside Milwaukee, proclaiming dual loyalties—or, perhaps closer to the truth, a single loyalty in two manifestations. The dining rooms in many working- and middle-class Catholic households piously displayed both a crucifix and a framed portrait of President Kennedy. Thus it was, as Dan Berrigan would later observe, that the FBI agents from Fordham chased the political radicals from Columbia.[18]

"Good" Catholics—that is, Catholics who regularly attended Mass, did their Easter Duty, and made sure that their children attended Catholic school (or at least Confraternity of Christian Doctrine classes)—could also be counted on to dutifully pay their taxes, show respect to police officers, and send their sons to fight America's wars. Innumerable parochial organizations stretching across the nation—Knights of Columbus chapters and Holy Name Society groups, men's sodalities and retreat programs—were named after parish or local heroes who had fallen in combat, bearing witness to the seemingly self-evident truth that American Catholics were the most loyal citizens of the most blessed nation on earth, as well as members of Christ's One True Church. The fact that the papal flag and the Stars and Stripes hung on either side of the altar in Catholic churches was so much a part of the givenness of parish architecture, literally part of the furniture of the place, that most parishioners never noticed them until the late 1960s, when there was debate about removing them as potentially embodying conflicted loyalties. To many American Catholics, the very possibility of such a rearranging of ecclesiastical furniture smacked more of treason than of sacrilege.[19]

Such loudly trumpeted patriotism was of course elicited by a genuine regard and affection for a country that had enabled Catholic immigrants from Ireland, Germany, Italy, and a host of other cultures to rise into middle-class affluence within three generations. America was, as the British Catholic visitor G. K. Chesterton correctly observed, "a land too easily loved" by those on whom it showered its blessings, among whom were generations of Catholic immigrants. But such devotion was elicited as well by the attempt to compensate, perhaps overcompensate, for centuries-old Protestant accusations of Catholic "otherness" in a land founded by Puritans and largely shaped by Protestants, at least until the end of the nineteenth century. It was therefore not surprising that by the mid-twentieth century Catholic leaders in the style of New York's Cardinal Francis Spellman proclaimed themselves, and were viewed by others as, overwhelming supporters of the nation's crusades. In the case of Spellman this claim was quite literal, as he and his successors served as official chaplains to the Armed Forces of the United States, traveling to the far-flung battlefields of Korea to bless with holy water the bayonets of servicemen fighting communism. And thus it was also not surprising to learn that the chief guarantor of American identity and values against real and perceived threats of communist infiltration during the first decade of the cold war was an Irish Catholic senator from Wisconsin (Joe McCarthy), aided by the legal counsel of another Irish Catholic, from Massachusetts (Robert Kennedy).[20]

The actions of the Catonsville Nine announced the severing of that century-old and carefully woven cord that tied being a "good" Catholic to respect for law and order and an unhesitating support of U.S. foreign and military policy. A new cultural identity was born in Catonsville, and the fact that so many of the Catonsville protesters were priests or religious played an important part in legitimating that new identity. Priests and nuns were by definition good Catholics; indeed they were super Catholics because of their lives of heroic celibacy. How could good American Catholics destroy government property? How could good American Catholics act as though U.S. foreign policy was something to be questioned, much less protested against? How could good American Catholics call civil service workers, many of them Catholics themselves, "orderlies in the front parlor of the charnel house"? A new kind of good American Catholic was thus revealed in the actions of the Catonsville Nine, as well a new kind of Catholic past. After the burning of the draft files with homemade napalm, the past wasn't what it used to be.

The Berrigans and their good Catholic co-conspirators quite dramatically made available a different past. Catholic Christianity, a complex and ancient brand of Christianity, had always contained within itself two distinctive, some would say opposing strands of identity.

On the one hand, Roman Catholicism embodied a Constantinian tradition of public religion, named after the fourth-century emperor Constantine, who had legalized Christianity in the Roman Empire. This strand of Catholicism offered firm support to both human culture and human culture's demands of political stability, economic flourishing, and group safety. This face of Catholicism embodied the advice of Jesus to his disciples: to render unto Caesar that which was Caesar's. That included paying taxes, respecting rulers (even unjust rulers), and, eventually at least, supporting the state in its military undertakings. St. Paul advised the early Christian communities scattered around the Mediterranean to be notable among their fellow neighbors for their model lives of sobriety, diligence, and faithful citizenship. Even if Christians finally had "here no lasting city, but seek one which is to come," they were nonetheless called to be faithful citizens of the earthly cities in which they lived.[21]

This ancient and revered side of the Catholic tradition developed strategies for compromise (in an ideologically neutral sense of the word, meaning only a realistic appraisal of how to witness to the Word) between the absolutist demands of Jesus in the Sermon on the Mount and the realities of living in a fallen world. Thus the Constantinian side of the Catholic tradition sought to keep its faithful from prophetic zeal and from attacking the established political and economic order of things, even though Jesus himself was described in the gospel records as a prophet more often than any other label and was himself eventually put to death for precisely attacking the very foundations of Roman political rule.[22]

Over against the Constantinian impulse within Roman Catholicism there emerged very early in its history another impulse, a prophetic and profoundly *destabilizing* vision of reality that viewed the very ideas of political compromise, economic success, and even family stability as, at best, irrelevant to the message of Jesus, and as, at worst, tending to sell out Jesus' vision of the Kingdom of God to the forces of darkness. "Whoever loves father or mother more than me," Jesus had warned his disciples, "is not worthy of me." This radical, prophetic, and world-denying side of the Catholic tradition sought to offer believers a life much like that lived by Jesus and his first disciples. Compromise was to be eschewed whenever and wherever possible in favor of witnessing to the stark but clear demands of Jesus himself about how his disciples should live their lives. Christian (and Catholic) discipleship was therefore about poverty, not material affluence ("Give no thought to what you are to eat and drink"). It was about service, not hierarchical office, as the measure of Christian distinction ("Listen to those who sit on the Chair of Moses, but do not emulate them . . . for they are whited sepulchers"). It was about absolute pacifism in the face of aggression, not strategies of countercoercion to protect the weak and defenseless ("If someone strikes you on the right cheek, turn to him the other also"). *Real* Christianity—not the domestic form of semi-Christianity offered to the masses who were only superficially cleansed of their paganism—was not and could not be a "mass religion," the religion of the mob. Jesus himself had, finally, found only eleven to be his disciples. His followers should not hope for greater success than their Master.[23]

This side of the Christian message was channeled fairly early in the evolution of the Catholic tradition into the reasonably safe form of monasticism and religious life, in which those who desired lives of discipleship more closely modeled on those of Jesus and his apostles could do so safely out of public sight—originally in the safest place of all, the desert. Dozens, and then hundreds of fervent believers followed St. Anthony of the Desert (usually credited as the founder of Catholic monasticism) out of the cities and into the barren wilderness of Egypt, eager to give all they had to the poor and follow Jesus, just as the Master had bidden his own disciples to do.

This prophetic impulse bid the truly serious followers of Jesus to turn their backs on the world, the devil's playground ("Little children, do not love this world, which is passing away"). True believers were called to freely renounce three of the most basic goods associated with human flourishing: to renounce family in a vow of chastity, the ownership of goods in a vow of poverty, and freedom of choice in a vow of obedience. This prophetic side of the Catholic tradition was revered and even celebrated by the official Church and among the laity who had no desire to leave their comfortable lives to live like hermits in the wilderness. Thus though it remained a numerically insignificant movement within the Catholic tradition, it never disappeared, even in America. Indeed it could never even be directly attacked by the mainstream (Constantinian) tradition of Catholicism because of the grudging recognition that it probably embodied far more faithfully the vision and lifestyle of Jesus and his earliest disciples than did the world-affirming message of the mainstream Church after the fourth century. To that extent this prophetic impulse within Catholicism always remained something like the ideal model, even among middle-class Catholics. Of course the majority of believers couldn't live like Jesus and his first disciples; there were the orthodontist bills to worry about, and getting the kids into a good college. But those few who did undertake such a life were to be respected as having chosen the higher path.[24]

This world-renouncing impulse within Catholicism was glimpsed in North America in the lives of the congeries of nuns and male religious who ran schools, orphanages, and hospitals across the land—respected figures within Catholic culture, even if the vast majority of American Catholics lived most of their lives quite contentedly within the Constantinian, "big church," tradition. This alternative prophetic impulse undoubtedly found its most famous lay incarnation in the Catholic Worker Movement started by Peter Maurin and Dorothy Day in 1933, a "Christian communist" movement dedicated to working with and among the poor. Both Day and Maurin described their movement variously as "anarchist," "communitarian," "pacifist," and "radical," and all of those words correctly described it at various stages of its development. Just like male and female religious, the Catholic Workers were radically committed to living "against the world, for the world," but without the traditional vows of poverty, chastity, and obedience. As both supporters and opponents of the Worker within the American Church always noted, it was the one place in the tradition where you could go as far left as secular radicals while still remaining a faithful Catholic. Just as passionately as any communist espousing the cause of the proletariat, Day and Maurin sought to take the side of the disenfranchised during the Great Depression. Over against their fellow Catholics, whom they took to be perhaps too much at ease in Zion, Day and Maurin saw capitalism, military coercion, and the government itself as something very close to a covenant with death. As Day (herself a convert) put it, "I first became a Catholic because I felt that the Catholic

Church was the church of the poor . . . the church of all immigrant populations that came over or were brought over for prosperous Puritan, money-making developers of this country, ravishers of it, you might say."[25]

Day, Maurin, and their few thousand followers quite proudly claimed to be (and were in fact) a "spectacle unto the world" to their Catholic coreligionists, who were busy fitting in and being accepted after riding the escalator to middle-class affluence. At its height in the 1950s and 1960s, the Worker movement claimed perhaps five thousand followers out of a total American Catholic population of tens of millions—in other words, a very small prophetic band within the country's largest denomination. The Catholic Worker Movement offers an analogue for understanding the historical importance of the Catonsville Nine.[26]

Very much like the Catholic Worker Movement (in which a number of them had been formed and from which some had crafted their Catholic identities), the Catonsville Nine offered a reminder that the *real* Catholic tradition, the one against which the much larger Constantinian impulse could and should be judged, was alive and well within the American Catholic community. Indeed their radical stance against the U.S. military system in general and the war in Vietnam in particular embodied to thousands of American Catholic young people a very different history of Christian discipleship, one that harkened back to the earliest Christian community in Jerusalem immediately after Jesus' death. In this understanding of Catholic Christianity the genuine history of discipleship had always been one of outsiders, like Anthony of the Desert, who eschewed the world and its pomp. It was defined by radicals like Francis of Assisi, who had renounced wealth and a worldly church for "Lady Poverty." It was distinguished by anarchists like the Brethren of the Common Life, who saw personal property as, at best, a form of temptation. It was peopled by pacifists who took Jesus at his own word ("Those who live by the sword will also die by the sword") in denouncing all forms of coercion, even the so-called just war tradition crafted by medieval thinkers. Such outsiders in fact were not external to the Catholic tradition: they *were* the Catholic tradition. For the Catonsville Nine, and for the thousands of supporters who clogged the main streets of Baltimore at their trial in October 1968, that genuine Catholic tradition had to be restored because death should have no dominion for Christ's followers, whatever J. Edgar Hoover or Lyndon Johnson thought. For Dan Berrigan and his faithful cohort, the real question for Christians was not whether their actions caused scandal among the world's people or fury among government workers. The real question, indeed the only question, was "being in the right place when Christ returns." Being in *that* place probably meant eschewing most of the institutional identities by which middle-class Catholics defined themselves, including especially the compromises the institutional Church had made with the state and its needs. The Catonsville Nine could thus take pride in causing the same discomfort to bishops and police officers that Jesus had caused to temple officials and Roman procurators: "I have come to send fire upon the earth, and how I am consumed until it is accomplished." *That* was a past considerably older than Constantine, one the institutional Church had done its best to domesticate. The fire fueled by the napalm in Catonsville could thus be traced to a first-century prophet from Nazareth.[27]

In the Catholic tradition, the Holy Spirit had always been identified with fire; that fire inspired the Catonsville Nine. They fought against an institutional Church that appeared to be complicit in sending young men off to their deaths in a land most Americans couldn't even identify on a map of the world; against Church leaders like Cardinal Shehan, who appeared to come very close to equating Christian discipleship with good citizenship and compliance with the draft system; and against a Constantinian tradition of "public religion" that sought to make Christianity and American democracy two sides of the same coin. The Catonsville Nine seemed to make the Christian message relevant (not yet a cliché in 1968) to a growing movement of young people and clergy who, perhaps correctly, felt that the Catholic Church had lost its fire in making peace with things as they are. Indeed the Catonsville Nine made that ancient prophetic message relevant in a way that many in the Baltimore courtroom, in the parish hall of St. Ignatius Church, and on the streets around the Baltimore Customs House saw as the *real* Christian message, the real record of the Christian past, inflamed with the fire of the Holy Spirit.

The unchallenged dominance of a safe American Catholic past—the past of fitting in, of being a dutiful citizen, of displaying the American flag with a statue of the Virgin Mary on the front lawn—had now been formally challenged by Catholic insiders, priests and former missionaries raised within the American Catholic community. A competing understanding of the American Catholic past was made relevant and compelling by charismatic prophets unafraid of witnessing to truths that transcended the Selective Service Act, ushering in a new American Catholic future.[28]

"AMERICA IS HARD TO FIND"

On October 10, 1968, to the surprise of no one, including those on trial, the Catonsville Nine were found guilty of the willful destruction of federal government property, the incineration of Selective Service files (a second federal offense), and deliberate interference with the efficient application of the Selective Service Act of 1967, for which they were all sentenced to jail. As each member of the jury was polled individually as to the verdict, however, one of the spectators in the packed but tensely silent courtroom called out, "Members of the jury, you have just found Jesus guilty." The speaker was Arthur Melville, a former Maryknoll missionary and the brother of one of the defendants. As other spectators rose to their feet to loudly denounce both the jury and a legal system that could sponsor such a miscarriage of justice, an infuriated Judge Thomsen called out for order in his courtroom. But order he did not, and would not, get. Pandemonium spread from the courtroom itself to supporters of the Nine standing outside, waiting with lighted candles. Things, it would seem, were very quickly getting out of hand, so Thomsen called on Frank Udoff, a U.S. marshal posted to the courtroom in the very likely event that just such chaos would break out, to clear the courtroom completely.[29]

To the sound of hundreds singing "We Shall Overcome" outside the courthouse, the Nine were released on bail, save for Phil Berrigan and Tom Lewis, who were both already serving six-year jail terms for pouring blood on draft files the previous fall. Berrigan and Lewis went from the courtroom back to jail, each with an additional three and a half years of jail time, to be served concurrently with the sentences they were already serving. Dan Berrigan, Tom Melville, and George Mische (as ringleaders) were each given three years; David Darst, John Hogan, Marjorie Melville, and Mary Moylan were each sentenced to two years. The seven were allowed to stay out of jail on bail, pending the legal appeal of their case, but travel restrictions were imposed on them, limiting their movements to areas of their work and home. Further, Judge Thomsen explicitly warned the seven (as part of the conditions of their bail) to avoid giving public speeches of any kind and to also avoid encouraging others to participate in such protests. But it was one thing to command compliance; it was quite another to get it.[30]

Dan Berrigan returned to Ithaca, New York, where Cornell, in response to a petition signed by fourteen hundred students and faculty, reinstated him as a chaplain to the university, despite his having been found guilty of a federal offense. The university declared that the Catonsville incident was Berrigan's personal affair, not involving Cornell in any way. But Berrigan had not returned to bucolic Ithaca to flee from his war activities, nor did he want the students there to feel too comfortable about their lives of comparative privilege. On hearing the news of his reinstatement, he observed that he felt relieved that Cornell had welcomed him back: "Catonsville was my way of striving to speak to the Cornell community. I wished, by placing my future in jeopardy, to raise questions connected with the very existence of the university."[31]

On April 9, 1970, a year and a half after the verdict, all appeals were formally denied. To the grief of the others, David Darst had died in a car crash in October 1969. Tom Lewis and John Hogan surrendered to begin their prison terms. George Mische had intended to continue organizing resistance to the government but was arrested by the Chicago police on May 16. Marjorie and Tom Melville were granted a ten-day stay of freedom to sit for examinations for their master's degrees at American University in Washington, D.C.: "We took our final exam and went to prison. Civil disobedience is civil disobedience. You take what the law says. That's a major principle." But the Berrigan brothers and Mary Moylan refused compliance with what they considered an unjust sentence by an unjust government, disappearing into the dense social network known simply as "the underground." Phil Berrigan successfully eluded capture for ten days; Dan led the police on a wild goose chase for four months before his capture in August 1970. Mary Moylan, dying her red hair black, disappeared into the underground for an entire decade, finally surrendering to police authorities in 1978.[32]

Dan Berrigan's four-month hide-and-seek game with the FBI incensed the federal authorities, as the fugitive priest seemed to be thumbing his nose at law enforcement officers. This sense was played out in a number of incidents. At a Cornell University weekend event called "America Is Hard to Find" Berrigan suddenly appeared before ten thousand students celebrating a "Freedom Seder" in his honor a week after he disappeared. In addition to the Cornell students present, hundreds of young people from as far away as California had hitchhiked to Ithaca to hear the rock groups that were going to perform. As Berrigan strode onto the stage of the gym to the cheers of thousands of young people who recognized him, many of the young women present hugged each other and cried, and a young man rushed to the platform to shake Berrigan's hand. "Bless you, bless you, Father Dan," he said to the priest. Arthur Waskow, who was conducting what the *New York Times* termed a "modified and political Passover service," took the microphone and directed students to block the entrances to the stage. "We have been joined by those who are pursued by the police and are in need," he announced, a somewhat politicized riff on the Passover directive to engage in hospitality with the needy in celebrating the seder. Berrigan told the surprised but delighted students, "[It is] no more logical that a war resister obey a government order to surrender to American justice, than that an American youth appear for induction into the military. I hope that I can, by example, encourage people to do what we did—to break the law in a way that is politically significant."[33]

FBI agents assigned to the event resolved to arrest Berrigan in the gymnasium with as little drama as could be arranged under the circumstances—surrounded, as they were, by thousands of Berrigan supporters. But this was not to be. Shortly before 11 p.m. the house lights in the gym went off while a rock group continued to perform onstage in the spotlights. In the dark the priest calmly climbed inside a giant papier-mâché figure of an apostle used by a theater troupe participating in the event. Fifteen minutes later, when the house lights were turned on again, the agents discovered that the apostle (and the prophet inside) had simply walked out of the gym to the panel truck outside used to haul props, and was driven away.[34]

The very next week a seemingly relaxed Berrigan was interviewed by *Times* reporter Thomas Brady in the Manhattan apartment of friends. Sitting on a couch in the living room, Berrigan told Brady that he was still in full communication with superiors in the Jesuit order and discussed the two books he had just published; one, *The Catonsville Nine*, published by Beacon Press, was being dramatized by Gordon Davidson to be produced as a play in Los Angeles. Berrigan also told Brady that his mother thoroughly approved of what he and his brother, Phil, were doing to stop the war in Vietnam: "My two sons are right," Berrigan reported his mother as saying. "This is what priests should be doing." Asked about the heavy responsibilities his flight imposed on those who were helping him elude arrest, Berrigan observed that his arrest would undoubtedly take a burden off the network of his friends who were helping him. Then he added:

> But it is proper that they should share my burdens if my burdens are useful. They're not just sitting up with a cancer patient. Maybe they're sitting in a delivery room, midwifing the future. My being outside must radicalize my friends. They can't help me without putting

themselves in legal jeopardy. I don't long for arrest. I long for one more useful day.[35]

The FBI, reportedly incensed by Dan Berrigan's "Cornell escapade," resolved to take no chances with his brother. Phil Berrigan had resolved to hand himself over to the authorities on the evening of April 21 at the end of an antiwar rally at St. Gregory the Great Catholic Church on Manhattan's Upper West Side. In fact he had told the authorities where he would be so that the arrest could take place without incident. But the FBI agents assigned to St. Gregory's, stung by the Cornell episode, arrived hours before the scheduled rally, surrounded the church, and undertook a room-to-room search of the parish rectory next door. While they were pounding the doors inside the rectory, shouting "Father Dan, Father Phil, are you there?" the church's pastor, Henry Browne, suggested they look under the beds as well. After smashing down the locked door to the pastor's study, the agents did in fact find both Phil Berrigan and David Eberhardt (of the Baltimore Four) hiding in the room's closet. That night dozens of FBI agents, mingling with the crowd outside the church, hoped to catch a glimpse of Dan Berrigan, but without success.[36]

Dan eluded the FBI until August 11, staying with thirty-seven different families in eleven cities, most in the Northeast; at least one of his hiding spots was as far away as the San Francisco Bay area. But what is striking about Dan Berrigan's four-month flight from the authorities—striking, at least, from the vantage of almost forty years—was how public was the underground that sheltered him. During those four months Berrigan was interviewed regularly by major journals and television stations (the *New Yorker*, NBC, the *New York Times*, and educational television), and his poetry and essays were published in *Saturday Review* and *Commonweal*. He even managed to show up at a Methodist church in the Germantown section of Philadelphia one Sunday to preach a sermon to an astonished but delighted congregation. Agents of the FBI, perhaps understandably, came to believe that the Jesuit was purposefully underscoring their incompetence by so blithely moving among the lawyers, professors, physicians, and Catholic antiwar activists who constituted his vast support network. Piecing together the entire four-month affair a year later, John Kifner wrote:

The F.B.I. searched for him frantically, raiding the wedding of a former priest—Anthony Scoblick, later named a defendant—and a former nun, showing up at the opening of his play [*The Catonsville Nine*] in Los Angeles, staking out the Syracuse hospital where his mother lay ill, visiting the parents of a Cornell friend, searching churches and a nunnery in the Bronx. But, at best, they were always a step or two behind.[37]

Berrigan was finally run to ground by FBI agents at the Block Island home of the poet Anthony Towne and William Stringfellow, he of the "Death shall have no dominion!" pronouncement in Baltimore a year and a half earlier. As Berrigan was handcuffed and taken into custody, one of the agents (undoubtedly Jesuit-trained) muttered the Jesuit motto "Ad majorem Dei gloriam" ("For the greater glory of God") under his breath. It would later be revealed that three days before his arrest Berrigan had recorded a message in Stringfellow's house for the Weathermen—a far more radical and overtly coercive underground group similarly organizing resistance to government policy—pleading with them to return to nonviolent protest methods: "No principle is worth the sacrifice of a single human life." But neither the Weathermen nor the FBI gave much heed to Berrigan's thoughts on principled nonviolent resistance to the Vietnam War. The Weathermen resorted to increasingly violent measures in the 1970s, and Berrigan was sent off almost immediately to the federal penitentiary in Danbury, Connecticut, where he began serving the three-year sentence handed down in Baltimore.[38]

THE DANGEROUS MEMORY OF JESUS

The action of the Catonsville Nine, one in a much longer series of political actions undertaken against the Vietnam War in 1968, was hardly the most publicized protest event of that interesting year. The press all but fell over itself in reporting the student protests in April at Columbia University and in May at the Sorbonne. Both sets of student protests made it to the front pages of the *New York Times,* which neither the burning of the draft files in Catonsville nor the trials and appeals that followed it managed to do. Nor did the action in Catonsville generate the level of student protests that other events did, despite the busloads of hundreds of Cornell students who traveled south to support Dan Berrigan on the streets of Baltimore. The clashes between police and student protesters in Grant Park and on the streets of Chicago during the Democratic National Convention in August

1968 drew thousands of student protesters from across the country, generating as well one of the most famous rock anthems of the decade, Crosby, Stills, Nash, and Young's "Chicago/We Can Change the World." Even William Stringfellow's memorable apocalyptic judgment on the forces of darkness (i.e., the draft boards) during the Baltimore trial—such good copy, one would have thought, for reporting on the apocalyptic denunciations of the young against the draft and all its works—went unreported in the secular press.[39]

The events surrounding the burning of the draft files in Catonsville was a critical moment in the sixties for Catholics in the United States. The Catonsville Nine, both the actual participants in the events and the political meanings that event took on after 1968, represented the moment when the American Catholic engagement with history, and particularly the Catholic place in American history, entered into an identity crisis from which it has yet to fully emerge. The Catonsville events served to catalyze that identity crisis because it pluralized how, and in what ways, one could be a good American Catholic.

The events at Catonsville, undertaken by "good Catholics"—among them priests and missionaries whom rank-and-file Catholics had always been taught to revere—opened the possibility of a new American Catholic identity because it witnessed to a different history of Catholic Christianity, one that evoked the "dangerous memory" of Jesus. This kind of remembering of Jesus, who he was and what he did, did nothing whatsoever to shore up the connection between Christian discipleship and U.S. citizenship. Being a citizen of the Kingdom of God did not mean being a complacent and dutiful citizen of the United States. On the contrary, this memory of Jesus militated against all those American flags next to statues of the Virgin Mary in front yards across the land.

It was the great German political theologian Johann Baptist Metz who first wrote about the "dangerous memory of Jesus." Metz wrote that memories give human beings their historical identities; memory allows human beings to wake up every morning and (more or less) know who and where they are. Therefore, Metz argued, all human experience is ultimately grounded in the narration of memories: "[Historical] identity is formed when memories are aroused."[40]

Metz argued that memory generally falls into one of two major categories. In the first, memory is simply the recollection of the past as the "good old days," a recollection in which "the past becomes a paradise without danger, a refuge from our present disappointments." In this form of memory the horizons of the real world are simply "the way things are," so that the status quo on every level—cultural, political, religious—goes unquestioned. "This is how the church is, because it has always been this way. This is how being a Christian relates to being a good citizen, because it has always been this way." When memory functions in this way, history (reality, the way things *really* are) goes on as it always has. The state or the Church or any institution has remained ever the same: what Jesus did, and what contemporary religious leaders do, are on the same continuum. Catholic reality, like every other kind of reality, forms a continuous stream of actions and truths. The past, in this form of remembering, not only does *not* challenge us to reexamine the present arrangements of human culture: it forms a solid support for the status quo. To that extent remembering is "safe."[41]

But Metz also observed that this kind of remembering represents "the history of the successful and the established. There is hardly any reference in this history to the conquered or defeated, or to the forgotten or repressed hopes of our historical existence." This first kind of remembering is thus "selective memory." It creates a false history by ignoring those who challenged the status quo. This form of remembering offers us security and peace of mind at the price of historical veracity. It does indeed offer us a safe past, but it is a past that never existed, or at least existed only for a select few. By this logic Catholics should have obeyed Cardinal Shehan's exhortation to support the war effort in Vietnam as a just cause worthy of religious, no less than political, devotion. They were obliged to follow his advice because the Church had a "just war" tradition and Vietnam was an application of this theory. Or because good Catholics should *always* obey duly constituted authority, because that's what the Catholic tradition had always enjoined on the faithful. Or because American Catholics had *always* been America's most faithful citizens and soldiers. American Catholics were part of an unbroken tradition, stretching back to the apostles, of being faithful Catholics by being faithful citizens. Thus it was, is now, and ever shall be. Amen.[42]

But for Metz there was another kind of memory, the kind that shocks us out of the safe certainty of the past. This form of remembering is not safe and does not support the status quo. Metz said that this form of remembering offers us "dangerous memories" because it radically challenges the notion that the way things are automatically has God's blessing. Indeed this form of remembering "reveals new and dangerous insights for the present" because it recognizes that the status quo might very well be made up of institutions that Christians are not only free to oppose, but indeed *must* oppose. This kind of remembering sees in the current power arrangements of the "real world" a strange resemblance to the corrupt political and religious establishments of Jesus' day, against which the prophet from Nazareth railed. "Brood of vipers" is what Jesus called the religious authorities of his day. "Whited sepulchers, full of uncleanness" is how Jesus described the duly constituted authorities. It is this sense of discontinuity between what Jesus had in mind for the citizens of his Kingdom and the current political and religious establishments that makes "remembering Jesus" so dangerous and so subversive. Such remembering "illuminates for a few moments, and with a harsh and steady light, the *questionable nature* of the things which we have apparently comes to terms with."[43]

Through this lens the "things as they are," which the Constantinian tradition of Catholicism had labored for so long, and at times so brilliantly, to enshrine, making citizenship in the Kingdom of Heaven and citizenship in Caesar's kingdom easily reconcilable loyalties, perhaps does not sit so easily with Christian discipleship. Indeed this second kind of memory raises the very likely possibility that the present authorities are strikingly similar to those of Jesus' day, by whom the first disciples were (according to tradition) put to death. And Christian memory, if anything, becomes even more dangerous when human suffering is brought into the equation, for the entire Christian scripture would seem to bear witness that if God is to be found anywhere, it is on the side of the suffering poor, because that is where Jesus took his stand against the religious and political leaders of first-century Palestine. Scripture would seem to be replete with such dangerous memories. Arguably the most famous of these, or at least among the most widely recognized, is the hymn sung by Mary, the mother of Jesus, as recorded in the first chapter of the gospel according to Luke, which the Catholic tradition has appointed to be sung at Evening Prayer for every day of the year: "He has cast down the mighty from their thrones, and has lifted up the lowly. He has filled the hungry with good things, but has sent the rich away empty."[44]

"The dangerous memory of Jesus," then, demolishes assumptions about power and who should possess it; it shatters assumptions about government-sanctioned violence and whose right it is to use it; it attacks, at its very base, the easy belief that it is religion's duty to make peace with political realities simply because that is how the world is, and it has always been so. Most dangerously, it recalls Jesus' personal stance with and for the poor against the religious and political leaders of his day.[45]

Precisely because Jesus stood in a very specific stance vis-à-vis the political and religious authorities, Metz maintained, *all* genuine Christian theology is political—or at least all genuine Christian theology has obvious political ramifications. Further, Metz argued that Christians who sought to keep their political and religious loyalties in safely isolated separate categories miss the entire meaning of "remembering" in its Christian sense. Indeed remembering the Christian past in a way that isolates political loyalties is actually a form of forgetting. For Metz—and for many Catholic and Protestant theologians after him—"remembrance" in its overt Christian sense ("Do this in memory of me") places radical political and social duties on individual believers. Just because others "over there" are suffering because of actions for which we are not directly responsible as citizens does not mean that we are morally free of concern about them, especially if we are part of a system that is causing suffering among them. Politics, in this sense, has overt moral and religious meanings, just as religion has clear political obligations. "Others" (like the Vietnamese) cannot therefore ever be simply an "anonymous mass":

> Christians will come to have a conscience not only about what they do or do not do to others, but also about what they let happen to others. On a political level, solidarity with those who suffer means a radical questioning of the structures of socio-political power that are usually taken for granted. In light of the Christian memory of suffering, it is clear that social power and political domination continually have to justify themselves in view of actual suffering. The social and political power of the rich and the rulers must be open to the question of the extent to which it causes suffering.[46]

The meaning of the Catonsville Nine for the American Catholic engagement with their own past during the 1960s becomes clearer: the Nine offered to their fellow believers a very different and far more dangerous understanding of what it meant to be a "good Catholic" in the United States. Good Catholics could not simply dismiss the sufferings of Vietnamese peasants half a world away as necessary political fallout for an anonymous mass of political enemies. The demands for patriotic loyalty in such a context did not, and should not, be taken as having divine authorization. To the contrary, the authorities who demanded compliance in causing such suffering to others had to "justify themselves in view of the actual suffering." And if they could not offer morally believable justifications for their actions, they had to be disobeyed. Indeed they had to be actively opposed. This was not primarily a political duty, but a Christian moral duty.

The dangerous memory of Jesus opened up a new past in which real Christians (and therefore by definition "good Catholics") could not assume that obeying government authority was the morally correct thing to do, a situation that many opponents of the Berrigans in 1968 would have to grapple with themselves just a few years later, after *Roe v. Wade*. What the Catonsville events sacramentalized was the ancient but largely buried Christian tradition of civil disobedience to Caesar in order to render unto God that which was God's. Such disobedience made many authorities—draft board officials, federal judges, archbishops—deeply angry, just as it had infuriated Roman governors and first-century religious authorities. But such anger, though understandable, could not deter Christians from their duty, which was to be in the right place when Jesus returned. After the Catonsville Nine the American Catholic past wasn't what it used to be.

Avery Dulles and the Law of Unintended Consequences

Father Dulles is now largely thought by friend and foe alike to be one of the most forceful voices for a renewed orthodoxy in the Church. Liberals see him as having turned his back on his younger radicalism; like many an older man, they suggest, he has grown more conservative with age. His experiences with certain forms of liberal Catholicism, while not changing his ideas about the Church, seemed to have alerted him to their potential for disaster.
—Robert Royal, "Avery Dulles' Long Road to Rome," *Crisis*, 2001

A "HEALTHY PLURALISM"

While the Catonsville Nine were energizing lefties on the streets of Baltimore, a somewhat more sedate revolution was taking place in, of all places, the theology department office of a son of the East Coast establishment. Avery Cardinal Dulles was probably the most institutionally lauded Catholic theologian in the United States in the last quarter of the twentieth century. The author of twenty-four books and more than eight hundred articles, Dulles was widely known and respected well before receiving his red hat in February 2001. A scholar with a voluminous knowledge of the history of his craft, he was known as well for his carefully calibrated evaluations of theological positions and a rare ability to see and understand many sides of a theological argument. Both those who agreed with his theological opinions and, tellingly, those who did not respected him as a fair and engaging conversation partner, even during the rough-and-tumble debates that defined the Catholic "long sixties."

Dulles began his long path to a cardinal's hat as a Presbyterian child of the East Coast diplomatic establishment. Both his great grandfather, John W. Foster, and his great uncle, Robert Lansing, served as secretaries of state to U.S. presidents. That position seems to have become something of a family heirloom. His own father, John Foster Dulles, served as secretary of state to Dwight Eisenhower, and his paternal uncle, Allen Dulles, was a founder of the Central Intelligence Agency. If he had done nothing else, given his family pedigree Dulles's conversion to Roman Catholicism at the end of his first semester as a student at Harvard Law School would have made news.[1]

But Avery Dulles's family pedigree was the least of his achievements. After entering the Society of Jesus in 1946 and earning a doctorate in theology at the Jesuit Gregorian University in Rome, he joined a succession of theology faculties: Woodstock College in Maryland, the Catholic University of America, and Fordham University. Many of his books appeared on standard reading lists for doctoral students in theology. *The Catholicity of the Church, The Assurance of Things Hoped For, The Craft of Theology, The Splendor of Faith*, and *A History of Apologetics* were sometimes called "Dulles's Greatest Hits." He received almost all of the awards and accolades possible for an American Catholic theologian over the course of his long career: the Cardinal Spellman Award, the Campion Prize, the Cardinal Gibbons Award, and many more. But his single greatest hit of all was undoubtedly *Models of the Church*, published in 1974 and instantly acclaimed a classic work by theologians in the United States and abroad. *Models* earned Dulles both fame and a mind-numbing list of speaking engagements in North America and Europe. Indeed such was his renown that in February 2001 he became the first American nonbishop to be named a cardinal, making him (in the argot of Catholicism) a "Prince of the Church" while allowing him to remain a working theologian, free of diocesan oversight and fund-raising concerns. But this prince's life became contested territory for the factions battling for the soul of American Catholicism. Both the left and the right wings of American Catholicism have offered considered judgments as to the meaning and trajectory of Dulles's theological career.[2]

As arguably the most visible and unarguably the most honored American Catholic theologian by the end of the twentieth century, Dulles was virtually the embodiment of American Catholic theology itself. Some in the Catholic academy have cast him as a theological liberal who, as a result of the seeming chaos of the Catholic sixties, lost the faith and joined the other side: an increasingly conservative Vatican leadership seeking to correct an overly radicalized reading of the documents of Vatican II. Others, perhaps less charitably, portray him as an independent thinker who, as a result of ecclesiastical honors bestowed on him considerably before he received the cardinal's hat, became enamored of Roman recognition and so increasingly espoused the party line. Still others have asserted that Dulles never really changed his theological opinions; it was the American Catholic community itself that lurched to the left, a move that made Dulles appear to become more conservative while in fact remaining fairly stationary.[3]

Two of the most perceptive readings of Dulles's career have been offered by Joseph Komonchak, professor of theology at the Catholic University of America, and Anne-Marie Kirmse, Dulles's research assistant at Fordham University. In February 2001, at the time of Dulles's elevation to the College of Cardinals by Pope John Paul II, Komonchak observed (with his usual deft command of complex issues) that Dulles tended "to be a conservative among liberals and liberal when among conservatives." He thus contended that Dulles's seeming theological movement from left to right might be better understood by conceiving of his entire career as a "commitment to conversation" from a centrist position so that his conversation partners largely determined his specific positions. In this reading of his career, Dulles was "a good listener, first, in the sense that he has attended to the voices of the past in large works on the history of theology, to separated Christians in several ecumenical dialogues, and to fellow Catholics in analyses of postconciliar church life and theology." Komonchak opined that Dulles had learned his art of conversation from the *Spiritual Exercises* of St. Ignatius Loyola, the founder of his order, and had incorporated this Ignatian tradition into a quite distinctive theological method for doing Catholic theology. The focus of that distinctive method was to be found in Dulles's penchant for models, arguably most famously expressed in his magisterial work, *Models of the Church*.[4]

For Dulles the *seeming* differences of opinion among Catholic theologians actually reflected far more basic *preconscious* understandings of how the real world operated. Theologians therefore needed to address those (largely buried) preconscious models, and in the process they could discover that there was more wisdom in others' theological positions than they had previously thought. His lifelong exploration of these deeper models, in Komonchak's estimation, thus performed a double service to Catholic theology: it encouraged a salutary modesty in undercutting the claim of any single model to explain the great Mystery at the heart of the Christian gospel, and it promoted mutual understanding and communication between theologians who saw things differently, allowing them to agree to disagree while remaining members of the same Household of Faith. In Dulles's irenic and brilliant approach, "none of the models is dismissed out of hand, each having its strengths; [but] none becomes all-determining, each having its weaknesses."[5]

In Komonchak's reading, Dulles's theological career was marked by a decidedly centrist base of operations, making forays to the left and to the right, as time and Church need dictated. If he appeared to be making more forays against the left by the end of the twentieth century, "that is probably in part because he thinks that it is certain liberal [models] that most need to be challenged, at least in theological circles."[6]

Anne-Marie Kirmse agreed with Komonchak that Dulles's models approach was central to understanding the trajectory of his long and distinguished career, but she also emphasized his commitment to maintaining a healthy pluralism in Catholic theology as the hallmark of his thought. Dulles always maintained that "the various models used to illustrate a theological concept must be kept in dialectical tension with each other, and that each should be used to critique and complement the others. To choose only one as paradigmatic would lead to distortion."[7]

Kirmse's recognition of this tension at the heart of much of Dulles's theology is especially helpful in evaluating his supposed "lurch to the right" during the final decades of his career. If Kirmse is right, then students of Dulles's career must never lose sight of the strategic nature of his thinking. His firm belief that reality was more complex than any single model we can construct to explain it thus helps us to understand his famous remark that theological models "are neither true nor false, but only apt or inept." In other words, Dulles believed that no model, however lucid or sophisticated, could do complete justice to that Divine Reality at the heart of things. Rather than conceiving of some models as right and others as wrong he argued that all models are more or less helpful in explicating the Mystery (i.e., "apt or inept"). In such an approach to doing Catholic theology, the task of the theologian was to craft a more "apt" model (or more likely, models in the plural) for understanding the great Mystery to which such theology bore witness. In other words, pluralism was built into the very process by which Dulles approached the craft of theology.[8]

Kirmse wrote that Dulles's commitment to a plurality of models helped Catholicism to avoid canonizing any one model as *the* crucial one, "as if no other time had anything to contribute to our understanding of revelation." She agreed with Komonchak that such pluralism helped to keep theologians (including Dulles) humble in their system-building efforts, knowing that their efforts would not be the last word but would contribute to a different synthesis to meet the unforeseen necessities of the future. A truly effective theology for the Church could never be constructed by offering a frozen, unchanging model of some perfect Church achieved in the past. Indeed it was precisely *against* such an understanding of theology that Dulles maintained a

✓ mediating position between conservative and liberal viewpoints. He has attempted to present a balanced view of the issues at hand, describing the assets and liabilities of each side. He is grieved by the polarization which has occurred since Vatican II, and he has tried to escape being labeled as either a conservative or a liberal.[9]

Both Komonchak and Kirmse offer valuable insights for understanding a theological career that produced so many articles over the course of five decades. Indeed it would seem that anyone attempting to interpret the sheer mass of scholarship produced by America's first cardinal-theologian must begin with these two protean interpretations. But there is another factor to be considered, one that helps to explain why both liberals and conservatives sought to interpret the meaning of a centrist theologian who produced such a radical work as *Models of the Church*. And that is the law of unintended consequences.

Although Dulles had a strategic and mediating style, the pluralism inherent in his models approach had some radical effects, The Christian past, as Dulles so brilliantly described it, appeared to show that the Church had defined itself in many ways over the long course of its history, so that a monolithic vision of its core identity appeared to be both historically baseless and theologically improbable. In a word, Dulles's very lucidity and command of the sources gave birth to a quite robust historical consciousness that was independent of his intentions in writing *Models of the Church*.

This pluralism, and the historical-mindedness that accompanied its recognition, was especially troubling for traditionalist Catholics in the United States, who believed, as many Catholics had believed before reading Dulles's book, that the institutional model was the core model for Catholic Christianity. The True Church, in this model, was indistinguishable from the visible institutional structures of the Catholic Church. In this understanding of Catholicism, the Church was marked by the values of strict hierarchy; by (perhaps overly) legal understandings of both the sacraments and mass attendance (it "counted" if you arrived before the Offertory); by careful attention to a vast array of institutional minutiae, from how to correctly fold one's hands during prayer to the color of nuns' habits; by a deeply ingrained belief that it was easy to tell who was in the Ark of Salvation, and who was not. Catholicism was, in this view, alarmingly concrete, embodied, and legal.

But as Dulles so deftly illustrated, though such an institutional emphasis had indeed been present in Catholic Christianity for centuries, it had also been considered the *least important* way of talking about the Church by the early Church Fathers and by the giants of the tradition, Augustine and Aquinas. A number of other models—the Church as the sacramental embodiment of Christ's presence in history, the Church as the herald of the Good News to the marginalized, the Church as the servant of all humanity, and not just of Catholics—had far more stature than the institutional model. And Dulles, ever the meticulous scholar, backed up that pluralistic claim with innumerable examples from the Christian and Catholic past.

To explain the meaning of Dulles's career, then, by reading his work from the early 1970s as embodying the kind of liberal premises that he later came to regret (from whatever set of motives) is to attribute both considerably more and less to the intentionality of scholars than seems warranted by the historical record: *more* because it presumes that important works of theology will always be read with the intention the authors had in mind in writing them, and *less* because such an evaluative approach seems to presume that authors of such important works had a single (or at least easily identifiable) motive in writing them. *Models of the Church*, in a more serendipitous reading of history, was the right work at the right time, by a respected scholar noted both for his careful research and for his balanced presentation of the Catholic tradition. Whatever Dulles's intentions in writing it, the book took the historical awareness already introduced into the North American Catholic community, by the changes in the liturgy, by the debates over artificial contraception, and by the battles over reforming religious life, and added to it the roots of a pluralistic understanding of the Church itself. And along with that pluralism came a historical recognition—perhaps with shock, perhaps with relief, perhaps with wonder—that things were more complicated than they had at first seemed.

THE CRAFT OF THEOLOGY

In a 1971 work definitively announcing his presence as a theological voice
to be reckoned with, *The Survival of Dogma*, Avery Dulles observed that in
the century between 1868 and 1968, that is, roughly the period between the
First and Second Vatican Councils, the Catholic hierarchy, and especially
Vatican officials in Rome, had been particularly vigilant in scrutinizing the
orthodoxy of theologians. This vigilance, however well intentioned, had
unfortunately resulted in the "suppression of ideas which later proved [to
be] sound and useful." With the Church threatening a return to the bad
old days, Dulles dryly observed that such suppression of ideas hardly
offered a helpful approach to the present. Given the prominence that many
of the ideas that had been condemned in the early twentieth century had
achieved at Vatican II, he argued that a renewed attempt at suppression of
theological debate, rather than dialogue, might very well contribute to an
already growing decline of respect for the teaching authority of the institutional Church itself. Indeed Dulles noted that many of the Catholic faithful
and theologians already believed that some members of the hierarchy were
better middle managers than theologians, far better at balancing spread-
sheets than for their "outstanding capacity in doctrinal matters." The
result, he argued, had been for some bishops to resort to the least convincing kind of argument, that from authority ("Do this because I tell you
to"), when confronted by challenges to their interpretation of the tradition
by theologians or uppity lay people. But such an appeal to authority—even
to one, like Dulles, who himself always evinced the greatest respect for duly
constituted Church authority—was problematic at best. In discussing the
theological acumen of some Catholic bishops, Dulles noted:

> The gulf between intellectual competence and decisive power has
> become, at times, too wide for comfort. . . . In this situation, little is
> gained by passionate insistence on "religious submission of mind
> and will." The *precise* point at issue is whether such submission is
> morally responsible and whether the alleged charisms of the episco-
> pal office (to which appeal is made) can in fact compensate for the
> apparent lack of professional competence. The plea for obedience
> often fails to answer this question, for it overlooks the fact that
> assent to teaching cannot normally be a matter of sheer voluntary
> obedience. As an intellectual act, it demands grounds for honest
> conviction.[10]

The unspoken presence in Dulles's analysis of the debates raging within the American Catholic Church was, of course, Paul VI's 1968 encyclical on artificial contraception, *Humanae Vitae*. Dulles thus situated the reception of that document within the larger frame of what he took to be the primary challenge facing the postconciliar Church: finding the proper relationship between the well-defined power of bishops to teach in the name of the Church and the "equally undeniable right of the faithful in general, and competent experts in particular, to exercise" *their* responsibility to teach the faith. In Dulles's estimation the apparent decline in respect for the bishops' teaching authority—for which *Humanae Vitae* formed the flashpoint—could be seen as "partly due to the fact that the universal episcopate has not yet achieved a satisfactory working relationship with the intellectuals and prophets in the Church."[11]

Dulles therefore sought a mediating answer about who had teaching authority in the community, while also arguing that bishops could not claim for themselves the "totality of teaching power." Bishops were certainly mandated by canon law to teach in the name of the Church, but the Catholic tradition had also consistently recognized throughout its history that there were "other teachers, including charismatics (prophets) and scholars (such as theologians)," who reliably taught in the name of the Church. In Dulles's estimation both bishops and theologians had a divine mandate, which had been recognized by the Church itself, to offer different kinds of teaching for the good of the entire community. Indeed a careful study of the Catholic past showed clearly that doctrine did *not*

> in every case, flow down to theologians and the laity from the top officials of the Church. If the Spirit dwells in the entire Body, enlivening all the members, doctrinal initiatives can begin from below as well as from above. . . . The theologian, then, cannot be rightly regarded as a mere agent of the hierarchical teaching authority. His task is not simply to repeat what the official magisterium has already said, or even to expound and defend what has already become official teaching, but, even more importantly, to discover what has not been taught.[12]

But while arguing for this broader understanding of who could teach in the Church, Dulles also observed that theologians should not seek to substitute *their* charism for that of the bishops, because the tradition clearly expressed the authority, and duty, of bishops to provide clear teaching to the faithful.

Although there certainly existed other sources of teaching in the Church, none of these could replace the episcopacy as an authoritative source of teaching. But bishops did have to pay more careful attention to the work of theologians as "rightful participants in passing on the tradition of the community" before pronouncing on doctrinal or disciplinary questions. This was especially important in Catholic Christianity, which had consistently held that bishops' powers to teach had "no charism that operates mechanically or magically." Instead a study of the past showed that bishops, and indeed the pope himself, had an obligation to bring the best and most accessible theological talent to bear in offering official teaching; no magical understanding of how the episcopacy arrived at their teaching, he argued, could substitute for good theological advice.[13]

Dulles's argument on what would come to be called the "two magisteria," that is, on the twofold teaching obligations of both bishops and theologians, was taken by many in the American Catholic community to be a theological position well left of center. Such an impression might be supported by the perception that the hardest sayings in his book seemed addressed to bishops, reminding them that there were other legitimate teachers in the community and that they needed to be wary of claiming anything like a "totality of teaching power."

But in fact a careful reading of Dulles's book gives the impression of a decidedly centrist work of theology, deeply rooted in the historical evolution of a complex theological tradition. What Dulles found in the Catholic past, and especially in the High Middle Ages, where the term *magisterium* had initially been used almost exclusively to refer to the work of theologians and not to the teaching authority of bishops, was that the very concept of teaching authority was multivalent. That is, his deep immersion in the development of Catholic theology led him to believe that there was a healthy pluralism with regard to teaching in the name of the Church. Abbots and mendicant friars, lay mystics and university theologians, no less than bishops and popes, had all pronounced in the name of the Church and had all been heeded as official teachers at different points and in various circumstances. Over against the kind of uniformity and theological cleanness of line that many twentieth-century Catholics took to be normative, Dulles found a theological tradition in which "manyness" was not only tolerated, but even celebrated. Thirteenth-century nominalists and realists, seventeenth-century Dominican "rigorists" and Jesuit "laxists," twentieth-century devotees of the *Nouvelle théologie* and neo-Thomistic scholastics—all of these fought like theological cats and dogs in their respective eras. But all considered themselves (and their debate partners in often fierce exchanges) to be Catholics holding a common faith, despite the very different epistemologies and models of Church that informed their common faith. What Dulles had found in his (sometimes awe-inspiring) mastery of the history of Catholic theology was that the tradition had always, wisely, allowed various theological emphases to flourish within its own household.

History, then, and not liberal ideology, served as the reservoir for Dulles's argument. Further, and equally to the point, in the course of making his argument Dulles had sought to remind theologians that their contributions toward explicating the theological tradition could in no way replace the authority of the bishops' teaching office within their dioceses nor that of the Bishop of Rome within the universal Church. The duty of theologians in elucidating church teaching was not to replace episcopal authority, but to inform and complement it through dialogue, debate, and rigorous scholarly research.

Balance, nuance, and a deep respect for (and astounding knowledge of) the historical record had led Dulles to the belief that the past did not support the univocal and one-sided positions of some theologians and bishops in the present. The evidence of history, in other words, seemed to condemn both members of the hierarchy who believed that they alone possessed the authority to pronounce on disputed theological issues, and theologians who seemed to argue that their academic expertise could substitute for the teaching office of bishops. History itself appeared to demolish the monolithic arguments offered by both sides of the debates in 1971.

Models of the Church, published three years later, would go even further toward elucidating a pluralist theological past. In that book Dulles argued that Roman Catholicism was indeed catholic (in its Greek root meaning of "universal") precisely because its theological tradition sought to balance various models of religious community that had evolved over time. Indeed he claimed that it was this very pluralism in ecclesiology—conceiving of the Church as both sacrament and herald, servant and institution—that made the Church both catholic and apostolic.[14]

In Dulles's opinion, the model of the Church privileged after the sixteenth-century Council of Trent was that of a "perfect society" in history. In this model, which had dominated Catholic theological discussion in the four centuries after the Reformation, the very structures of the institutional Church were equated with features of the Kingdom of God itself. And the privileging of that institutional model had come to color the popular conception of Catholicism as well: "In the popular mind the Catholic Church is identified with what I describe as the institutional model of the Church. Catholics, therefore, are commonly thought to be committed to the thesis that the Church is most aptly to be conceived as a single, unified, 'perfect society.'" But this popular misconception was problematic for twentieth-century believers: "I hold that Catholics today should not wish to defend a primarily institutional view of the Church." Indeed he confessed that he had taken a "deliberately critical stance toward those [models of church] that are primarily or exclusively institutional." Thus of all the models presented in his book "one of the models cannot properly be taken as primary— and this is the institutional model." This was so, he argued, because institutions are, "of their very nature, subordinate to persons":

> Structures are subordinate to life. "The Sabbath was made for man, not man for the Sabbath" (Mark 2:27). Without calling into question the value and importance of institutions, one may feel that this value does not properly appear unless it can be seen that the structure effectively helps make the Church a community of grace, a sacrament of Christ, a herald of salvation, and a servant of mankind.[15]

In his 1974 book Dulles presented five major approaches, or models, for understanding the Church: the Church as "mystical communion," which included both the older metaphor of the Christian community as the *mystici corporis* (Christ's "mystical body" in history) as well as Vatican II's preferred metaphor of the Church as the "People of God"; the Church as the sacrament of God's encounter with humanity, both in its specific sacraments and more broadly through its embodiment of grace in observable forms; the Church as the prophetic herald of the Good News to humanity; the Church as the servant of both God and humanity through its care for the marginalized and poor; and the Church as the institutional continuation of Christ's message and witness through its offices, hierarchical figures, and formal protocols.[16]

Dulles's (perhaps surprising) denigration of the institutional model proceeded not from progressive loyalties, as some conservative and liberal theologians would later argue, but rather from his belief that pluralism and not homogeneity, tension and not uniformity, marked the Catholic theological tradition throughout its history. This tradition, as he understood perhaps better than any other Catholic thinker of his generation, called for the dominance of this or that particular model of the Church at different points, depending on time and circumstance. He allowed that there might have been good contextual reasons in the sixteenth century for the Church to have emphasized its institutional reality over against a perhaps over-spiritualized understanding of the Church on the part of some Protestant reformers. But the overemphasis on that institutional model had served its purpose, perhaps too well, and it was imperative to restore a more balanced (and thus more Catholic) appreciation of the many-sided nature of Christ's Church:

> A balanced theology of the Church must find a way of incorporating the major affirmations of each basic ecclesiological type. Each of the models calls attention to certain aspects of the Church that are less clearly brought out by the other models. . . . The most distinctive feature of Catholicism, in my opinion, is *not* its insistence on the institutional but rather its wholeness and balance. I am of the opinion that the Catholic Church, in the name of its "catholicity," must at all costs avoid falling into a sectarian mentality. Being "catholic," this Church must be open to all God's truth, no matter who utters it.[17]

Dulles thus offered a sober caution about absolutizing any one model in ranking the importance of the various models: the community of believers, in its pilgrimage toward that Kingdom that stood beyond history, was not, and could not be, encapsulated by any single model of what the "one, holy, catholic and apostolic church" could be. Some theologians, he warned, quite mistakenly tended to assume that the essence of the True Church

> somehow exists, like a dark continent, ready-made and awaiting only to be mapped. [But] the Church, as a sociological entity, may be more correctly viewed as a "social construct." In terms of sociological theory, one may say that the form of the Church is being constantly modified by the way in which members of the Church externalize their own experience and in so doing transform the Church to which they already belong. Within the myriad possibilities left open by the Scripture and tradition, the Church in every generation has to exercise its options. . . . The future forms of the Church lie beyond our powers to foresee. The Church will have to make adjustments in order to survive in the society of the future and to confront the members of that society with the challenge of the gospel.[18]

As Dulles presented what he took to be the genuinely catholic take on the reality of the Church, the tradition could be defined as an ongoing tension between unity and pluralism, between "oneness" and "manyness," between the institutional protocols (which were certainly necessary) and the theologically more important metaphors that pointed to the Church's transcendent reality beyond history. In this creative tension, the pluralism does (and should) remain as real and determinative as the unity. As he saw it, the *real* Catholic past was far more diverse, pluralistic, and messy than many in the twentieth-century Church understood or desired. Those who sought to constrain that broad tradition into any single model—but especially into the institutional model—were betraying the tradition, not restoring it: "Much harm is done by imperialistically seeking to impose some one model as the definitive one." Each model of the Church should interpenetrate and mutually qualify the others. Such a "profuse mixing of metaphors reflects not logical confusion, but theological vitality."[19]

If any of the models were to be privileged in the context of American Catholicism in the last quarter of the twentieth century, Dulles believed that the "communion" model had "special merit." This was so because it preserved the institutional realities of Catholicism within a much larger set of loyalties: the external offices and laws were important not in themselves, but because they served as a "vivid sign" to a deeper community of shared love and compassion (*agape* in the New Testament) that transcended laws, officers, and rituals. Indeed if the Church ceased to be a community of love, then the external signs were simply dead letters. The communion at the heart of the Church gave legitimacy and life to its offices and rituals, and not the other way around. To insist on external conformity to the institution and its rules—as one so often encountered in the old Catholic question "Does this count?" regarding keeping the rules of fasting and ritual observance—while ignoring the more important mystical and affective bonds that legitimated them, was to completely misapprehend Catholic Christianity itself.[20]

In expanding on this argument, Dulles made several points that undoubtedly disquieted critics of the messy Catholic sixties, soon to be termed conservatives or traditionalists. Their own efforts to highlight an institutionally defined and centered understanding of Catholicism was understandable, he allowed, given the public debates and battles then being waged at every level of the American Catholic community. It was completely understandable why some American Catholics looked longingly back to a more stable, institutionally defined definition of what Catholicism was about, a definition that specified everyone's place clearly, according to their (literally) ordained roles. If only everyone would obey the rules that applied to them within the institution; if only everyone would listen to duly constituted institutional authority and stop second-guessing Church officials, from the pope to the local pastor; if only the laity would return to their older agreement to "pay, pray, and obey" Christ's vicars on earth, then all would return to normalcy—or at least to that normalcy that had defined the post–Vatican I Church in the United States.

But the entire point of Dulles's book was that such Catholic "normalcy" was actually quite anomalous when viewed against a wider, deeper, and richer understanding of the tradition of Catholic Christianity. What one actually encountered in the theology and practice of the early Church, in the theological schools and ritual practices of the Middle Ages, and in the rich and ancient traditions of Catholics in the "oriental churches" was an understanding of Catholicism that made nineteenth- and early twentieth-century American understandings of their faith seem pale and thin indeed. And what Dulles had discovered in the rich but messily pluralistic past was that returning to an older set of definitions—with their clearly demarcated boundaries between "us" and "them," between clear rules and messy mixings, between the safely parochial (in every sense) and the dangerous (and seemingly secular) demands of history—would only constrict what Catholicism was really about and make it less able to meet the demands of the fractious present. Such a constriction would simply shelve contemporary Catholicism's engagement with its own rich past for yet another generation, as it had in the early twentieth century.

The danger in pluralizing the definition of Catholicism, as Dulles recognized so brilliantly, did not come from outside the Church at all. The fractious debates over Church authority, theological formulations, and witnessing to gospel values (most particularly with regard to Vietnam) just then roiling the American Catholic community, and which some felt could only be the work of radicals undermining the Household of Faith (or at least of liberals loosening the bonds of authority within that household), found rich support in the Catholic past itself.

The pluralisms of Dulles's models bespoke a master narrative marked *not* by monolithic answers or unified understandings of authority and power. On the contrary, the models Dulles offered to understand the mystery of the Church demonstrated that the tradition had opted for different, sometimes even contradictory ways of conceiving itself, depending on the context and the audience. One might argue that what Dulles offered his readers in *Models of the Church* was the shocking but nonetheless true realization that Catholicism offered master narratives (in the plural) rather than a single master narrative. Part and parcel of that realization was that the Church had *changed* its dominant model at different periods of its history. Such a realization, though seemingly unexceptional in the abstract, actually contained the seeds of crisis within itself, as Garry Wills would memorably observe during those same years. In 1971, the very year Avery Dulles emerged on the national Catholic stage as a major theological presence with the publication of *The Survival of Dogma*, Wills discerned such seeds of crisis in a new dirty little secret: that the Church itself changed, a recognition that many Catholics experienced as a form of personal crisis.[21]

THE VARIETIES OF (CATHOLIC) RELIGIOUS EXPERIENCE

Much like Wills, but in more academic form and with less rhetorical flourish, Dulles presented an understanding of Catholicism in which change and pluralism played starring roles. This seemed obvious to Dulles and to others who had studied the tradition, if not as carefully and deeply as he, at least in a similarly sustained way. To some, however, such an understanding of Catholicism came as a shock to the system.

Dulles, hardly a thoroughgoing theological liberal, believed that he was offering an insight intrinsic to the Catholic tradition itself, one that the Church's greatest thinkers and intellects—St. Paul, St. Augustine, and St. Thomas Aquinas, Bishop Bousquet and John Henry Newman, Yves Congar and Karl Rahner—had written about for centuries. That insight seemed beyond dispute simply because of its ubiquity and pedigree. And that insight was simply that *no* single metaphor or model could contain or fully express the truth of God's rich dealings with humanity in and through the Church. Thomas Aquinas, Catholicism's greatest medieval thinker, had argued in the thirteenth century that the more metaphors, the better. He argued that talking about God required metaphors rather than description, analogy rather than data collection. His own preferred designation for the Holy One in the *Summa*, "Qui Est," usually translated as "the one who is," or into its masculine form, "He who is," was itself a metaphor. Thomas's insight transcends gender: God is neither male nor female, but simply "is." And thus Thomas, arguably more subtle than some of the "neo" Thomists who claimed to be his intellectual followers, might have been less disconcerted than they when twentieth-century Catholic feminists started translating his phrase as "She who is," a construction that, however unsettling, is both grammatically correct and in line with Thomas's argument about the mysteriousness of the Holy One.[22]

Most Catholic theologians after Thomas took his insight regarding the benefit of multiple metaphors in talking about God as simply part of the furniture of their shop, which they inherited from the great Catholic minds who came before them. The more metaphors to talk about God and God's dealings with humanity, the better, for (on one level, anyway) all the metaphors were true. By the same token, all were incomplete and partial, and each needed to be corrected ("aptly," as Dulles put it) by others. Many models thus served the task far better than reliance on any single construct, however excellent.

No one knew this better than Avery Dulles, from first to last a dutiful son of the Church, and neither conservative nor liberal, at least not as those political monikers are used to designate party allegiances. However brilliant his utilization of the models approach in talking about the Church, Dulles was simply doing for the twentieth century what Thomas had done for the thirteenth: presenting multiple models for understanding the complex reality that was Catholicism—certainly an institution, but vastly more than an institution. And Dulles offered this pluralism not to minimize the importance of the institutional Church in any way, but rather to link it with realities that transcended institutional loyalties.

But in the very process of showing how and in what ways the tradition had thought about the Church, Dulles's book leaked what Wills recognized as the "dirty little secret" of modern Catholicism: that the Church had changed its preferred metaphor for thinking about itself over the course of its history. Its various preferred models had not displaced each other, at least in the sense of erasing earlier models as viable options. Rather the Catholic tradition had allowed many metaphors to stand in tension with each other—the institutional reality of the community sometimes supporting its prophetic, diaconal impulses, and sometimes not; the sacramental sometimes balancing the necessity of preaching the Word, and sometimes displacing it. This field of tension demonstrated the disconcerting truth that Catholicism wasn't simply a *single* stream, but multiple streams mingling in a deep and wide tradition. The very pluralism of the models bore powerful witness to the fact that manyness and tension were as intrinsic to the community of the faithful as were uniformity and docility.

The trajectory of Dulles's decades-long career after 1974 makes it highly unlikely that he ever sought to pour fuel on the fires raging within the American Catholic community during the "long sixties," which stretched from Vatican II well into the 1970s. In a real sense those who posit such a change of heart on his part fail to understand one of the core theses of his supposedly liberal book: that pluralism wasn't a partisan thing at all; it was a Catholic thing. Further, those who posit a dramatic change of heart to explain his career disregard his own witness at the end of his career: that his theology had changed very little over the course of five decades.

But to say all of this is not to deny that his 1974 work played an important part in nurturing a historical consciousness already let out of the bag. *Models of the Church* in fact did lend aid and comfort to those who found the static model of post-Tridentine classical theology both confining and unconvincing. No, these institutional discontents argued, such an understanding of Catholicism was both stunted and ahistorical, and Dulles had the goods proving them to be correct:

> The Church of Christ could not perform its mission without some stable organizational features. Throughout its history, from the very earliest years, Christianity has always had an institutional side. All of this is fitting and proper. . . . [But institutions] do not necessarily imply institutionalism, any more than the papacy implies papalism, or law implies legalism. By institutionalism we mean a system in which the institutional element is treated as primary. Institutionalism is a deformation of the true nature of the Church.[23]

Catholic theology in the Patristic period, in the Middle Ages, down through the great Scholastic doctors of the thirteenth century, and until the nineteenth century was relatively free of institutionalism, Dulles asserted. He offered a brilliant short course on over a millennium and a half of theological discourse to prove just that. For Dulles the Catholic past offered little comfort to those who sought to return to some "purer" model of Church, centered on obedience and docility to institutional protocols. For critics of the Catholic sixties who believed that a reassertion of institutional order and hierarchical power was the needed antidote to the seeming chaos raging around them, Dulles appeared to be a publicist for the other side of a family feud just then veering toward domestic violence. But Dulles himself never put much stock in identifying serious theologians—least of all himself—in such polarized terms. And it is precisely here that the law of unintended consequences provides such a handy tool for understanding his crucial role in abetting the growth of historical consciousness among his fellow American Catholics.[24]

Dulles, ever the balanced and dispassionate thinker, who sought to give every model in his argument its due, might best be understood as the author of an apolitical and sophisticated work of theology that had unintended consequences in its time. His very mastery of the dense and complex history of Catholic theology militated against an institutionalist understanding of Catholicism. Such an emphasis on Catholicism's laws and structures in order to hold things together, though understandable, had little foundation in the actual history of the Catholic theological past. Dulles's very brilliance in presenting the many models of the Church confounded the effort to hold up just one of those models as normative or defining. In other words, the very things that made *Models of the Church* so brilliant—his impressive mastery of the past, his catholic willingness to engage so broad a spectrum of Catholic thinkers in conversation, his lucid arguments, which even nonspecialists could understand—made his work a classic in the historicist canon. Things change, including how the Church thinks and teaches about itself; that, Dulles thought, was very good news indeed. Those on what would become known as the Catholic Right, who would later seek to claim him as one of their own, thought otherwise. But it is possible to understand his 1974 classic as an important theological work in its own right, a work that sought to make no political statement at all, but that ineluctably contributed important theological heft to the burgeoning awareness of pluralism in the Church—not pluralism as threat or pluralism as disobedience, but pluralism as the most Catholic stance of all. Such were the unintended consequences of *Models of the Church*.

8

Things Change

"CHANGE AS A FORM OF PERSONAL CRISIS"

Christians, especially Catholic Christians, have an ambivalent relationship with historical change. One of the more arresting examples of this ambivalence came in an address Pope Benedict XVI delivered in an allocution on December 22, 2005, to Roman curial officials. Benedict argued that the Second Vatican Council did not represent any kind of "rupture" with previous ecumenical councils of the Church. This was the case, he observed, because, in all of its essential details, the Church cannot change. Whatever Benedict's intention in making such a claim, on one level at least his assertion is surprising given the dramatic theological and liturgical changes that Christianity underwent during its long history.[1]

The original followers of Jesus of Nazareth, all Jews in the first Christian community in Jerusalem, came to realize shortly after his death that their purchase on the faith of Abraham, Isaac, and Jacob had been radically reshaped by Jesus' teaching and life. Thus, within two generations of Jesus' death, the Jewish scriptures became an "old testament," retained as revelation, yes, but now supplemented with newer testimonies and letters, through which the ancient Hebrew texts would be radically reinterpreted. Indeed one could argue that the first three Christian centuries were a time of constant change, a radical shift in believers' views both of the past and of a future that would end with Jesus' return in glory.[2]

Perhaps the single most arresting evidence of this willingness to not only recognize but to celebrate historical change was the Christian community's decision to renumber time itself. Time was no longer to be measured by the years since the creation of the world (as in the Jewish calendar), nor by the number of Olympiads held (as in the Greek calendar), nor by *ab urbe condita,* "since the founding of the City [of Rome]" (as in the Roman calendar). After 523 the common calendar of both Europe and the Christian East counted time from the purported date of Jesus' birth in Bethlehem. Thus AD (*anno domini*, "in the year of our Lord") came to precede the date listed on the cornerstones of public buildings and official documents. Viewed from this vantage Christianity (and Catholic Christianity, which was emerging as a distinct tradition within it) was grounded in a dramatic historical disjunction: Jesus' presence in history changed everything.[3]

Jesus being put to death by Roman soldiers for appearing to threaten the political status quo of first-century Palestine changed everything: how we measure time, why our actions in history are important, and where time was going. Christianity, so understood, was radically wedded to events in time and space. And those events often represented dramatic historical disjunctures and interruptions. History, in important ways, changed before and after Jesus' birth and death. Viewed from such a Christian understanding of history, time was *not* an unbroken stream, and grace often manifested itself in these "in-breakings" that separated one historical moment from another. Thus the big stuff in Christian theology and worship—sin and death, grace and redemption, Christmas and Easter—was *not* timeless or free of historical context. On the contrary, the big stuff was profoundly determined by historical occurrences: when and where Jesus was born (and what land was to be called holy); how and why he died (and thus the cross, and not the empty tomb, as the chief iconic symbol for Christianity itself); Jesus' promise to return and end time itself (and therefore the Christian confidence about what would happen when time stopped: the resurrection of the dead). History itself therefore defined how and why Christians were different from other believers—from, say, the Jewish people, our forebears in the faith.[4]

But viewed from another vantage, Benedict's assertion that the Church cannot change is understandable. St. Paul himself and other leaders of the early Christian community sought to emphasize continuity with the revelation delivered on Mt. Sinai and to the prophets. The Holy One of Israel, Paul reminded his readers, does not revoke promises once made to the Hebrew people; such assurance witnessed to the happy fact that the Holy One remained faithful, even if God's people failed to be faithful to the covenant.[5]

Not all early Christians bought this argument about the continuity between the old and the new law, as various movements from Gnosticism to Marcion witnessed. These sectarian movements emphasized Christian revelation as something radically new, superseding the outdated promises made to Israel (even, in the case of Marcion, positing the Father of Jesus as a new god, not the god of the old covenant). But what emerged by the sixth century as the Orthodox and Catholic traditions of Christianity made these continuities the normative position. From the perspective of Orthodox and Catholic Christians it was necessary to downplay the discontinuities between Judaism and the message of Jesus (ministers as "priests"; the eucharist as "sacrifice," etc.) even if there remained elements of the Christian message, such as St. Paul's observation that "no one is saved by the works of the Law [of Moses]," that made such continuity more like an uneasy truce than an unconditional surrender.[6]

Other factors certainly contributed to the Catholic tradition's profound wariness about celebrating, or even recognizing, historical change and discontinuity. The Christian theological reliance on Greek philosophy (especially on Plato and Aristotle) during the Middle Ages sought to reconcile Athens and Jerusalem, an important aspect of which was making sense of the historically bound consciousness of Jesus with the Greek notion of divinity as timeless and eternal. From the standpoint of the Athenian side of the conversation, precisely because Jesus' message purportedly derived from the Holy One, both it and the messenger who delivered it had to be "impassable," that is, eternal and free of historical change. The Church Fathers (and Mothers) from both the East and the West tended to emphasize the unchanging and unchangeable nature of the Christian message, its transcendence of historical context and mutability.[7]

Another episode confirming Catholic uneasiness with the possibility of historical change or even development in Church teaching occurred in the sixteenth century, during the Age of Reform. Scholarship on the Reformation Era has moved the emergence of the reform impulse back from the sixteenth to the fifteenth (and in some cases, even the fourteenth) century, and thus well before Luther's famous debate with Rome over indulgences, which began in 1517. But what has not been disputed by scholars is the traumatic reaction of the Roman Catholic hierarchy to various reformers' charges that there was radical change and discontinuity in the Christian community between the age of the Apostles and their own. Indeed these "protestants" argued that much Church teaching of the previous one thousand years represented a corrupt departure from the purity of Jesus' gospel and the faith of the early Church.[8]

The decrees produced at the Council of Trent between 1545 and 1563, which defined a Catholic "counter" reformation against the challenges produced by Luther, Calvin, and Zwingli, attested to the quite robust and profoundly ahistorical hierarchical position that sixteenth-century

Catholic belief and practice were simply the contemporary versions of the very same beliefs and practices the first apostles taught. Catholic Christians in Europe and in the far-flung New World could (and should) believe that what they did on Sunday mornings was the very same liturgical act that the early Christians performed in the catacombs of Rome and in the house churches of those brave believers who gathered during the fearsome Roman persecutions of the second and third centuries. Further, this Tridentine brand of Catholicism posited the Church as a perfect society founded by Jesus and entrusted to St. Peter during Christ's earthly ministry: a society complete and perfect from its inception, remaining largely untouched by history and by the historical cultures in which it found itself. St. Peter was portrayed in church art holding the keys to the very same hierarchical power and to the Kingdom of Heaven, as was held by the popes who commissioned those artworks.[9]

This ahistorical, post-Tridentine strand of Catholicism was confirmed and further buttressed in the nineteenth and twentieth centuries, first in the declaration of papal infallibility at the First Vatican Council in 1870, and then in the Roman denunciation of modernism in two papal documents in 1907. In fact the Catholic Church's engagement with modernism in its own house offers the best insight into why the reforms of the Second Vatican Council, and the broader events of the sixties in which that Council took place, caused such a crisis for so many American Catholics during the 1960s and 1970s.

Students of Catholic modernism are largely skeptical of Vatican charges that modernism was an organized movement, largely because of the disparate scholarly agendas of its purported ringleaders. The papal syllabus denouncing the errors of the modernists in July 1907 (*Lamentabili Sane*) never mentioned the names of George Tyrell, Alfred Loisy, or Maurice Blondel, usually considered the leaders of the movement. But it did present certain aspects of each one's scholarship as the strategic maneuverings of an organized cabal, despite the incompatibility of many of their ideas. What is very prescient in the papal denunciation, despite its highly unlikely assertion of an organized plot, is its detection of a pattern in the modernists' thinking that can in fact be read as the intellectual glue holding them together. And that intellectual glue was a belief about human ideas, institutions, and beliefs that is usually called *historicism*.[10]

Christian thinkers who challenged the "timeless" truths taught by the Church before the modernist episode in 1907 tended to argue either that they had received new insight or revelation from God (the Gnostics of the early Church and the Albigensians of the Middle Ages) or that the original meaning of the gospel had been lost or buried over time and now needed to be restored (Luther and Calvin). But the group labeled modernist by Rome in 1907 undertook something totally new. They appeared to argue that *both* the traditional teaching of the Church *and* their new (contradictory) take on Christian truth were correct—each in their own place and time. It was this emphasis on historical context and development that signaled to the pope and to others that something radically new was afoot in the "pernicious ideas" of modernist scholars like Loisy and Tyrrell.[11]

Something troubling *could* be discerned below the surface of the pope's haphazard charges in his "Syllabus" of errors—troubling at least for those who believed that Catholicism *had* to be timeless in order to be true. Along with condemnations of positions that none of those accused of modernism actually held (number 65: that "modern Catholicism can be reconciled with true science only if it is transformed into a broad and liberal Protestantism") were glimpses of a worldview that *was* informed by a new historical consciousness that directly assailed the static presuppositions of Tridentine Catholicism. For instance, number 40 in the "Syllabus" elucidated the historicist understanding of Loisy and Tyrrell (and of many post–Vatican II sacramental theologians as well): that "the Sacraments have their origin in the fact that the Apostles and their successors, swayed by circumstances and events, interpreted some ideas and intentions of Christ." Likewise, numbers 22 ("The dogmas the Church holds out as revealed truths have not fallen from heaven"), 44 ("There is nothing to prove that the Sacrament of Confirmation was employed by the Apostles"), and 53 ("The organic constitution of the Church is not immutable, [but] is subject to perpetual evolution") *did* elucidate a new awareness of the historically conditioned nature of Catholic belief and practice that most of those accused, like most Catholic scholars after Vatican II, simply accepted as part of the mental furniture of the modern world.[12]

Pius X's "Syllabus" thus put the modern world on notice that Catholic doctrines and practices existed above the battle-scarred plains of history and were therefore free of historical development or mutability. What Jesus and the apostles believed and did was precisely what contemporary Catholicism believed and did, nothing more and nothing less. Indeed the very name used to denounce this "sum of all heresies" (modernism) excoriated the modern intellectual climate itself, which encouraged the false doctrine that could assail such self-evident truth. But viewed from the events of the Catholic sixties, modernism can be fruitfully understood as the first sustained Catholic institutional engagement with a broad and deep intellectual movement that would sweep through American Catholicism in the 1960s. Pius X was in fact largely successful in halting Catholicism's engagement with that intellectual movement, save for pockets of intellectual rebellion like the French *Nouvelle théologie* movement in the 1930s and 1940s. But whatever one thinks today of the purported "system" denounced by Pius, he was not far off the mark in believing that a new understanding of history and historical consciousness had arisen among Church historians and biblical scholars by the early years of the twentieth century, a consciousness that posed an unprecedented challenge to the way Catholics had understood their faith for millennia.[13]

THE ORGANIC UNITY OF HISTORY

What Pius X sensed as something new and deeply troubling in the writings of Loisy, Tyrrell, and others in the early years of the twentieth century was but the tip of a much larger and deeper intellectual iceberg that had emerged in Germany in the eighteenth century. The papal condemnation of modernism, viewed thus, was a somewhat delayed and tardy recognition of an intellectual movement that by 1907 had largely become the predominant worldview among German, British, and American scholars. At heart this new worldview was not about science (Darwin), nor about scripture (the "higher criticism" practiced by Julius Wellhausen and Alfred Loisy); it was focused on new thinking about history itself. It was a new way of historical thinking—with a tendency to explain reality in all of its forms in terms of past development—that caused an intellectual revolution that finally reached the doors of the Vatican. Darwin's new twist on the idea of evolution (itself an idea as old as Aristotle) might have required no more dramatic measure of accommodation on the part of believers than a reinterpretation of the creation story had not the very idea of "transcendent revelation in history" itself become problematic. Thus the new historical consciousness made Darwin possible, not the other way around.[14]

Historismus, usually translated in the United States as "historicism," emerged in Germany in the eighteenth century as one of several components in the larger intellectual project of German Romanticism, which attacked the classical, static categories of Enlightenment thought in favor of more fluid, "realistic" categories in which history itself played the leading role. The special object of this Romantic movement's wrath was Enlightenment thought's reliance on "natural law," the belief that at its core the real world and its values rested on an eternal, unchanging law, unchanging because its author was God. By the eighteenth century natural law had achieved normative status in many European intellectual traditions, not least in the theology of the Roman Catholic Church. Whereas Protestant natural law, perhaps most famously embodied in the thought of John Locke, drew on classical philosophy by way of the Cambridge Platonists and Hugo Grotius, Roman Catholic natural law rested on a much older authority: the thirteenth-century "angelic doctor," Thomas Aquinas. But both the Protestant and Catholic streams agreed that "human nature" and "right action" were *givens*, things that remained the same from age to age. It was this very heart of natural law thinking—that human beings and their codes of right and wrong remained the same over time—that was assailed by the new understanding of history and historical context.[15]

In place of the eternal, unchanging categories offered by natural law, scholars pressing the new historical consciousness posited a developmental understanding of the real world: everything—ideas, institutions, and human beings themselves—evolved over time, changing beliefs, laws, and even categories of right and wrong to fit new historical contexts. This new understanding of time and history was perceived as, and to a large extent was, a direct attack on the older static and timeless categories of thought that had shaped Christian theology from Augustine to Pius X. For that latter tradition of theology, the ends of political, philosophical, and religious action remained ever the same, allowing for small adjustments to specific needs of geography and local custom. It was against this set of presuppositions that historicism was set, and it was because of the persistence of the old thinking that one of the most perceptive students of the new historical movement, Friedrich Meinecke, could claim that historicism was "the greatest spiritual revolution which Occidental thought has undergone" since Moses and Aristotle. By the second half of the nineteenth century, in fact, this new way of understanding reality had created a humanly centered world. Indeed Carl Becker, one of the most famous students of Enlightenment thought in the twentieth century, claimed such historicism as one of the requirements of modernity: "What is peculiar to the modern mind is the disposition and the determination to regard ideas and concepts, the truth of things as well as the things in themselves, as changing entities, as points in an endless process."[16]

First spelled out by Johann Gottfried Herder in 1774, historicism was a worldview in which social institutions, intellectual and spiritual beliefs, and even logical categories were immersed in the stream of history itself. The history of any phenomenon, Herder's argument went, was a sufficient explanation of it, and all human institutions and belief systems could be understood and evaluated through the discovery of their historical origins and development. Herder offered a worldview, which most scholars after him equated with modernity itself, in which life and reality were synonymous with history and history alone, and in which all notions of truth had to be examined and explained as realities forged within the historical process.[17]

While Herder and other thinkers spelled out the intellectual foundations of this new approach to history in the eighteenth century, its widespread acceptance among historians, theologians, philosophers, and scientists occurred in the nineteenth. Ludwig Feuerbach began to use the word *historicism*, along with *empiricism*, to describe a new critical openness to reality as it presented itself to human perception, in the process laying the philosophical groundwork for much of modern science as we know it. Physical reality, Feuerbach argued, can and should be measured and analyzed, so that the physical causes of scientific realities might be explained and controlled. Physical diseases weren't caused by divine displeasure, but by physical causes like germs and viruses. In a similar way in the mid-nineteenth century K. F. Eichorn established the historical school of law by applying Herder's theories to various legal traditions, jettisoning natural law theories of jurisprudence in favor of explaining the "ends of justice" in terms of the social parameters of specific cultural and national groups. The very same pattern of accepting historicist presuppositions as the foundation of modern, disciplined thinking occurred in linguistics (Lachmann and the Grimm brothers—yes, the fairy tale ones), economics (Knies and Schmoller), the new discipline of sociology (William James and Emile Durkheim), and philosophy (Karl Marx).[18]

But it was the historical studies of Leopold von Ranke that established the new historical consciousness as received truth. Von Ranke insisted that the past must be rigorously examined so that scholars could describe it *wie es eigentlich gewesen* ("as it really happened"). For von Ranke history and history alone—not abstract systems of thought—could provide the most reliable guide to questions of human meaning and flourishing.[19]

Given its presuppositions about reality, the philosophy of history advanced by Herder implied that if God were to be talked about in any kind of believable way, She or He had to be radically imminent *within* the evolving historical process itself. Any discussion of the divine predicated on a two-story universe—with God "up there" and humanity "down here"—now became intellectually problematic for anyone attempting to make peace with the new worldview. Immanence therefore became the trademark of what, by the end of the nineteenth century, would become known as theological liberalism or modernism. Precisely because language was a construct to describe events in time and space, scholars, applying historical critical methods to the records of the religious past, thought those records revealed at least as much about the human response to an encounter with an Other as about anything outside the historical process. The record of Jesus' words and deeds as narrated in the gospels, so understood, was as much a Christian second- or third-generation reflection on Jesus' earthly ministry as it was a biography of Jesus. Creedal statements were to be analyzed as symbolic monuments offering parameters of belief rather than propositional information about the Holy One. The Bible was therefore poetry, not prose, symbolic and not descriptive, subjunctive rather than declarative.[20]

THE MEANING OF THE CATHOLIC SIXTIES

Pius X's attack on the modernist threat, perceived by him as the Trojan horse threatening to spirit historical consciousness into the Catholic Church, appeared at the time to be successful, frightening Catholic scholars for half a century and freezing Catholic scholarship in (strangely medieval) scholastic categories in which historicism was not even a remote intellectual option.

But however successful Pius X may or may not have been in extirpating the heresy, historical consciousness did not go away. Thus the Catholic Church after 1907 became notable as the single largest institution in Western culture that resolutely set its face against dealing with historical change as part and parcel of its teaching and worship. It was only a matter of time before the Church would have to deal with change, and this was because the Catholic tradition itself is resolutely public. That is, Catholic theology from at least the Middle Ages had always engaged mainstream culture and its ideas, in a sense baptizing them for its own institutional purposes. To that extent, Catholicism has always represented the big tent in Western Christianity, interacting with cultural presuppositions and welcoming a broad variety of ideas, traditions, and cultural stances. As James Joyce supposedly noted (correctly, in this case), "Catholicism means 'here comes everybody.'" Unlike sectarian groups (such as the Amish and Mennonites) that sought to stand apart from a fallen world, the mainstream Catholic tradition had always sought engagement and conversation with a redeemed but sinful world. The clock was ticking, and chimes sounded in 1964.

Thus, however shocking it might have been to the bishops who voted for the reforms of Vatican II, it should come as no shock at all to students of the history of ideas that historical consciousness and the critical methods that applied it, so successfully contained in 1907, were at last set loose within the Church by the Second Vatican Council. Ecumenical councils, by their very nature, deal with the big stuff on the plate of the world's largest religion, and between 1907 and 1965 historical consciousness had grown to be the eight-hundred-pound gorilla in the chapel. Whatever the intentions of the pope and the good bishops gathered in Rome in 1962–65, the very vibrancy and size of Catholicism made dealing with historical consciousness necessary. And the reforms mandated by the council offered the first opportune moment in half a century to do just that.

Indeed the council's own stated intent of "returning to the sources" made the emergence of historical consciousness not only possible but likely. What canon lawyers, historians of liturgy, and theologians found in those original sources demonstrated that things had indeed changed— sometimes for the better, sometimes not. The council's directive to return to those sources made it likely that Cardinal Newman's famous observation would come to be widely understood within the Church: "To live is to change; and to live long is to have changed often." Such a realization contained within it the seeds of revolution made all the more dramatic by being pent up for half a century. Such was the result of the law of unintended consequences, which makes living in history so exciting and so unnerving.

Similarly Paul VI's effort to hold the line on Catholic teaching on marriage and human sexuality, quite ironically, had the opposite effect from the one intended. Far from calming the waters of the faithful by assuring them that magisterial teaching on such matters *would* not change because it *could* not change, the encyclical unleashed widespread dissent within the community, partly no doubt because of media fanning the flames of a complex and nuanced moral question. But the dissent also was fueled by the recognition, both among moral theologians and many lay people, that the timeless categories of natural law—categories that had served the Church so well in the past—now appeared dated or (even more troubling) implausible. The static worldview that the language of natural law presumed seemed to contradict the lived experience of many modern believers. However untutored in historicist thinking, many Catholics lived so much of their lives in the world which that thinking had created that the Church's (classical) pronouncement about sexuality and birth control now made no sense. The Church was, almost literally, making them an offer they couldn't understand.

Moral theologians, such as Charles Curran who attempted to show how and why Catholic theology was put in an impossible situation when the best modern thought was perceived as a challenge to established doctrinal positions, were dealt with as disloyal, or even heterodox. But the resulting theological situation put even loyal supporters of Paul VI's condemnation of birth control in the uncomfortable intellectual position of supporting the teaching of the encyclical while attempting to find better theological arguments to buttress its teaching than the static, implausible ones it offered. The resulting intellectual scramble to prove (or disprove) that teaching offered a short course on precisely what Paul VI had wanted to avoid. It showed that Catholic theology (including moral theology) evolved and developed over time.

The Vatican directive asking religious orders such as the Los Angeles IHMs to return *ad fontes*—to the original historical springs that had produced them—in order to achieve a faithful renewal of religious life in and for the Church revealed that many accretions had developed over the centuries, some of which were in flat contradiction to charismatic and apostolic purposes for which their orders had originally been founded. Whatever one thinks of the resulting nature of religious life for men and women after those reforms—some tending to think contemporary religious life more authentic, others arguing that the massive loss of nuns and male religious proves its bankruptcy—the very effort to carry out the directives promulgated by the pope and the bishops of the Church showed that religious life changes and evolves. Part and parcel of that recognition was the accompanying realization that religious life had never achieved a golden moment when it had gotten everything so right that there was no need for a critical scrutiny of their lifestyle and apostolic work. However appropriate cloister, wimples, and veils might be in one place and time, the likelihood that such practices could be frozen in place forever seemed, by the second half of the twentieth century, anyway, highly unlikely. Though this point might sound like a penetrating glimpse of the obvious, it was actually a quite revolutionary insight for Catholics unaccustomed to thinking in historical categories. And it most certainly *was* revolutionary for certain bishops who wanted nuns to look, live, and act as they had in the past.

The same story of how Christian identity and worship change over time applies as well to the stories of the Catonsville Nine, and even to Avery Cardinal Dulles (however unlikely such a point may seem to some fans of his theology). Pluralism implies different answers for different times, places, and people; and different answers brings with them an implied (and sometimes an overt) challenge to the idea that there is only one way of living the Christian life, ready-made for every situation, everywhere and at all times. Pius X's model of the Perfect Church, standing above the battle-scarred plains of history and free of its vicissitudes, was not to outlast the twentieth century. Perhaps because the Holy Spirit has a sense of humor, that model was subverted by an ecumenical council of the Church itself. Certainly Catholic Christians in the United States, where historical consciousness had won the day in so many parts of the culture—in science, technology, historical and social scientific scholarship—were ready when what Garry Wills termed the "dirty little secret," that the Church itself changes, was let out of the bag. The very enthusiasm evinced by many, arguably most American Catholics in embracing the changes and rejecting the attempt by some in the Church to identify past models and answers as unchangeable witnessed to the fact that they had been waiting for precisely that little secret for some time.

It would seem that there are at least three lessons to be learned from the Catholic sixties in the United States, although there might very well be others that will manifest themselves as the fruits of that decade continue to unfold. First, it seems highly unlikely that historical consciousness—the awareness that everything, including the Church, changes as history unfolds—can ever be effectively explained away again. True, some whom the secular press term traditionalists have been attempting that very thing since shortly after the Second Vatican Council closed. Those on the extreme end of these efforts view Vatican II as an anticouncil; that is, they see that event of 1962–65 as not being a real council of the Church at all, but rather an event abetted by the Forces of Darkness against the Fortress Church of Pius IX and Pius X. This group has always constituted an interesting but numerically insignificant group of Catholics.

More numerous—and more influential, at least in Europe—are those Catholics who even in the 1960s and certainly in the contemporary Church wish to claim Vatican II for the side of continuity and ahistorical Catholic truth: no "rupture" did—or could—emerge from the implementation of the reforms of the council because the Church cannot change. But more to the point, they argue, is the fact that the council fathers implementing the reforms intended no such rupture with previous councils or Church practice. The efforts of this group—some in key hierarchical positions of authority—to ignore the genie let out of the bottle, or at least to act as though that genie offered nothing new and important, have found powerful spokespersons in the highest levels of Church government. But their arguments ignore the perspicacious law of unintended consequences, a law provable to the extent that it provides intellectual clarity on what in fact happened in the Catholic sixties. Mainstream Catholics in the United States, after the sixties, have come to understand their own revered brand of Christianity as having undergone historical development and change. The law of unintended consequences goes a long way in explaining why that perception has triumphed so broadly in the American Catholic community. Whatever the strengths of the arguments offered by the group attempting to claim Vatican II for the side of continuity, their failure to take into account the clear results of that law undercuts important aspects of their position. *Whatever* the intentions of the bishops passing the conciliar decrees, the resulting documents sponsored a revolution that took on a life of its own, just as all events in history have a tendency to do. Intent is largely irrelevant as an explanatory factor.

Second, the widespread acceptance of the seemingly self-evident truth that things change will make it increasingly difficult to propound or defend Church teaching and practice by appealing to timeless, static categories of propositional truth. This applies most particularly to the intellectual tradition of scholastic natural law, which the Catholic tradition has relied on for presenting its most important teachings since the thirteenth century. The fractious nonreception of Paul VI's encyclical on birth control, if nothing else, illustrates this with startling clarity. Whatever the truth of Paul VI's teaching, the massive noncompliance accorded his encyclical shows that the great majority of American Catholics did not form their consciences along the lines of such moral reasoning, and have not since. There are of course many possible reasons for this lack of compliance on the part of the vast majority of practicing Catholics on an issue that the hierarchical Church has termed "serious matter." Some of those reasons may indeed involve personal ignorance, sinful willfulness, or just plain selfishness. But an important reason for that noncompliance, what I would label as the main reason, is that the classical unchanging world it presupposes no longer makes sense to the vast majority of the faithful in the United States.

What Bernard Lonergan so elegantly called the "transition from a classicist world view to historical mindedness" in fact describes the intellectual revolution that mainstream Catholics underwent during the sixties.

Whatever the strengths of that older classicist worldview—and it served the Catholic Church extraordinarily well for centuries—it can no longer provide plausible explanations for Church teaching. Such a function is crucial for teaching doctrine and ethical practice, as the Catholic theological tradition has always argued that Church leaders have the obligation to explain *why* they offer specific teaching in terms that are both accessible and convincing to the faithful. The inability to do this, or the inability to do this effectively and believably, risks reducing Catholic teaching to mere hierarchical edicts whose authority rests on the weakest argument of all, the argument from authority: "Do this because I say so." This would be a profound betrayal of the Catholic theological tradition, which has always believed that faith and reason are not oppositional but rather work together for the glory of God in the world. The "rational plausibility" offered to explain why specific teachings fit into the larger framework of belief are, to that extent anyway, crucial in the Catholic tradition of theology. The older intellectual categories of scholastic natural law, first enunciated so brilliantly by St. Thomas Aquinas in the thirteenth century, appear unable to accomplish that now. Perhaps the intellectual justification offered in its place to explain Catholic teaching will represent the most important long-term fruit of the intellectual revolution sponsored by historical consciousness in Catholic Christianity. Time will tell.

Third, the events of the Catholic sixties in the United States have given rise—problematically, I think—to factions that are labeled by commentators both inside and outside the Church as liberal and conservative. There are perhaps understandable reasons why such labels emerged in the first place and are now taken to be self-evidently appropriate. There is, most assuredly, a certain intellectual ease in using the same labels in reporting Church feuds as the secular media use in narrating political debates. Perhaps this very ease appealed to Catholics, who were actually rather new to the game of talking about parties within the household of faith, as until the early 1960s there were only two kinds of Catholics: faithful and lapsed.

But the result is a situation in which Catholics, then and now, who supported the changes sponsored by the Second Vatican Council are designated liberals, while those who opposed or questioned those changes are termed conservatives. There were (and are) salient alliances between opponents of the council with strategies of political and social conservatism advanced by specific political parties in the United States, just as some supporters of the reforms allied themselves with left-leaning political causes.

But the story of the American Catholic revolution I have offered also illustrates why such designations are problematic, and, indeed, obscure at least as much as they reveal. The awareness that things change—though arguably quite radical in its implications for understanding the religious past and present—is not intrinsically liberal in any meaningful sense, at least as that word has been understood in its North American political context. The very person who first described the revolution from classicism to historical consciousness, Bernard Lonergan, remained resolutely above the fray when it came to battles over liturgy, birth control, and the reform of religious communities, and remained somewhat traditional in piety to the end of his life. Some, like Avery Cardinal Dulles, have become contested icons in the years after the sixties precisely because of the inability of such left and right labels to satisfactorily explain their role in the events of that decade. How could one who was perceived to be (and was) so resolutely conservative in his support for the traditional structures of the institutional Church produce such a radical work as *Models of the Church*? Surely there had to have been a change of heart to explain such a contradiction, at least if one accepts the left/right, liberal/conservative axis of religious identity as determinative.

But Dulles was neither mistaken nor disingenuous in asserting that he had never changed course in his theological career. He was neither a liberal who repented of his ways nor a conservative who saw the light. He was instead a profound thinker who recognized that pluralism was, in itself, a profoundly Catholic value, and he found that pluralism in the history of the Catholic tradition itself.

If *liberal* is construed to mean capitulating to secular standards by betraying ecclesiastical ones, or ignoring the record of the historical tradition in favor of modern notions, then it is difficult to see how it applies in any meaningful sense to activists like the Berrigan brothers and the Catonsville Nine, who resolutely set their face against the secular political and military justifications for U.S. military involvement in Vietnam. Indeed their dramatic actions against the entire draft system represented, in their own understanding at least, a profoundly *Catholic* no to a course of foreign policy that, they felt, violated ancient Christian principles of compassion and concern for others. Similarly Charles Curran found his original voice as a moral theologian by studying St. Alphonsus Liguori, the patron saint (literally and figuratively) of confessors looking for conservative and reliable pastoral advice in hearing cases of conscience. What he found in the writings of that deeply pious and conservative eighteenth-century saint was a wise respect for sharp disagreements among reliable Catholic moral teachers about the gravity and even moral meaning of certain acts. The past of Catholic moral theology, as Curran learned while writing his dissertation at a pontifical (and thus officially papal) university in Rome, was considerably less tidy and uniform than he had been led to believe by some of his seminary professors. It is, again, difficult to see how extrapolating from the moral reasoning of such a traditional thinker as Liguori can be construed as liberal in any way, theological or otherwise. The same radical appreciation of how things change—learned precisely as the result of a return to the historical records of the Catholic tradition itself—illumines the stories of Frederick McManus and the Los Angeles IHMs as well.

What the category of historical consciousness allows us to see is that none of these figures can be appropriately understood by the application of political labels. What they had in common as central players in the socioreligious drama I've termed the Catholic sixties was a deep appreciation of how the religious tradition to which they all belonged had undergone historical evolution and change. That appreciation was as Catholic as it was modern, in the sense that Pius X so feared. At its core was the radical recognition that what faithful Christians did and believed in the mid-twentieth century was not always a faithful replication of what the early Christians and the medieval builders of the great cathedrals had done and believed. Sometimes this recognition was good news; sometimes it was a cause for reform; sometimes it embodied a complex combination of both. But at its root was an appreciation of disruption, discontinuity, and evolution as part of the very fiber of the Catholic tradition. Change was not foreign to the Catholic tradition: it defined it.

The recognition that the Christian life here below meant living faithfully amid the constant flux of change did not emerge in the decade between 1964 and 1974. Nor was it unique to the lively cultural experiment of the United States. St. Paul reminded his first-century Christian readers of just this truth in exhorting them to keep in mind, "We have here no lasting city, but seek one that is to come." Paul's exhortation to pilgrim believers living in the pluralistic and confusing culture of the far-flung Roman Empire of the first century seems as timely today as it was twenty centuries ago.

ACKNOWLEDGMENTS

Writing projects are always collective endeavors involving authors with a broad network of other people who cannot, technically speaking, be repaid for their many kindnesses, but only acknowledged. Such is certainly the case for the project that produced this book.

A number of my colleagues at Fordham University made the project itself possible. Terry Tilley, indefatigable chair of the fine Theology Department that I call home; Brennan O'Donnell, the talented dean of Fordham College; Bob Himmelberg, dean of faculty; David Stuhr, associate vice president for academic affairs; and Stephen Freedman, academic vice president, were consistently supportive and helpful in setting up the 2008–9 academic year, during which most of this book was written. Maria Terzulli, administrator of the Curran Center at Fordham and (truth be told) queen of all she surveys, wisely discerned the information that was necessary for me to know in my absence from that wonderful center and shielded me from other information going on at Fordham that would have distracted me. Angela O'Donnell, associate director of that center, ran the far-flung lectures, conferences, and student seminars that are a regular feature of our institutional life elegantly and efficiently. Patrick Ryan, the McGinley Professor of Religion and Society at Fordham, read through the entire manuscript and made many helpful suggestions about style and content.

T. Frank Kennedy, S.J., rector of the Jesuit community and director of the Jesuit Institute at Boston College—and very funny lunch companion—approached me several years ago to offer the considerable resources of that institution's Gasson Chair to me, which made my year among the talented scholars there both productive and pleasurable. The chair of theology, Ken Himes, O.F.M., and Boston College's energetic provost Bert Garza eased my entry into a new academic context with kind attentiveness. Likewise Toni Ross and Gloria Rufo, executive assistants in BC's Theology Department, offered invaluable local knowledge about a host of issues, from computer glitches to actual names in Accounts Payable that made my time there so enjoyable. To all of them I offer a heartfelt thanks.

A number of talented scholars read parts of the manuscript as it was being written. Massimo Faggioli, the research fellow in Boston College's Jesuit Institute for the 2008–9 academic year, read several parts and offered helpful critiques over lunches and dinners. I am especially grateful to him for his sage advice regarding the reception of Vatican II, a topic he took up years ago under the tutelage of his mentor, Giuseppe Alberigo. Three fellow Jesuits who are themselves respected theologians and historians—Jim Keenan, Bruce Morrill, and John O'Malley—all read chapters at various stages of writing, offering suggestions that saved me from making mistakes of fact or interpretation. To them I acknowledge my gratitude while also confessing that any remaining errors in the book are all, alas, my own.

Five students aided me in the course of this project. Jen Sawyer and Angelique Rivard (indispensable presences at Fordham's Curran Center) undertook research for me during the summer of 2008, unearthing more about birth control and the Catonsville raid than they ever thought they wanted (or needed) to know. Much of the newspaper coverage utilized in this work is the result of their spending beautiful summer afternoons in the basement of Fordham's library, going through reels of microfilms. Brian McGovern, a graduate assistant at the Curran Center, uncomplainingly reformatted the entire manuscript, as well as making insightful suggestions as to content. My two research assistants at Boston College, Jason Donnelly and Matt Sherman, both very talented doctoral students in BC's Theology Department, uncomplainingly welcomed late Sunday night emails requesting research data for early Monday morning and offered helpful suggestions based on the research they undertook on my behalf—this while both were engaged in writing their own dissertations. My editor at Oxford University Press, Theo Calderara, played a crucial role in shaping the present work at a very early stage in its production; his prescient advice and acute editorial skills (combined with his long-suffering patience) helped in critical ways in bringing the project into what I hope is a compelling historical narrative. To all of these I confess my debt.

Ruby Hugh, a good friend from my Harvard graduate school days, helped to keep me sane by regular visits to Boston's impressive spectrum of Chinese restaurants and by regular showings of the BBC's *Prime Suspect* TV series. I will dearly miss those evenings of pork-fried rice.

Finally, this book is dedicated to Nick Lombardi, a close friend and fellow Jesuit, who listened to me speculate about this project years before I sat down to write it and helped to keep me on track during trying moments in its writing by suggesting a drink on the back porch of the Jesuit residence at Fordham. I gratefully acknowledge him with the title that the founder of the Jesuit order, Ignatius Loyola, reserved for his closest friends and advisors: *amicus in Domino*, "friend in the Lord."

NOTES

Preface

1. *Information Catholique Internationale* 183 (January 1, 1963), 1.

2. Examples of this "history of ideas" approach is Charles Taylor's brilliant reconstruction of the idea of reform stretching back into the late Middle Ages in *A Secular Age* (Cambridge, MA: Belknap Press of Harvard University Press, 2007), and Bernard Bailyn's magisterial reconstruction of the ideas that made possible the political and social arguments of the colonial leaders in *The Ideological Origins of the American Revolution* (Cambridge, MA: Belknap Press of Harvard University Press, 1992).

Chapter 1

1. *Information Catholique Internationale* 183 (January 1, 1963), 1.

2. James D. Crichton, *Changes in the Liturgy: Considerations on the Instructions of the Sacred Congregation for Rites for the Proper Implementation of the Constitution on Sacred Liturgy, Issued on September 26* (Staten Island, NY: Alba House, 1965), 4–6; *Information Catholique Internationale* 183 (January 1, 1963), 1.

3. George Devine, *Liturgical Renewal: An Agonizing Reappraisal* (New York: Alba House, 1973), 45; Frederick McManus, "The New Rite of Mass," *Worship* 39 (February 1965): 69; Luis Maldonado, "Liturgy as a Communal Enterprise," in *The Reception of Vatican II*, ed. Giuseppe Alberigo et al. (Washington, DC: Catholic University of America Press, 1987), 309–21; John Henry Newman, *The Letters and Diaries of John Henry Newman*, ed. C. S. Dessain and T. Gornall (Oxford: Oxford University Press, 1979), 25:175.

4. On Pius V's 1570 Missal (the *Missale Romanum*), see Bard Thompson, *Liturgies of the Western Church* (New York: New American Library, 1961), 42–49. For a critical (revisionist) interpretation of the standardization of Pius's missal, see John Bossy, "The Counter-Reformation and the People of Catholic Europe," *Past and Present*, May 1970, 51–70. Quote from Alberigo, foreword to *The Reception of Vatican II*, vii.

5. This paragraph has been shaped by Garry Wills's brilliant reconstruction of the reaction to the new liturgy as mandated by the September 1964 Instruction in *Bare Ruined Choirs: Doubt, Prophecy and Radical Religion* (Garden City, NY: Doubleday, 1971), 2, 21.

6. "Vernacular Warning: Scandal in Hurried, Undignified Use," *National Catholic Reporter*, November 4, 1964, 3. See also Robert Hvoda, "The Mass of the Future," *The Critic* 23 (1964): 29.

7. Wills, *Bare Ruined Choirs*, 65; Dale Francis, "The Mood of the Laity: How Are Catholics Reacting to the New Liturgy?" *The Critic* 24 (February/March 1965): 57.

8. This paragraph is based on my *Catholics and American Culture: Fulton Sheen, Dorothy Day, and the Notre Dame Football Team* (New York: Crossroad Press, 1999), 160–61. McManus, "The New Rite of Mass," 65–76; Frederick McManus, "The Implementation and Goals of Liturgical Reform," *Worship* 39 (October 1965): 480–485, 482.

9. Massa, *Catholics and American Culture*, 161; Jim Castelli and Joseph Gremillion, eds., *The Emerging Parish: The Notre Dame Study of Catholic Life Since Vatican II* (San Francisco: Harper & Row, 1987), 129.

10. Dale Francis, "The Mood of the Laity: Confused, Frustrated, and Bewildered," *The Critic* 24 (February/March 1965): 56. Pastor's quote from Devine, *Liturgical Renewal*, 48. Massa, *Catholics and American Culture*, 62–63.

11. "Backlash Gets Organized: Ask Referendum on Liturgy," *National Catholic Reporter* 1 (April 1 1965): 1.

12. Larry Michaels, "Commotion about the New Mass?" *National Catholic Reporter* 1 (April 28, 1964): 4; Msgr. J. D. Conway, "Question Box," *National Catholic Reporter* 1 (November 25, 1964): 4.

13. John W. O'Malley, "Vatican II: Did Anything Happen?" in *Vatican II: Did Anything Happen?* ed. David Schultenover (New York: Continuum, 2007), 64. O'Malley convincingly argues that the primitivist origins of at least some of the reformist energies at Vatican II rested in the essentially conservative *resourcement* theology of figures like Jacques Maritain (63–67). For a fuller account, see John W. O'Malley, *What Happened at Vatican II?* (Cambridge, MA: Belknap Press of Harvard University Press, 2008), 36–43.

14. O'Malley, "Vatican II: Did Anything Happen?" 58.

15. Paul B. Marx, *Dom Virgil Michel and the Liturgical Movement* (Collegeville, MN: Liturgical Press, 1957), 36–37, 73–74, 87–88; Annibale Bugnini, *The Reform of the Liturgy, 1948–1975*, trans. Matthew J. O'Connell (Collegeville, MN: Liturgical Press, 1990), chapters 1–3; Nicola A. Montini, introduction to *The Saint Gregory Hymnal* (Philadelphia: St. Gregory Guild, 1940); Pietro Marini, *A Challenging Reform: Realizing the Vision of the Liturgical Renewal* (Collegeville, MN: Liturgical Press, 2007). Quote from Wills, *Bare Ruined Choirs*, 21, italics in original. Miss Havisham, one of the central characters in Charles Dickens's *Great*

Expectations, was jilted by her intended groom and left standing alone at the altar on her wedding day. To forever mark that betrayal, she stopped all the clocks in her mansion, Satis House, and kept the banquet table with her wedding cake just as it was.

16. Cardinal Bellarmine's classic institutional, papal-centered model of the Church can be found in his *Disputationes de Controversiis Christianae Fidei adversus huius temporis haereticos* (Ingolstadt, 1586). See also John Hardon, *A Comparative Study of Bellarmine's Doctrine of the Relation of Non-Catholics to the Catholic Church* (Rome: Gregorian University, 1951).

17. "Dogmatic Constitution on the Church," in *Documents of Vatican II*, ed. Walter Abbott (New York: Guild Press, 1966), chapter 2, "The People of God."

18. Bernard Lonergan, "The Transition from a Classicist World View to Historical Mindedness," in *Law for Liberty: The Role of Law in the Church Today*, ed. James E. Biechler (Baltimore: Helicon Press, 1967), 127.

19. Ibid., 127, 128.

20. Ibid., 130.

21. Ibid., 129.

22. Ibid., 129.

23. Ibid., 130.

Chapter 2

1. An earlier version of this chapter appeared in *Worship*, March 2007, 121–41. *Lumen Gentium, Vatican II: The Conciliar and Post Conciliar Documents*, ed. Austin Flannery, (Northport, NY: Costello, 1980), chapter 2, "The People of God," chapter 3, "The Church Is Hierarchical."

2. "Between 85 and 87 percent" from Andrew Greeley, William McCready, and Kathleen McCourt, *Catholic Schools in a Declining Church* (Kansas City, MO: Sheed and Ward, 1976), 130. Conversation with Andrew Greeley at the National Opinion Research Center, July 2005. Greeley's data are presented in *The American Catholic: A Social Portrait* (New York: Basic Books, 1977), chapter 7, "Changes in the Church," see especially table 7.7 on 138.

3. Paul B. Marx, *Virgil Michel and the Liturgical Movement* (Collegeville, MN: Liturgical Press, 1957), 73–74; Hubert Jedin, *A History of the Council of Trent*, trans. Dom Ernest Graf (St. Louis: B. Herder, 1957), volume 1, book 1, chapter 1, "The Victory of the Papacy over the Reform Councils."

4. Quote about *Orate Fratres* in Marx, *Virgil Michel*, 407.

5. Biographical information from "Frederick R. McManus: In Service to God's People," *The Jurist* 48 (1988): 415–16. Michael Davies, "The ICEL Betrayal," *The Angelus* 3 (July 1980), at www.sspx.ca/Angelus/1980_July/ICEL_Betrayal.htm.

6. Among the many monographs published by McManus between the 1950s and 1980s were the translation and commentary on *Pontifical Rite of the Restored*

Order of Holy Week (1958), an edited guide to *Parish Ritual* and *Handbook for the New Rubrics* (both in 1961), *Sacramental Liturgy* (1967), *The Rite of Penance: Understanding the Document* (1975), and an edited collection of commentaries near the end of his active career, *Thirty Years of Liturgical Renewal: Documents of the Bishops' Committee on the Liturgy* (1987).

7. "Frederick McManus: In Service to God's People," 415–16; R. Kevin Seasoltz, "Monsignor Frederick R. McManus, 8 February 1923–27 November 2005," *Worship* 80 (March 2006): 98–101.

8. Seasoltz, "Monsignor Frederick R. McManus," 99–100; "Frederick R. McManus," 416.

9. Frederick R. McManus, *The Ceremonies of the Easter Vigil* (Patterson, NJ: Saint Anthony Guild Press, 1953); *The Rites of Holy Week* (Patterson, NJ: Saint Anthony Guild Press, 1956); *The Peoples' Holy Week* (Patterson, NJ: Saint Anthony's Guild Press, 1957); *Pontifical Rite of the Restored Order of Holy Week*, translated and with an introduction by McManus (Patterson, NJ: Saint Anthony Guild Press, 1958).

10. Marx, *Virgil Michel and the Liturgical Movement*, 73–74, 407.

11. Frederick R. McManus, "Scripture Readings in English," *Worship* 32 (1958): 48–51.

12. Frederick R. McManus, "Communion Song," *Worship* 32 (1958): 510–13.

13. Statistics on *Worship*'s circulation from *Ulrich's Periodical Dictionary* (New Providence, NJ: R. R. Bowker, 1963, 1966, 1968). Similar advice can be found at Frederick R. McManus, "Responses," *Worship* 31 (1957): 560–62; (1958): 48–51, 108–10, 260–62; (1959): 66–69, 123–25, 188–92; (1960): 50–52, 107–10, 167–69, 227–30, 282–85, 353–56, 414–16.

14. Frederick R. McManus, "Mass Facing the People," *Worship* 33 (January 1959): 123–25.

15. Frederick R. McManus, "The New Code of Canon Law," *Worship* 34 (November 1960): 637–41.

16. Frederick R. McManus, "Vatican Council II," *Worship* 37 (December 1962): 2–11.

17. Frederick R. McManus, "The Constitution on the Liturgy: Commentary, Part I," *Worship* 38 (1964): 314–374.

18. Frederick R. McManus, "The Constitution on the Liturgy: Commentary, Part II," *Worship* 38 (1964): 450–496.

19. Ibid., 457, 459, 460.

20. Ibid., 463, 464. McManus himself uses the word "insists" with regard to the Prayer of the Faithful at the bottom of 463.

21. Frederick R. McManus, "The New Rite of Mass, Part I," *Worship* 39 (1965): 66–165.

22. Frederick R. McManus, "The Implementation and Goals of Liturgical Reform," *Worship* 39 (1965): 480–87.

23. John Henry Newman, *An Essay on the Development of Christian Doctrine* (originally puplished in 1878), 6th ed. (Notre Dame, IN: University of Notre Dame Press, 1989), 40.

Chapter 3

1. Paul VI, *Humanae Vitae* (Washington, DC: U.S. Catholic Conference, 1968). The three quotations in the first paragraph are taken from Articles 2 (first quote), 3 (second quote) and 4 (third quote) of the encyclical.

2. The letter first uses the phrase "responsible parenthood" in quotation marks in Article 7. The quotation is from Article 10, which is itself titled "Responsible Parenthood."

3. Article 10.

4. Article 14. For the sides of the debate over the encyclical, see Richard McCormick, *Corrective Vision: Explorations in Moral Theology* (Milwaukee: Sheed and Ward, 1994), 10; John Ford and Germain Grisez, "Ordinary Magisterium," *Theological Studies* 39 (1978): 258–312; William H. Shannon, *The Lively Debate: The Response to "Humanae Vitae"* (New York: Sheed and Ward, 1970), chapters 5, "The Second Phase of the Debate over the Pill," chapter 6, "The Widening of the Debate over the Pill."

5. *Humanae Vitae*, Article 12. I follow William Shannon's argument very closely here: see *The Lively Debate*, 108–9.

6. "Theologian Discusses Encyclical," *The Tablet* 222 (September 1968): 924; "Statement Accompanying the Encyclical *Humanae Vitae*," *Catholic Mind* (1968): 49–57.

7. John Lynch, "Notes on Moral Theology," *Theological Studies* 25 (1964): 223–53.

8. Ibid., 235.

9. John Courtney Murray offered a classic form of this kind of natural law approach to understanding reality: "The doctrine of natural law has no Roman Catholic presuppositions. Its only presupposition is threefold: that man is intelligent, that reality is intelligible, and that reality, as grasped by intelligence, imposes on the will the obligation that it be obeyed in its demands for action or abstention." *We Hold These Truths: Catholic Reflections on the American Proposition* (Kansas City, MO: Sheed and Ward, 1960), 109.

10. By "moral naturalism" I mean an approach to morality that sees moral guidelines as being implanted in nature itself, so that one could prove the truth of any moral position in a way analogous to a scientist proving scientific theorems by appealing to the workings of the physical universe. In such an understanding of morality, the rules for human action were (almost literally) built into the structure of nature itself. See Richard McCormick, "Moral Theology from 1940 to 1989: An Overview," in *Corrective Vision: Explorations in Moral Theology* (Milwaukee, WI:

Sheed and Ward, 1994), 1–7. The quote about the "objective moral order" is from E. A. Ryan and J. Blett, "The Nature and Destiny of Man," *Theological Studies* 5 (March 1955): 77.

11. On physicalism, see *Cambridge Dictionary of Philosophy*, 2nd ed., ed. Robert Audi (New York: Cambridge University Press, 1999); *Routledge Encyclopedia of Philosophy*, ed. Edward Craig (London: Routledge, 1998).

12. On Baconian science, see Theodore Dwight Bozeman, *Protestants in an Age of Science: The Baconian Ideal and Ante-Bellum Religious Thought* (Chapel Hill: University of North Carolina Press, 1977).

13. John T. McGreevy, *Catholicism and American Freedom: A History* (New York: Norton, 2003), 242–43.

14. John T. Noonan Jr., *Contraception: A History of Its Treatment by Catholic Theologians and Canonists* (Cambridge, MA: Belknap Press of Harvard University Press, 1965), 532; Ford to Archbishop Vagnozzi, 6 April 1964, folder 5, box 86, General Secretary's Files, National Catholic Welfare Conference, Washington, D.C.

15. Germain Grisez, *Contraception and the Natural Law* (Milwaukee, WI: Bruce, 1965), 78–80, 81. See also Richard McCormick, "Notes on Moral Theology," *Theological Studies* 26 (1965): 640.

16. Grisez, *Contraception and the Natural Law*, 78.

17. My own construal of Grisez's model of natural law rests on Robert George's very fine exposition in *In Defense of Natural Law* (Oxford: Oxford University Press, 1999), chapter 3.

18. See Robert George's excellent analysis of Grisez on this phenomenological line of argument (ibid.). George goes on to note, "The natural law theory originally proposed by Germain Grisez, and developed and defended over the past 25 years by Grisez, John Finnis, Joseph Boyle, William May, and Patrick Lee, among others, has been sternly criticized by many philosophers who are sympathetic to natural law. Some of these critics suggest that Grisez's view of the relationship between morality and nature disqualifies his theory as a theory of natural law. . . . Lloyd Weinreb maintains that . . . natural law theories such as Grisez's differ from theories of classical and medieval law theories insofar as [they] dispense with the idea of a 'normative moral order.' They are theories of 'natural law without nature'" (83).

19. Richard McCormick, "The Encyclical *Humanae Vitae*," in "Notes in Moral Theology," *Theological Studies* 29 (1968): 728, 729.

20. Ibid., 731.

21. Ibid., 731–32, 737.

22. Ibid., 732, 733.

23. Joseph A. Komonchak, "*Humanae Vitae* and Its Reception: Ecclesiological Reflections," *Theological Studies* 39 (1978): 221–51.

24. Ibid., 234–35.

25. Ibid., 234; Paul VI, *Gratia domini, Acta Apostolicae Sedis* 61 (1969): 715.

26. Komonchak, "*Humanae Vitae* and Its Reception," 252.

27. Ibid.

28. Janet Smith, "Pope John Paul II and *Humanae Vitae,*" in *Why "Humanae Vitae" Was Right: A Reader,* ed. Janet E. Smith (San Francisco: Ignatius Press, 1993), 234. Smith observed, "Phenomenology is one of the modern schools of philosophy which is largely distinguished for its method; it does not use the tight definitions of Thomism or any other tradition, but attempts to use common language to analyze human experience and by means of this analysis to unfold basic truths of existence. . . . Phenomenologists are concerned to provide accurate descriptions of the way things are, of the nature of reality—descriptions not pre-determined by definitions, but rooted in common experience" (234, 235). See Karol Woityla/John Paul II, *The Acting Person* [1969], translated by Andrzej Potocki (Dordrecht, Holland: D. Reidel, 1979); Hans Kochler, "The Phenome-nology of Karol Woityla: On the Problem of the Phenomenological Foundation of Anthropology," *Philosophy and Phenomenological Research* 42 (1982): 326–34; Kevin P. Doran, *Solidarity: A Synthesis of Personalism and Communalism in the Thought of Karol Woityla/John Paul II* (New York: Peter Lang, 1996); Samuel Gregg, *Challenging the Modern World: John Paul II and the Development of Catholic Social Teaching* (Lanham, MD: Lexington Books, 1999).

29. Smith, "Pope John Paul II and *Humanae Vitae,*" 234.

30. Ibid, 237–38, 239.

31. On the "paranoid style of history," see Richard Hofstader, "The Paranoid Style in American Politics," *Harper's,* November 1964, 77–86: "I call it a para-noid style simply because no other word adequately evokes the sense of heated exaggeration, suspiciousness, and conspiratorial fantasy that I have in mind. I am not speaking in a clinical sense, but borrowing a clinical term for other purposes" (77).

Chapter 4

1. The title of this section is taken from two works widely read: Charles Cur-ran's own *Loyal Dissent: Memoirs of a Catholic Theologian* (Washington, DC: Georgetown University Press, 2006), and from "The Response to Human Life," *America,* September 7, 1968, 162–65, which offered the individual responses of twelve members of the Jesuit faculty of Alma College, a seminary in California.

2. My account of the events on July 29 and 30, 1968, closely follows those of-fered by William H. Shannon in *The Lively Debate: The Response to "Humanae Vitae"* (New York: Sheed and Ward, 1970), 147–48, and as reported in the *New York Times,* July 31, 1968, 1.

3. "Text of the Statement by Theologians," *New York Times,* July 31, 1968, 16. *Magisterium* (from the Latin *magister,* "teacher") refers to the formal teaching of

the Catholic Church. As originally used in the Middle Ages it referred to the teaching of theologians on the faculties of universities; in the modern period it has come to be used primarily for the pronouncements of popes and ecumenical councils.

4. On the "classicist universe," see chapter 1. The historical examples are offered at the end of the second paragraph of "Text of the Statement by Theologians," *New York Times*, July 31, 1968, 16.

5. "Text of the Statement by Theologians," *New York Times*, July 31, 1968, 16, paragraphs 3 and 4.

6. Ibid., paragraphs 6 and 7.

7. Mary McGrory, "Dilemmas of Pope and President," *America*, August 17, 1968, 91; John T. Noonan, quoted in cover story, "On the Pope's New Encyclical," *National Catholic Reporter*, August 7, 1968, 1.

8. Patrick Crowley, quoted in "On the Pope's New Encyclical," 1; Michael Novak, "Frequent, Even Daily Communion," in *The Catholic Case for Contraception*, ed. Daniel Callahan (New York: Macmillan, 1969), 94.

9. Gregory Baum, "The Right to Dissent," *Commonweal* 88 (August 23, 1968): 553–54; John Haughey, "Conscience and the Bishops," *America* 119 (October 12, 1968): 322; Daniel Callahan, "An Alternative Proposal," *Commonweal* 88 (August 23, 1968): 558–60; James Hitchcock, "The Church as Tradition and Institution," *Continuum* 6 (Spring 1968): 60–71; Bernard Haring, "The Encyclical Crisis," *Commonweal* 88 (September 6, 1968): 588–94; William Clancy, "The Troubling Spirit," *Commonweal* 88 (August 23, 1968): 560–62.

10. The classic study positing this factor as contributing to the Salem witch trials of 1691–92 is Paul Boyer and Stephen Nissenbaum's *Salem Possessed: The Social Origins of Witchcraft* (Cambridge, MA: Harvard University Press, 1974). Boyer and Nissenbaum's point is that, due to the absence of a colonial charter in Massachusetts at the time of the witchcraft outbreak, the tensions in Salem Village moved from being political to being "demonic" (literally). Because no one in authority was able to explain the real sources of the strange behaviors inflicting certain members of the town (in the estimation of the authors, disputes over land), participants searched for cosmic explanations; the devil, many believed, made them do it. I am not using the phrase "witch hunts" in the literal sense in which Boyer and Nissenbaum used it, but rather to explain metaphorically a sense widely shared by Church leaders that something far more sinister than simply alternative theological worldviews was going on in the revolt represented by the Mayflower Statement and needed to be uncovered and punished.

11. Curran, *Loyal Dissent*, 3, 6.

12. Ibid., 7–8, quote on 8. Curran recalled that one of his other professors at the Gregorian, the American Jesuit Edwin Healy, once told his class that he held a certain interpretation of moral teaching "even though Father Hurth holds the opposite—although he writes occasionally under the name of Pius XII" (8).

13. Ibid., 10.

14. Ibid., 11, 13–14. See Bernard Haring, *The Law of Christ*, vol. 1: *General Moral Theology*, trans. Edwin G. Kaiser (Westminster, MD: Newman Press, 1961), part 2, "The Subject of Moral Values in Theological Anthropology," part 3, "The Moral Duty of the Disciple of Christ." "Unfortunately, in popular preaching bodily concupiscence is often depicted as the most grievous consequence of original sin and the root of all evil. . . . A greater and more perilous source of evil is pride rooted in our spiritual nature. This may be called spiritual concupiscence" (part 2:64).

15. Ibid., part 2:15; Charles Curran, "Invincible Ignorance of the Natural Law According to St. Alphonsus: An Historical-Analytic Study from 1748 to 1765," STD dissertation, Academia Alfonsiana, Rome, 1961.

16. Haring, *General Moral Theology*, part 2:17–18.

17. Ibid., 20–22.

18. Ibid., 24–25.

19. Ibid., 29.

20. Charles Curran, "Masturbation and Objectively Grave Matter: An Exploratory Discussion," *Proceedings of the Twenty-first Annual Convention of the Catholic Theological Society of America* (Yonkers, NY: St. Joseph's Seminary, 1967), 21:95–112. See also Charles Curran, *Christian Morality Today: The Renewal of Moral Theology* (Notre Dame, IN: Fides Press, 1966), 13–26, 67–76, 107–19, 121.

21. Curran, *Loyal Dissent*, 32.

22. B. Olmstead, "Father Curran in, out as Theological Society Officer," *National Catholic Reporter* 3 (June 28, 1967), 1. Among Curran's articles, see Charles E. Curran, "Dialogue with Joseph Fletcher," *Homiletic and Pastoral Review* 67 (July 1967): 821–29; "The Ethical Teaching of Jesus," *Commonweal* 87 (November 24, 1967): 248–50; "Masturbation and Objectively Grave Matter"; "Sexuality and Sin: A Current Appraisal I," *Homiletic and Pastoral Review* 68 (September 1968): 1005–14; "Sexuality and Sin: A Current Appraisal II," *Homiletic and Pastoral Review* 69 (October 1968): 27–34.

23. Curran, *Loyal Dissent*, 34. For a close reconstruction of the events, see Robert B. Townsend, "Culture, Conflict, and Change: The '67 Strike at Catholic University," at http://mason.gmu.edu/-rtownsend/67strike.Intro. See also Albert C. Pierce, *Beyond One Man: Catholic University, April 17–24, 1967* (Washington, DC: Anawim Press, 1967); Francis Connell to Archbishop Vagnozzi, December 1, 1966, Connell Papers, Holy Redeemer College Archives, Washington, DC.

24. Francis Connell to Archbishop O'Boyle, April 16, 1966, Connell Papers, Holy Redeemer College, Washington, DC; Samuel J. Thomas, "A Final Disposition . . . One Way or Another: The Real End of the First Curran Affair," *Catholic Historical Review* 91 (October 2005): 714–42; Curran, *Loyal Dissent*, 34–35.

25. Jean R. Hailey, "Groups Protest Priest's Ouster: Contract Expires August 31. Liberal vs. Conservative," *Washington Post*, April 19, 1967; William R. MacKaye,

"Father Curran's Hazardous Theological Specialty: No Specifics—Three Negatives," *Washington Post*, April 20, 1967.

26. Curran, *Loyal Dissent*, 37; Jean R. Haley, "Full Boycott Called at CU after Ouster: Boycott to Protest CU Dismissal," *Washington Post*, April 20, 1967.

27. Gerald Grant and William R. MacKaye, "Bishops Voted to Fire Curran with 1 Dissent: Only 1 of 24 Bishops Opposed Firing of Curran at Secret Session. Previous Firings Cited 'Heretical Teachings.' Ouster Recommended. 2 Bishops Present," *Washington Post*, April 21, 1967; Curran, *Loyal Dissent*, 38.

28. Jean R. Haley, "Faculty Backs Ouster Protest: Student Protest Closes Catholic U.," *Washington Post*, April 21, 1967; William R. MacKaye, "Impact of Vatican II Is Seen in Walkout: News Analysis," *Washington Post*, April 22, 1967; Jean R. Haley, "Catholic U Rebellion Laid to Faculty: They Made Mistake," *Washington Post*, April 22, 1967; John Carmody, "O'Boyle Summons CU Faculty," *Washington Post*, April 24, 1967; Jim Hoagland, "Catholic University Boycott Goes on without Break," *Washington Post*, April 23, 1967; Jean R. Haley, "Catholic U Reinstates Fr. Curran: Priest Promoted. Classes for 6600 to Resume Today," *Washington Post*, April 25, 1967; Gerald Grant, "Fight for Academic Freedom Still Wide Open at Catholic U: News Analysis," *Washington Post*, April 26, 1967.

29. Catholic University's new statutes described in Curran, *Loyal Dissent*, 41, 49. In a lecture delivered at the Masonic Temple in Boston titled "The Conservative," Ralph Waldo Emerson referred to the "irreconcilable antagonism [between] the opposition of Past and Future, of Memory and Hope." Emerson implied that the "Party of Hope" usually won these ongoing battles, if only because the Party of Memory died first. See http://infomotions.com/alex2/authors/emerson-ralph/emerson-conservative-730.

30. Curran, *Loyal Dissent*, 56, 58.

31. "News Release by Carroll A. Hochwalt, Chairman of the Board of Trustees," in John F. Hunt et al., *The Responsibility of Dissent: The Church and Academic Freedom* (New York: Sheed and Ward, 1969), 206–7. See also 23–29, 39.

32. Curran, *Loyal Dissent*, 62.

33. The report of the inquiry board can be found in Charles Curran, Robert E. Hunt, et al., *Dissent in and for the Church: Theologians and "Humanae Vitae"* (New York: Sheed and Ward, 1969), 221. See also Curran, *Loyal Dissent*, 63.

34. Curran, *Loyal Dissent*, 66.

35. Ibid., 64–65.

36. Ibid., 65–66.

37. National Catholic News Service (domestic), June 17, 1969; Joseph Byron, "The Case of the Washington Nineteen: A Search for Justice," in *Judgment in the Church*, ed. William Bassett and Peter Huizing (New York: Seabury, 1971), 104–12.

38. Andrew Greeley, *The Catholic Myth: The Behavior and Beliefs of American Catholics* (New York: Charles Scribner's Sons, 1990), 91, 92.

39. Andrew Greeley, *Crisis in the Church: A Study of Religion in America* (Chicago: Thomas More Press, 1979), 13. The question that was posed for approval or rejection to the Catholics polled in the national survey was: "A married couple who feel they have as many children as they want are really not doing anything wrong when they use artificial means to prevent conception" (table on 40). Greeley referred to the archdiocese of Chicago as "particularly devout" because of the high percentage (17) of Catholics under the age of thirty who self-identified as such (13n). In the *National Survey of Family Growth*, published by the U.S. Department of Health, Education and Welfare in 1970, it was reported that 11 percent of Catholic couples practiced birth control by female sterilization (compared to 13.6 percent of Protestants and 4.7 percent of Jews); 34 percent used the pill (compared to 36 percent and 30 percent, respectively); 15 percent used condoms (12 percent and 20 percent); 8 percent through male sterilization (13 percent and 10 percent); 5 percent utilizing foam (5.2 percent and 2.5 percent), and 8.3 percent practiced rhythm (2.5 percent and less than 1 percent). "Contraceptive Utilization," *National Survey* (Hyattsville, MD: Office of Health Research, Statistics, an Technology, 1979), series 23, no. 2, table 18 on 32.

40. Greeley, *Catholic Myth*, 95.

Chapter 5

Much of the material in this chapter is based on chapter 8, "To Be Beautiful, Human, and Christian: The IHM Nuns and the Routinization of Charisma," in my book *Catholics and American Culture: Fulton Sheen, Dorothy Day, and the Notre Dame Football Team* (New York: Crossroad, 1999), 172–94. The epigraph is from Dunne's rollicking review in the *New York Review of Books* 45 (May 28, 1998): 17, of Monsignor Francis J. Weber's two-volume biography of Cardinal McIntyre, *His Eminence of Los Angeles, James Francis Cardinal McIntyre* (Mission Hills, CA: St. Francis Historical Society, 1997). Among the background data Dunne highlighted in explaining McIntyre's contentious episcopacy was that, while the cardinal (like most American bishops) came from working-class parents born in Ireland, he had also worked in a Wall Street brokerage house before entering the New York archdiocese's Dunwoodie Seminary (18). The Roman emperor Caligula reportedly made his horse a consul of Rome.

1. Dan L. Thrapp, "Order of Nuns Here Plans to Modernize Dress and Ideas," *Los Angeles Times*, October 18, 1967. The story was later picked up on the East Coast; see "Reforms Planned by Nuns on Coast," *New York Times*, October 27, 1967. Harvey Cox, "Corita: Celebration and Creativity," in *Sister Corita*, ed. Corita Kent and Harvey Cox (Philadelphia: Pilgrim Press, 1968), 17.

2. Thrapp, "Order of Nuns Here." See also "California Order Tests Liberal Rules That Would Let Sisters Pick Their Jobs," *National Catholic Reporter* 4 (October 25, 1967): 7.

3. Thrapp, "Order of Nuns Here," 1.

4. "Decree on the Appropriate Renewal of Religious Life" (*Perfectae Caritatis*), in *The Documents of Vatican II*, ed. Walter Abbott (New York: Herder and Herder, 1966), 466–85. See especially part 3: "The manner of living, praying, and working should be suitably adapted to the physical and psychological conditions of today's religious, and also, to the extent required by the nature of each community, to the needs of the apostolate, the requirements of a given culture, [and] the social and economic circumstances anywhere" (469).

5. Mary Augusta Neal, *Catholic Sisters in Transition: From the 1960s to the 1980s* (Wilmington, DE: Michael Glazer, 1984), 18, 20; Mary Ewens, "Women in the Convent," in *American Catholic Women: A Historical Exploration*, ed. Karen Kennelly (New York: Macmillan, 1989), 25–35; Mary Schneider, "The Transformation of American Women Religious: The Sister Formation Movement as Catalyst, 1954–64" (Working Paper Series 17, no. 1, Cushwa Center for the Study of American Catholicism, University of Notre Dame, 1986); "Decree on the Renewal of Religious Life" (Vatican II), no. 17 (478), no. 20 (479–80).

6. "Decree on the Renewal," 478, italics added.

7. Ibid., 479–80. For reflections on the changes by Caspary, precisely in light of Paul VI's "Norms for Implementing the Decree on the Up-to-Date Renewal of Religious Life," issued a year after the close of the Second Vatican Council on August 6, 1966, see Anita M. Caspary, *Witness to Integrity: The Crisis of the Immaculate Heart Community of California* (Collegeville, MN: Liturgical Press, 2003), 21–23.

8. Thrapp, "Order of Nuns Here," 1, 8.

9. "Told to Quit Schools, L.A. Nuns Say," *National Catholic Reporter*, January 17, 1968, 1, 7.

10. Ibid.; "Archdiocese Silent on Report Nun Teachers Will Be Fired," *Los Angeles Times*, November 7, 1967, section 2, p. 1; "Nuns Debate with Cardinal Explained by Head of Order," *Los Angeles Times*, November 11, 1967, 1, 14; "McIntyre Looks to Rome in Nun Dispute," *Los Angeles Times*, November 18, 1967, 3.

11. "New L.A. Lay Association Sides with Nuns in Dispute," *National Catholic Reporter*, January 24, 1968, 5.

12. "13 Jesuits Praise L.A. Nuns' Renewal," *National Catholic Reporter*, January 31, 1968, 10.

13. "Nuns Appeal to Pope to Press Liberal Practices," *New York Times*, March 12, 1968, 37; "Fighting Nuns," *Newsweek*, April 1, 1968, 100; "What to Wear?" *Newsweek*, February 16, 1968, 73; "Vatican Is Entering Dispute over Nuns on Coast," *New York Times*, April 17, 1968, 53; "Answer to Petition," *New York Times*, April 17, 1968, 53.

14. "Vatican Rules against IHM Nuns on Changes Opposed by McIntyre," *National Catholic Reporter*, March 13, 1968, 1, 12.

15. "IHM Nuns Put Off Compliance; Other Sisters Organize Support," *National Catholic Reporter*, March 20, 1968, 1, 6; "3000 Sisters Support IHMs," *National Catholic Reporter*, March 27, 1968, 1, 12.

16. "IHM Split Authorized, Sisters to Pick Group," *National Catholic Reporter*, June 19, 1968, 3; "Ultimatum to Nuns," *Newsweek*, June 21, 1968, 61.

17. "Whatever Happened to the IHMs?" *National Catholic Reporter*, April 7, 1971, 1, 8.

18. A second order is a group of religious women whose rule is modeled on that of a first order of men (in women's groups like the Benedictines, Dominicans, and "Poor Clare" Franciscans). All of these second orders were cloistered and avoided direct contact with the outside world. See Ewens, "Women in the Convent," 24–25.

19. Ibid., 24–25.

20. Ibid., 26, 32–33.

21. Marian Sharples, *All Things Remain in God* (Los Angeles: privately printed, 1963), 48; Caspary, *Witness to Integrity*, 15–16.

22. Caspary, *Witness to Integrity*, 16.

23. Ibid.

24. Sharples, *All Things Remain in God*, 180–210; Caspary, *Witness to Integrity*, 17.

25. A vote taken among all the sisters of the California Province showed that 97 percent wanted to separate from their Spanish counterparts; as a result five of the California sisters chose to return to the original community in Spain. Sharples, *All Things Remain*, 105, 205, 208, 213–14; Caspary, *Witness to Integrity*, 17–18.

26. Caspary, *Witness to Integrity*, 19. Dorothy Day was the founder, with Peter Maurin, of the Catholic Worker Movement, sometimes referred to as a movement of "Christian communism." Mother Madeleva Wolffe, as the third president of St. Mary's College in Notre Dame, Indiana, made it the first Catholic college in the United States to grant theology degrees to women. Maisie Ward, with her husband Frank Sheed, established an internationally known publishing house committed to making classic Catholic works available in print. Claire Booth Luce, a famous convert of Fulton J. Sheen, was a New York journalist and playwright whose play *The Women* won both popular and critical acclaim.

27. "Decree on the Up-to-Date Renewal of Religious Life" (*Perfectae Caritatis*), in *Vatican II: The Conciliar and Post-Conciliar Documents*, ed. Austin Flannery (Northport, NY: Costello, 1981), no. 4, 613, italics added.

28. Caspary, *Witness to Integrity*, 24.

29. Michael V. Gannon, "Before and after Modernism: The Intellectual Isolation of the American Priest," in *The Catholic Priest in the United States: Historical Investigations*, ed. John Tracy Ellis (Collegeville, MN: St. John's University Press, 1971), quote and Murnion interviews on 355. On the larger intellectual context of American seminaries, see John Tracy Ellis, "The Formation of the American Priest: An Historical Perspective," in the same collection.

30. Thomas J. Shelley, *Dunwoodie: The History of St. Joseph's Seminary* (Westminster, MD: Christian Classics, 1993), 213. See also John Cooney, *The American Pope: The Life and Times of Francis Cardinal Spellman* (New York: Times Books, 1984), 78.

31. Cooney, *American Pope*, 88–90; George Barry Ford, *A Degree of Difference* (New York: Farrar, Straus & Giroux, 1969), 105, 108–13. See also Caspary, *Witness to Integrity*, 59. This paragraph follows Caspary's arguments very closely.

32. McIntyre's departure from the New York archdiocese seems to have been greeted with something approaching universal relief among its priests; many priests referred to the "freedom train" that carried McIntyre west to his new position, freeing *them* of his presence. John Cooney, in his biography of Cardinal Spellman, expressed the sentiments of many of the New York clergy in describing the departing chancellor as a "mean-spirited, vindictive man who rationalized his conduct as always being for the good of the Church." Cooney, *American Pope*, 78; Ford, *A Degree of Difference*, 158.

33. Vincent Yzermans, ed., *American Participation in the Second Vatican Council* (New York: Sheed and Ward, 1967), 11. For McIntyre's difficulty with Latin, see Weber, *His Eminence of Los Angeles*, 1:11. For Hallinan's comment, see Shelley, *Dunwoodie*, 393, n. 26. Caspary, *Witness to Integrity*, 62. John Tracy Ellis later observed that McIntyre was "notoriously short-tempered and often prone to outbursts about matters on which he was less than well informed." Weber, *His Eminence*, 2:571.

34. "Pope Sees Cardinal McIntyre," *New York Times*, October 1, 1964, 25.

35. IHM General Chapter, 1963, "Recommendation #52 of the 1963 General Chapter," unpublished photocopy. See also "Basis for Changes and Adaptations of Customs Made by the Sisters of the Immaculate Heart, 1963–1965," unpublished photocopy, Archives of the Immaculate Heart Community, Los Angeles. Caspary, *Witness to Integrity*, 51–52.

36. "Minutes of the IHM General Council, November 12, 1965," Archives of the Immaculate Heart Community, Los Angeles; Caspary, *Witness to Integrity*, 67–68.

37. Caspary, *Witness to Integrity*, 69–70.

38. Ibid., 71.

39. "Minutes of the Meeting of Sister Elizabeth Ann and Mother Humiliata with Cardinal McIntyre, December 27, 1965," Archives of the Immaculate Heart Community, Los Angeles; Caspary, *Witness to Integrity*, 71–72.

40. Caspary, *Witness to Integrity*, 75. See also Letter of Cardinal McIntyre to Mother M. Humiliata, December 28, 1965, Archives of the Immaculate Heart Community, Los Angeles.

41. Letter of Cardinal McIntyre to Mother M. Humiliata, February 7, 1966 (a) and Letter of Cardinal McIntyre to Mother M. Humiliata, February 7, 1966 (b), both in Archives of the Immaculate Heart Community, Los Angeles; Caspary, *Witness to Integrity*, 78–79.

42. Letter of Cardinal McIntyre to Mother M. Humiliata, March 23, 1967, Archives of the Immaculate Community, Los Angeles; quote from Caspary, *Witness to Integrity*, 80.

43. Letter of Members of the Sisters of the Immaculate Heart to Cardinal McIntyre, April 2, 1967, Archives of the Immaculate Heart Community, Los Angeles.

44. Caspary, *Witness to Integrity*, 104.

45. Ibid., 105.

46. Ibid., 106; Thrapp, "Order of Nuns Here."

47. "Decrees of the Ninth General Chapter of the Sisters of the Immaculate Heart of Mary, October 1967," Archives of the Immaculate Heart Community, Los Angeles; Caspary, *Witness to Integrity*, 113.

48. Caspary, *Witness to Integrity*, 119–22. "Years after this eventful day I was approached by an auxiliary bishop in California who told me of his experience of being the young seminarian on duty as receptionist during this meeting. He stated that from a considerable distance he could hear the cardinal's voice reprimanding us" (120 n. 2).

49. Ibid., 122–23.

50. Previous accounts of the IHM story include Helen Rose Ebaugh, *Women in the Vanishing Cloister* (New Brunswick, NJ: Rutgers University Press, 1993), 139; Jo Ann McNamara, *Sisters in Arms* (Cambridge, MA: Harvard University Press, 1996), 640; John Seidler and Katherine Meyer, *Conflict and Change in the Catholic Church* (New Brunswick, NJ: Rutgers University Press, 1989), 80; James P. Shannon, *Reluctant Dissenter* (New York: Crossroads, 1998), 130; and my own "To Be Beautiful, Human and Christian: The IHMs and the Routinization of Charisma," in *Catholics and American Culture: Fulton Sheen, Dorothy Day, and the Notre Dame Football Team* (New York: Crossroads, 1999), 172.

Chapter 6

1. "9 Seize and Burn 600 Draft Files; 2 Priests among War Foes Arrested Near Baltimore," *New York Times*, May 18, 1968, 36; "Cardinal Scores Berrigan for 'Damaging' Acts; Shehan Rebukes Priest for Bloodying Draft Records, Says He Cannot Condone Destruction of Property," *New York Times*, May 27, 1968, 4; Sidney E. Zion, "Another 'No' to a Challenge on the Vietnam War," *New York Times*, October 13, 1968, E8 (this article includes a photograph of Phil and Dan Berrigan, both wearing Roman collars, setting fire to the draft files in Catonsville); Murray Polner and Jim O'Grady, *Disarmed and Dangerous: The Radical Lives and Times of Daniel and Philip Berrigan* (New York: Basic Books, 1997), 196–97. "The two parts gasoline provided the flames, and one part Ivory Flakes provided the adhesive so the jellylike substance would stick to the flesh" (196). Andrea Seabrook, "Echoes of 1968: Fire Sparked Push to End Vietnam War," *All Things Considered*, National Public Radio, May 17, 2008.

2. John Kifner, "The Berrigan Affair: How It Evolved," *New York Times*, February 21, 1970, A1; Seabrook, "Fire Sparked Push to End Vietnam War." Much of this and subsequent paragraphs have been shaped by David O'Brien's fine essay, "American Catholic Opposition to the Vietnam War: A Preliminary Assessment," in *War or Peace? The Search for New Answers*, ed. Thomas Shannon (Maryknoll, NY: Orbis Press, 1980), 119–50. See also Constance Rosenblum, "A History of the Vietnam Protest Movement," *Ave Maria*, December 1967, 1014.

3. Bart Barnes, "9 Convicted of Burning Draft Files. The Lord's Prayer. Records Burned. Charge Protested," *Washington Post*, October 11, 1968, A1; Richard Byrne Jr., "Revolution 9," (Baltimore) *City Paper*, January 9–February 4, 1993, 12–21; Ron Manuto and Sean Patrick O'Rourke, "Lessons from the Catonsville Nine," *Baltimore Sun*, May 17, 2008.

4. John Dear, "The Catonsville Nine 40 Years Later," *National Catholic Reporter*, May 20, 2008.

5. Profiles found online at "Fire and Faith: The Catonsville Nine File." Also "The Catonsville Nine," at www.jonahhouse.org. Philip Berrigan with Fred Wilcox, "Legionaries of the Lamb," in *Fighting the Lamb's War: Skirmishes with the American Empire* (Monroe, ME: Common Courage Press, 1996), 93–108. Dan Berrigan's rich use of biblical apocalyptic terminology can be found in his *Lights on in the House of the Dead: A Prison Diary* (New York: Doubleday, 1974). See also Bart Barnes, "Catonsville 9 Defend Burning Draft Files," *Washington Post*, October 10, 1968, A3.

6. Polner and O'Grady, *Disarmed and Dangerous*, 173. For a firsthand account of the impulses that motivated the group, see Daniel Berrigan, *To Dwell in Peace: An Autobiography* (San Francisco: Harper & Row, 1987), 219–22.

7. Loye Miller Jr., "Why Did Mild Phil Berrigan Turn Firebrand?" *Philadelphia Inquirer*, September 13, 1971. See also the Phil Berrigan interview in *From Camelot to Kent State: The Sixties in the Words of Those Who Lived It*, ed. Joan Morrison and Robert K. Morrison (New York: Times Books, 1987), 146.

8. Polner and O'Grady, *Disarmed and Dangerous*, 175–77.

9. Ibid., 177–78; Francine du Plessix Gray, *Divine Disobedience: Profiles in Catholic Radicalism* (New York: Knopf, 1970), 119–25; D. Berrigan, *To Dwell in Peace*, 210.

10. D. Berrigan, *To Dwell in Peace*, 206; Gray, *Divine Disobedience*, 203.

11. *Commonweal*, July 22, 1966; Polner and O'Grady, *Disarmed and Dangerous*, 201–2.

12. Philip Berrigan, *Prison Journals of a Revolutionary Priest*, ed. Vincent McGee (New York: Holt, Rinehard & Winston, 1970), 25; O'Brien, "American Catholic Opposition to the Vietnam War," 126; Polner and O'Grady, *Disarmed and Dangerous*, 201–2.

13. Kifner, "The Berrigan Affair"; "9 Seize and Burn 600 Draft Files," 36; Polner and O'Grady, *Disarmed and Dangerous*, 201–2.

14. Deidre Carmody, "9 War Foes Begin Baltimore Trial: 1500 Supporters Heckled as They Stage March," *New York Times*, October 8, 1968, 13; Deidre Carmody, "Defense Conceded Charges in Draft File Case: Judgment on Larger Issues Is Asked at Trial of Nine Catholics in Maryland," *New York Times*, October 9, 1968, 12.

15. Harvey Cox Jr., "Tongues of Fire: The Trial of the Catonsville Nine," in *The Witness of the Berrigans*, ed. Stephen Halpert and Tom Murray (New York: Doubleday, 1972), 22–23.

16. Gray, *Divine Disobedience*, 163–64; Polner and O'Grady, *Disarmed and Dangerous*, 204; Bill Wylie-Kellermann, "In One Another's Light: Reading King and Stringfellow," *Witness Magazine*, April 25, 2005; William Stringfellow, foreword to Melvin E. Schoonover, *Making All Things Human: A Church in East Harlem* (New York: Holt, Rinehart and Winston, 1969).

17. Michael Kaufman, *1968* (New York: Roaring Book Press, 2009), "Home Front," 21, "Columbia University," 43, "Chicago," 85; Fred W. McDarrah, *Anarchy, Protest, and Rebellion: The Counterculture That Changed America* (New York: Thunder's Mouth Press, 2003); Rebecca Jackson, *The 1960s: An Annotated Bibliography of Social and Political Movements in the United States* (Westport, CT: Greenwood Press, 1992), especially 124–28.

18. See especially the studies of Catholic culture in the "areas of second urban settlement": Jay Dolan, *The American Catholic Experience: A History from Colonial Times to the Present* (Garden City, NY: Doubleday, 1985), 361–83, 407–17; Dino Cinel, *From Italy to San Francisco: The Immigrant Experience* (Stanford: Stanford University Press, 1982), 125–30; Douglas T. Miller and Marian Nowak, *The Fifties: The Way We Really Were* (Garden City, NY: Doubleday, 1977), 133; William Halsey, *The Survival of American Innocence* (Notre Dame, IN: University of Notre Dame Press, 1973); Andrew Greeley, *The Church and the Suburbs* (New York: Sheed and Ward, 1959), 52.

19. For the special meaning of balancing the papal and American flags in Catholic churches in light of Joe McCarthy's anticommunism crusade, see Donald Crosby, *God, Church, Flag: Senator Joseph R. McCarthy and the Catholic Church* (Chapel Hill: University of North Carolina Press, 1978), chapter 1; I. F. Stone, *The Haunted Fifties* (New York: Random House, 1963), 39.

20. See my chapter "Oh, the Irony of It All," in *Catholics and American Culture: Fulton Sheen, Dorothy Day, and the Notre Dame Football Team* (New York: Crossroad, 1999), 1–20. Two classic works discussing the tradition of anti-Catholic cultural and political fears—and the perhaps overcompensation inspired among U.S. Catholics by those fears—are Ray Billington, *The Protestant Crusade, 1800–1860: A Study of the Origins of American Nativism* (New York: Macmillan, 1938), and John Higham, *Strangers in the Land: Patterns of American Nativism, 1850–1925* (New Brunswick, NJ: Rutgers University Press, 1955). See also the first chapter in my book, *Anti-Catholicism in America: The Last Acceptable Prejudice?* (New York: Crossroad, 2003).

21. Mircea Eliade, "Roman Catholicism," in *Encyclopedia of Religion* (New York: Macmillan, 1987), 12:431. Jesus' advice regarding rendering to Caesar can be found in Matthew 22:21. St. Paul's advice on faithful citizenship can be found at Philippians 5:6–8. "We have here no lasting city" is at Hebrews 13:14.

22. Jesus' radical standards of discipleship can be found in chapter 9 of St. Luke's gospel. "Compromise" in an ideologically neutral sense comes from Emile Durkheim's *Division of Labor in Society*, trans. W. D. Halls (New York: Free Press, 1984), 160: "But every decision of this kind can only be the result of a compromise, one that steers a middle course between the interests that are in competition and their solidarity with one another. It is a position of equilibrium that can only be found by a more or less laborious process of trial and error."

23. 1 John 2:14–17: "For all that is in the world, sensual lust, enticement for the eyes, and pretentious life, is not from the Father but is from the world. Yet the world and its enticements are passing away. But whoever does the will of God remains forever."

24. Eliade, "Roman Catholicism," 432.

25. James T. Fisher, *The Catholic Counter-Culture in America, 1933–1962* (Chapel Hill: University of North Carolina Press, 1989), 1. Day's quote from the broadcast script of "Still a Rebel," *Bill Moyer's Journal*, WNET, 1973. See also William D. Miller, *A Harsh and Dreadful Love: Dorothy Day and the Catholic Worker Movement* (New York: Liveright, 1973); Dorothy Day, "Who Are the Poor? They Are in Prisons, Too," *Catholic Worker* 22 (July–August 1955): 1.

26. Robert Coles, *A Spectacle unto the World: The Catholic Worker Movement* (New York: Viking Press, 1973). See also Coles's moving tribute to Day in "Remembering Dorothy Day," in *Harvard Diary: Reflections on the Sacred and the Secular* (New York: Crossroad, 1988), 5–6; Michael Baxter, "Notes on Catholic Americanism and Catholic Radicalism: Toward a Counter-Tradition of Catholic Social Ethics," in *American Catholic Traditions: Sources for Renewal*, ed. Sandra Yocum Mize and William Portier (Maryknoll, NY: Orbis Books, 1997), especially 53–55, 65–68.

27. "I may not be without blame. Even though we may be wrong, where we are is right. I'm not interested in this or that issue being right. I'm interested in being in the right place when Christ returns." Dan Berrigan, quoted in Polner and O'Grady, *Disarmed and Dangerous*, 214.

28. Paul Furfey, *Fire on the Earth* (New York: Macmillan, 1936), 117, describes those in the Catholic Worker Movement as espousing a "christologically shaped politics," a phrase appropriate to the Catonsville Nine as well.

29. Deidre Carmody, "Nine Found Guilty in Draft File Case," *New York Times*, October 13, 1968, A1; Deidre Carmody, "9 in Baltimore Get 2 to 3 ½ Years in Burning of Draft Records," *New York Times*, November 9, 1968, A13.

30. Carmody, "9 in Baltimore Get 2 to 3 ½ Years"; "Maryland War Foes Jailed When They Can't Post Bail," *New York Times*, December 14, 1968, 63.

31. Ellen Kirk, "Berrigan Given Option to Return," *Cornell Daily Sun*, May 12, 1969, 1.

32. Byrne, "Revolution 9," 18; Polner and O'Grady, *Disarmed and Dangerous*, 214–15.

33. Michael Kaufman, "Berrigan, Fugitive, Attends Festival Honoring Him," *New York Times*, April 18, 1970, 32.

34. Ibid.; Kifner, "The Berrigan Affair," 56.

35. Thomas F. Brady, "Antiwar Priest Sought by F.B.I. Says He Will Continue Defiance," *New York Times*, April 26, 1970, 78.

36. Kifner, "The Berrigan Affair," 56.

37. Ibid.

38. Ibid. The Weathermen, a splinter group of the Students for a Democratic Society (more commonly referred to as the SDS) became well-known in the mid-1970s for violence against the federal government. In 1970 the group issued a "Declaration of a State of War" against the U.S. government, focusing their attacks on federal office buildings and banks, but always preceded by evacuation warnings. On March 1, 1971, they set off a bomb in the U.S. Capitol ("in protest of the U.S. invasion of Laos"). Bombing the Pentagon on May 18, 1972, they stated that it was done "in retaliation for the U.S. bombing raid in Hanoi." On January 29, 1975, they set off an explosive device in the U.S. State Department building "in response to the escalation in Vietnam." Dan Berger, *Outlaws of America: The Weathermen Underground and the Politics of Solidarity* (N.p.: AK Press, 2006), 95; Lawrence Lader, *Power to the Left* (New York: Norton, 1979), 192.

39. David Bird, "300 Protesting Columbia Students Barricade Office of College Dean," *New York Times*, April 24, 1968, A1; J. Anthony Lukas, "Thousands March. Scores Are Arrested, Some Delegates. Tear Gas Is Used," *New York Times*, August 30, 1968, A1; Henry Tanner, "De Gaulle Sets a Referendum; Promises to Resign If He Loses; Asks Calm, but Fighting Flares," *New York Times*, May 25, 1968, A1. The lyrics to Crosby, Stills, Nash, and Young's "Chicago/We Can Change the World" served as something like a call to college students across the country to remember the events in Chicago and act on the principles that brought thousands of students to the Democratic National Convention in August 1968. The full lyrics can be found at www.lyricsdownload.com/crosby-stills-nash-young.com.

40. Johann Baptist Metz, *Faith in History and Society: Toward a Fundamental Practical Theology* (New York: Seabury Press, 1980), 66.

41. Ibid., 109, 110.

42. Ibid., 109.

43. Ibid., 200. See also Metz's "Communicating a Dangerous Memory," in *Love's Strategy: The Political Theology of Johann Baptist Metz*, ed. John K. Downey (Harrisburg, PA: Trinity Press, 1999), 137, and his "Christians and Jews after Auschwitz: Being a Meditation Also on the End of Bourgeois Religion," in

The Emergent Church: The Future of Christianity in a Postbourgeois World (New York: Crossroad, 1981), 17–33.

44. Metz, *Faith in History and Society*, 115. On how Metz's political theology is embodied in Catholic liturgy, see Bruce T. Morrill, *Anamnesis as Dangerous Memory: Political and Liturgical Theology in Dialogue* (Collegeville, MN: Liturgical Press, 2000). Mary's hymn, the "Magnificat," can be found at Luke 1:46–55.

45. Metz, *Faith in History and Society*, 229.

46. Michael J. Iafrate, "We Will Never Forget: Metz, Memory, and the Dangerous Spirituality of Post-9/11 America," at Catholicanarchy.org, 4. Iafrate is quoting from Metz's *Faith in History and Society*, 95, 115, in this paragraph.

Chapter 7

1. Avery Dulles, *A Testimonial to Grace* (New York: Sheed and Ward, 1946); Robert McFadden, "Cardinal Avery Dulles, Theologian, Is Dead," *New York Times*, December 12, 2008; John L. Allen, "Cardinal Avery Dulles, S.J., RIP," *National Catholic Reporter*, December 12, 2008.

2. Avery Dulles, *Models of the Church* (Garden City, NY: Doubleday, 1974). For contemporary reviews of this work, witnessing to Dulles's emergence as a player in the national church, see Jaroslav Pelikan, book review in *Commonweal*, April 25, 1975, 90–91; Gustav-Pierre Leonard, "That Unfaithful Woman: The Church," *Cross Currents* 25 (Spring 1975): 93–101; Patrick J. Burns, book review in *Theological Studies* 35 (1974): 563–65; Jerome Theisen, book review in *Worship* 8 (1974): 500–501; William Rademacher, "To Build Bridges," *Christian Century* January 29, 1975, 89–90; Avery Dulles, *The Catholicity of the Church* (Oxford: Clarenden Press, 1985); Avery Dulles, *The Assurance of Things Hoped For: A Theology of Christian Faith* (New York: Oxford University Press, 1994); Avery Dulles, *The Craft of Theology: From Symbol to System* (New York: Crossroad, 1992); Avery Dulles, *The Splendor of Faith* (New York: Crossroad, 2003). On the contested reading of Dulles's career, see Joseph Bottum, "One Establishment Meets Another," *Atlantic Monthly*, May 2001, 22–23: "Explaining the liberalism of Vatican II to an older generation that had experienced only the unified, pre-conciliar Church, [Dulles] became a leader for liberal Catholics in the 1970s. Explaining the conservatism of Vatican II to a new generation that had experienced only the fragmented, post-conciliar Church, he became something of a leader for conservative Catholics in the 1990s." For the sheer spectrum of interpretations of the trajectory of Dulles's thinking, see Richard McBrien, "Red Hat after Lurch to Right," *National Catholic Reporter*, November 15, 2002; Gill Donovan, "Cardinal Links Vocation Drop to Vatican II 'Myth,'" *National Catholic Reporter*, November 15, 2002; William F. Buckley, "On the Right—Execution Days Ahead? Opinions, Including That of Avery Cardinal Dulles, on Capital Punishment," *National Review*, April 16, 2001; "An Adult Faith Begins to Stir," *Catholic News Service*, November 6,

2005; Michael Gilcrest, "Cardinal Avery Dulles: U.S. Jesuits Need 'Wake Up Call,'" *AD2000*, July 2002, 10.

3. The interpretation that Dulles remained stationary while the Church moved to the left is my own in "Avery Dulles, Teaching Authority in the Church, and the 'Dialectically Tense' Middle: An American Strategic Theology," *Heythrop Journal* 48 (2007): 932–51. As will become obvious in the course of this chapter, I have since changed my mind about the interpretation I offered in that essay.

4. Joseph A. Komonchak, "All Dressed in Scarlet: Avery Dulles Goes to College," *Commonweal*, February 23, 2001, 9.

5. Ibid.

6. Ibid.

7. Anne-Marie Kirmse, "The Church and the Churches: A Study of the Ecclesiological and Ecumenical Developments in the Writings of Avery Dulles, S.J." (Ph.D. dissertation, Fordham University), 10. Kirmse adds in a footnote (20) that this "healthy pluralism" follows "in the tradition of Ernst Troeltsch and H. R. Niebuhr, and is in sharp contradistinction with David Tracy, who holds that models represent mutually incompatible options" (10).

8. Ibid., 23. The quote is from Dulles's *Survival of Dogma* (Garden City, NY: Doubleday, 1971), 196. "Lurch to the right" from McBrien in *National Catholic Reporter*.

9. Kirmse, "The Church and the Churches," 251. Kirmse's observation regarding Dulles's "mediating" position was seconded by William Bole in "A Moderate in a Disputatious Age," *Our Sunday Visitor*, May 25, 1997.

10. Dulles, *The Survival of Dogma*, 96–97.

11. Ibid., 100–101.

12. Ibid., 97, 98.

13. Ibid., 101–2, 103.

14. Avery Dulles, *Models of the Church* (Garden City, NY: Doubleday, 1974), 13.

15. Ibid., 14, 205.

16. Ibid., 39–44, 52–55, 68–73, 81–86, 97–101.

17. Ibid., 13–14.

18. Ibid., 205–6.

19. Ibid., 36.

20. Ibid., 204–5.

21. Wills, *Bare Ruined Choirs: Doubt, Prophecy and Radical Religion* (Garden City, NY: Doubleday, 1971), 20.

22. See, for example, Elizabeth Johnson's brilliant and prize-winning work, *She Who Is: The Mystery of God in Feminist Theological Discourse* (New York: Crossroad, 1992), especially chapter 1, "To Speak Rightly of God."

23. Dulles, *Models*, 40.

24. Ibid., 41.

Chapter 8

1. On Benedict XVI's attempt to claim the Second Vatican Council for continuity—over against the more common interpretation of that council as radically discontinuous with the previous two councils—see John W. O'Malley, *What Happened at Vatican II?* (Cambridge, MA: Belknap Press of Harvard University Press, 2008), 36–43, 299–302.

2. Jaroslav Pelikan, *The Emergence of the Catholic Tradition, 100–600*, vol. 1 of *The Christian Tradition: A History of the Development of Christian Doctrine* (Chicago: University of Chicago Press, 1971), 16–21.

3. Robert Hannah, *Greek and Roman Calendars: The Construction of Time in the Classical World* (London: Gerald Duckworth, 2005); Roger T. Beckwith, *Calendar, Chronology, and Worship: Studies in Ancient Judaism and Early Christianity* (Boston: Brill, 2005).

4. Especially helpful on all of this is Terrence Tilley's *History, Theology, and Faith: Dissolving the Modern Problematic* (Maryknoll, NY: Orbis Books, 2004).

5. Romans 11:29. Chapters 9 through 11 in Paul's letter to the Romans focuses on his argument about the irrevocable call of God to Israel.

6. Marcion (d. ca. 160) and his followers, excommunicated in 144, emphasized an extreme disjunction between Judaism and Christianity. Marcion's interpretation of the Apostle Paul led him to posit a great divide between the "god of love" of the New Testament and the "god of law" of the Old Testament. With a bible composed of ten Pauline epistles and an edited version of the Gospel of Luke, Marcionite Christians rejected the Old Testament completely. See "Marcion" and "Gnosticism" in *The Oxford Dictionary of the Christian Church*, 3rd ed. (New York: Oxford University Press, 1997). On the Gnostic anti-Semitic debates with mainstream Christianity, see Edward Kessler and Neil Wenborn, *A Dictionary of Jewish-Christian Relations* (New York: Cambridge University Press, 2005).

7. Jaroslav Pelikan, *The Spirit of Eastern Christendom, 600–1700* (Chicago: University of Chicago Press, 1974), 13. Pelikan is here explaining the theological position of the seventh-century church father Maximus the Confessor. On impassability, see Van A. Harvey, *Handbook of Theological Terms* (New York: Macmillan, 1964).

8. See, for example, Diarmaid MacCulloch, *The Reformation* (New York: Viking, 2003), 3–50, "The Old Church"; Steven Ozment, *The Age of Reform, 1250–1550: An Intellectual and Religious History of Late Medieval and Reformation Europe* (New Haven: Yale University Press, 1980), 22–72, "The Scholastic Traditions." For an argument that reform was a pan-Christian idea really rooted in thirteenth- and fourteenth-century Catholic piety, see Charles Taylor, *A Secular Age* (Cambridge, MA: Belknap Press of Harvard University Press, 2007), part 1, "The Work of Reform," especially 61–89.

9. Hubert Jedin, *History of the Council of Trent*, 2 vols., trans. Ernest Graf (St. Louis: B. Herder, 1957–61); John W. O'Malley, *Trent and All That: Renaming Catholicism in the Early Modern Era* (Cambridge, MA: Harvard University Press, 2000).

10. Klaus Schultz, *Papal Primacy from Its Origins to the Present* (Collegeville, MN: Liturgical Press, 1996), 128–74; Jeffrey von Arx, *Varieties of Ultramontanism* (Washington, DC: Catholic University of America Press, 1997); Alex Vidler, *The Modernist Movement in the Roman Church* (Cambridge, UK: Cambridge University Press, 1934); Bernard Reardon, *Roman Catholic Modernism* (London: A&C Black, 1970); Gabriel Daly, *Transcendence and Immanence: A Study of Catholic Modernism and Integralism* (Oxford: Oxford University Press, 1980).

11. Thomas Loome, *Liberal Catholicism, Reform Catholicism, Modernism: A Contribution to a New Orientation in Modernist Research*, at www.findarticles .com/articles/mi_hb050/is_200203.

12. Pius X, "Syllabus Condemning the Errors of the Modernists" (*Lamentabili Sane*), issued on July 3, 1907, at www.papalencyclicals.net/Pius10.

13. On the *Nouvelle théologie* movement, see James C. Livingston and Francis Schussler Fiorenza, eds., *Modern Christian Thought* (Upper Saddle River, NJ: Prentice-Hall, 2000), 2:198–205. On the static and ahistorical presuppositions of the prevailing neo-Thomism, see Gerald McCool, *Catholic Theology in the Nineteenth Century: The Search for a Unitary Method* (New York: Seabury Press, 1977), 216–40.

14. For a cogent argument against the idea of Darwinian natural selection being the culprit in the emergence of modernism, see James R. Moore, *The Post-Darwinian Controversies* (Cambridge, UK: Cambridge University Press, 1979), 12; Donald H. Meyer, "American Intellectuals and the Victorian Crisis of Faith," *American Quarterly* 27 (1975): 585–602; Paul Carter, *The Spiritual Crises of the Gilded Age* (DeKalb: Northern Illinois University Press, 1971), 14.

15. Sheila Greeve Davaney, *Historicism: The Once and Future Challenge for Theology* (Minneapolis: Fortress Press, 2006); Ernst Cassirer, *The Problem of Knowledge* (New Haven: Yale University Press, 1950), 170; R. G. Collingwood, *The Idea of History* (Oxford: Oxford University Press, 1946), 302; Charles Beard and Alfred Vaghts, "Currents of Thought in Historiography," *American Historical Review* 42 (1937): 460–87.

16. Friedrich Meinecke, *Historism: The Rise of a New Historical Outlook* (London: Routledge, 1972), 295; Carl Becker, *The Heavenly City of the Eighteenth Century Philosophers* (Cambridge, MA: Harvard University Press, 1932), 18.

17. On Herder, see Frederick M. Barnard, *Herder on Nationality, Humanity, and History* (Montreal: McGill-Queens University Press, 2003), 105–30; Hans Meyerhoff, *The Philosophy of History in Our times* (Garden City, NY: Doubleday, 1959), 10; Georg Iggers, *The German Conception of History* (Middletown, CT: Wesleyan University Press, 1968), 30.

18. Ludwig Feuerbach, *Sämtliche Werke*, 2 vols. (Leipzig: O Wigand, 1848–66), 2:143–44; Georg Iggers, "Historicism," in *Dictionary of the History of Ideas* (New York: Charles Scribner's Sons, 1973), 2:457; Meyerhoff, *Philosophy of History*, 12; Karl Marx, "Philosophical Manifesto of the Historical School of Law," in *Writings of the Young Marx on Philosophy and Science*, ed. Lloyd D. Easton and Kurt Guddut (Garden City, NY: Doubleday, 1967), 96–105.

19. Leopold von Ranke, *The Theory and Practice of History* (Indianapolis: Bobbs-Merrill, 1971), 5–23.

20. Willis Glover, *Evangelical Nonconformists and Higher Criticism in the Nineteenth Century* (London: Independent Press, 1954), 12–13; Moore, *Post-Darwinian Controversies*, 15.

INDEX